I0835820

**Previous books by the author**

*How to Plan Your Trip to Europe,* with Ray Gilden (1995)

*Tea & Bee's Milk: Our Year in a Turkish Village,* with Ray Gilden (2008)

*Camping With the Communists: The Adventures of an American Family in the Soviet Union* (2013)

*Life in Transition: Essays and Diversions* (2019)

EVE AND ME

Artha One Publishing, Portland Oregon.

ISBN 978-1-886922-09-9

No artificial intelligence (A.I.) was used in the writing or editing of this book.

KAREN GILDEN

# EVE AND ME

## THE SHADOW THAT SPANS 3000 YEARS

Artha One Press, Portland, Oregon

DEDICATED TO

Every woman who has suffered discrimination,
sexual abuse, assault, rape, or intimidation,
or who has been overlooked or ignored due to her sex.
With thanks to all who continue to work for the respect,
fair pay, and equal rights that every human deserves.

We are the daughters of mothers
from before charted time until the end of knowing.
We are the Earth Mother, the Great Goddess,
Mary the Virgin, and Mary the Whore.
We are the slaves and the sovereigns,
the wives and the lovers, the artists and their critics.
We are mothers, sisters, scientists, soldiers, and confidants.
We are the lady next door.
There is no end to our achievements,
nor to our promise.
We are woman.

# CONTENTS

# PREFACE

I'm not a historian but I do love history, and I've long been curious about why women are treated as they are, how they were treated in other centuries and other cultures, and whether it's reasonable to hope for a better future for our daughters. Like most writers I'm an observer, and during my long lifetime I've seen dramatic changes in the way women perceive and live their lives. Many of us are freer now than we've ever been, but the rules keep changing and so must we.

As a result of the "second wave" feminist movement in the 1960s and '70s, women have increasingly moved into men's roles, but we have not feminized those roles. We have taken the jobs, the titles, and the ambitions of men, often adapting our sexuality to male patterns of behavior. But feminism has not freed the world of poverty or hate, nor has it protected the planet from devastation. It has not taught us to think differently, only to move through life with more options. Is that all we're going to get?

*Eve and Me* is a personal view of women's history, an attempt to determine how that history influences us today. Clearly we live in a patriarchal society. Is patriarchy an inevitable outgrowth of history and culture? A natural human instinct? A bad habit? Did it have a beginning? Will it ever end? I wanted to know.

The book is in two parts. Part One covers the ancient world to the 19th century. Part Two begins with the fight for women's right to vote, and carries us to the present. Throughout, I've highlighted women who stood up for themselves—and often suffered for it—and women who personally interested me. Thanks to the internet you don't have to look hard to find women who have accomplished great things, often against great odds. But it wasn't always that easy. History has long ignored and downplayed female accomplishments.

Interestingly, even the *New York Times* has recognized their part in this failure. They have a section online called "Overlooked" that's defined like this: "Since 1851, obituaries in *The New York Times* have been dominated by white men. Now, we're adding the stories of other remarkable people."

For century after century women have been held back, dishonored and debased in ways that were aided chiefly by two things: religion's dependence on misogynistic myths, and male capitulation to the lure of power. They often go together. Though religion plays a largely negative role in this story I'm not against religion; I'm neutral. I know that religious belief is a source of inspiration for many, and a powerful support in time of need.

Neither am I anti-male, though men show up as detrimental to women far too often in these pages. Indeed, I like men and I respect those who support women, their rights, and their independence. I was married to such a man for 53 years; a kind, intelligent, courageous man who spent much of his time in determined activism.

One of the current president's first decisions in his second term was to declare that only two sexes exist. Why he thinks that's a president's prerogative is beyond me, but I believe gender is a spectrum and strict adherence to only two sexes ignores what are natural differences. Gender labeling deflects from the real issue, which is valuing individuals for who they are, however they are. Throughout the book I use the words *men* and *women* because those are the words in our current lexicon, though this is changing. My topic is women—however defined—and how they're treated through history. My pronouns are she and her.

The mythical story of Eve plays a crucial role in betraying women. Her shadow has cast a darkness that stretches across the globe. Eve is known almost everywhere, as if by osmosis. She was called evil incarnate, the original sinner, the wicked forebear of a cursed humanity. Those ideas and those words, whether believed or not, have cast a permanent shadow over every woman. It sneaks through the open doors of huts and flits effortlessly through the sealed windows of high-rises. The shadow Eve casts, however, is not her own. It emanates from the thoughts, words and deeds of others. I hope one day we will cast that darkness aside, and Eve and all her daughters will live in a world free of shadows.

# 1
# IN THE BEGINNING

I was 22 and single in 1963, sitting in my San Francisco apartment reading a magazine excerpt of Betty Friedan's new book, *The Feminine Mystique.* I was growing uncomfortable as I read; so uncomfortable in fact that I flung the magazine across the room in anger. Not because the situations she so admirably wrote about left me angry, but because she was, step by well-documented step, destroying the image of womanhood I had grown up with, the role I had prepared for, and the silent indoctrination I'd received from my mother, three aunts, friends, television, advertising, books, and the air I breathed. Was what she wrote true? I couldn't fathom it.

Conversations with roommates and friends soon followed, though none at that point had read the book and for most the topic held little interest. But I began paying attention to the voices coming out of New York and while I listened and read with interest, I remained skeptical. I was not alone.

Two years later I exchanged foggy San Francisco for sunny San Jose, intending to go back to school and finish my degree. Instead, I reluctantly agreed to go on a blind date and met my future husband;

a year later we married. Ray was a feminist, though that wasn't an idea either of us would have recognized. It was he who told me, a few weeks into our marriage, that I didn't have to try so hard; that everything didn't have to be perfect. That comment, which I remember so clearly, led to conversations that, over time, convinced me I could be more than "just" a wife and mother. To Ray it was obvious; he was a male, he could live as he wanted and make his own way. He showed me through his words and actions that I was no different; what I wanted from life was as valid as what he wanted.

It wasn't until the early '70s that I read Friedan's book and understood: Women's lives, especially after World War II, were defined only through their husbands and children—a situation that created widespread unhappiness and left women without a meaningful identity of their own. Friedan's clarifying exposure of that empty existence was a loud and uninhibited call to freedom.

By then I'd been part of a female support group that met weekly to share our histories and hopes and, of course, to complain. Thousands of such groups sprang up independently across the country in the '70s, all of us trying to rid ourselves of years of indoctrination, like brainwashed prisoners. Our group ran about a year, the meetings coming less frequently until there was no need or interest in continuing.

This "second wave" feminist movement (the first wave was the long struggle for the vote) influenced women across the country and parts of Europe, helped by the activist words of Betty Friedan, Gloria Steinem, Bella Abzug, and *Ms. Magazine.* Those three women, along with others, formed the National Women's Political Caucus in 1972 and led the way for the rest of us. The change that Friedan had called for wasn't immediate. It didn't reach every woman, or touch every heart. But even women like me, who had so much indoctrination to shed, began to see more clearly; and then we began to hope.

Many of us resolved to participate in the political realm. Political change was happening, and optimism prevailed. When Sandra Day O'Connor was appointed the first woman to sit on the U.S. Supreme Court in 1981, we cheered. "Finally!" And, without fanfare, I suddenly had the choice of a female doctor.

The war in Vietnam dampened some of that enthusiasm, but the anti-war movement that shook campuses proved that women could and would speak out and organize. While more young women were choosing college, others were looking around and saying to themselves, "I can do that. In fact I can do it better!" Women opened their own businesses, ran for local school boards, county and state offices, and finally for Congress. It was definitely progress.

Despite the hard work and advancements that women have achieved since *The Feminine Mystique* was published, as I write today it feels like women haven't progressed at all. The same issues remain, and so does the outrage.

From my first angry encounter with feminism in 1963 until today, life as a female has improved in many ways. We have no-fault divorce. I have my own credit. I can buy a house or start a business. But I have never received equal pay for equal work, nor have I enjoyed the certainty provided by the Equal Rights Amendment. We are now 25 years into the third millennium AD and women in the U.S. and around the world still suffer from patriarchal governance and misogynistic policing. Those are not my terms but Kate Manne's, writing in *Down Girl: The Logic of Misogyny.* She defines these concepts far more brilliantly than I could:

> "Misogyny upholds the social norms of patriarchies by policing and patrolling them; whereas sexism serves to justify these norms—largely via an ideology of supposedly 'natural' differences between men and women with respect to their talents, interests, proclivities, and appetites." More specifically, "Sexism taken alone involves believing in men's superiority to women in masculine-coded, high-prestige domains . . ." whereas "Misogyny taken alone involves anxieties, fears, and desires to maintain a patriarchal order, and a commitment to restoring it when it is disrupted. . . . Sexism has a theory; misogyny wields a cudgel."[1]

Thus patriarchy not only continues to exist, to the detriment of women, but is protected by those who benefit from it, i.e., not women.

Misogyny and sexism, in its many imaginative forms, remains and even blossoms today. Unwanted touching, abuse, violence, and rape still happen, and too frequently remain unreported out of fear of not being believed. But women and their supporters will never stop fighting. After all, E. Jean Carroll took Donald J. Trump to court and won. Twice.

# 2

## THE SECRETS RUINS HOLD

I've long been interested in ancient history, the more ancient the better. Excavations at Göbekli Tepe in Turkey started in 1995 and after stumbling across news of the findings I was immediately fascinated; especially after an early estimate suggested the site was 12,000 years old. Much older than the pyramids. That date has now been altered to about 9500 to 8000 BCE and the site has greatly expanded, but its strange stone monoliths remain a mystery.[1] And I love mysteries.

So when a second site came to light I was again captivated. Another unknown ruin, about the same age as Göbekli Tepe and in the same general area. But this site had no monuments, no towering monoliths. It had houses and remnants of people's lives, reflecting values that 21st century humans might do well to consider.

Imagine a room about 300 square feet (27 sq. meters). It's built of mud bricks over a framework of wood and covered, inside and out, with a thin layer of white limestone. On the south side of the room is a low platform with a hearth and an oven, built of the same material, with a storage area to one side. There are raised platforms on two or three sides of the room, maybe at differing heights, thought to be sleeping platforms or seating. Some walls are decorated with art—pictures of animals or designs in various colors. Imagine this is your home.

A ladder leads to a hole in the ceiling so you, and smoke from the fires, can exit. Climbing onto the roof you see that your home is one of hundreds, most sharing walls and built on top of older homes, just like yours. There are no streets per se; you move across the rooftops and ladders to reach the ground.[2]

This is the ancient village of Çatalhöyük in south central Turkey. It dates from around 7500 BCE to 5600 BCE. It was first discovered by James Mellaart who began excavations in 1961–63 and in 1965. From 1993 to 2018 British archaeologist Ian Hodder and an international team of archaeologists and other experts have carried out research and excavations at the Neolithic site. In 2018 the work was turned over to a Turkish archeologist.

Hodder, in a video lecture, described the village as one without any central governing structure, no central square or official building has been found, though some homes are slightly larger than others. He says that people lived in these houses for 50 to 100 years and then built new ones on top of the old. He also says they regularly replastered interiors with a thin layer of limestone. Artwork, and what he calls ritual features, were recreated in a new home in exactly the same positions as in the old.[3]

Among those artworks are hundreds of small carvings of women, described as older, with sagging breasts, stomachs, and bottoms. Some call these carvings goddesses. They vary in style, size, and the maker's skill, and are often found tucked into walls or near burials. I've found no mention of male figures, though they can't be dismissed. One important find is known as the Seated Woman of Çatalhöyük: a nude, heavy woman with sagging breasts and dimpled knees, who sits proudly upright in a chair with each hand resting on the head of a leopard. Is she a goddess? Some say yes. Others suggest she represents the elderly women who had achieved status in the community. Whoever she is, she now sits in the Museum of Anatolian Civilizations in Ankara, Turkey. (You can see her here.[4])

The bones of family members or friends are kept close, buried inside the homes, under the raised and sealed platforms. The bones are often passed around to others, especially skulls which are sometimes coated with plaster. Examination of the bones show "it's clear" that men and women were equally exposed to the smoke of the oven and hearth, that both men and women had the same diets, and both showed the same kinds of wear in their joints and bones. The skulls that were passed from home to home were equally male and female. Hodder emphasizes: there was no division by gender.

Nor does there appear any division by economic status. It's believed some residents grew crops in nearby fields, or cared for domestic animals, and some were hunter-gatherers. Whatever they did made no difference to the way they lived or ate. Hodder says there were very few bodies showing signs of violence, no arrows, etc. Nor is there a protective wall or border at the perimeter of the settlement. It's hard to imagine no central government, no central ritual, no economic status. Yet this community of 3000 to 8000 people survived for more than 1000 years.[5]

Çatalhöyük was named a World Heritage Site in 2012. The settlement has significance beyond its archeological interest. It's the first time my reading has shown me men and women living together in a settled place without either being dominant. No patriarchy. No matriarchy.

Did the people of Çatalhöyük believe in a goddess? Nothing is sure, though the many carved female forms suggest it. Belief in goddesses is supported by plenty of evidence, including the great temple of Artemis at Ephesus, one of the seven wonders of the ancient world. And in the Neolithic age a goddess made sense given the obvious exemplar: only women had babies, only women produced milk to feed them. Only women bled monthly and didn't die. Men couldn't do any of those things; of course the Creator must be a caring female, the Great Mother of us all.

Researcher and writer Barbara G. Walker, in *The Woman's Encyclopedia of Myths and Secrets,* writes "From the earliest human cultures, the mysterious magic of creation was thought to reside in the blood women gave forth in apparent harmony with the moon, and which was sometimes retained in the womb to "coagulate" into a baby. Men regarded this blood with holy dread, as the life-essence, inexplicably shed without pain, wholly foreign to male experience."[6]

## Marija Gimbutas

During the years the goddess reigned, some cultures might have been gynocentric (mother/woman centered), with children inheriting through their mother and women having equal roles in and out of the home. This idea is not universally held, however.

One of its proponents was Marija Gimbutas. She was born in 1921 in Lithuania, where she studied linguistics and archaeology and received her doctorate from the University of Tübingen. She moved to the U.S. in the 1950s and taught at Harvard and UCLA. Gimbutas spent decades directing major investigations at sites in the Republic of Macedonia and in Thessaly, Greece where she documented artifacts of daily life and religion reaching back to about 6000 BCE.[7]

She is best known for her Kurgen hypothesis, the name she gave Indo-European-speaking people, who she believed migrated to Europe from the eastern steppes of southern Russia and beyond, and carried their patriarchal culture into areas in Europe that had previously been peaceful societies that honored women, goddesses, and economic equality.

Mara Lynn Keller, a professor of religion and women's spirituality, is quoted saying that "Gimbutus fundamentally challenged the established view that European culture has always been male-dominant and that 'history' but not 'prehistory' was civilized."[8]

Like many women who challenge established wisdom, Gimbutas's work was often ignored, belittled, or dismissed. But with new innovations in archeology, including the use of DNA, views are beginning to shift in her favor.[9]

In the preface to *The Civilization of the Goddess* Gimbutas writes: "I reject the assumption that civilization refers only to androcratic [male dominant] societies. The generative basis of any civilization lies in its degree of artistic creating, aesthetic achievements, nonmaterial values, and freedom which make life meaningful and enjoyable for all its citizens, as well as a balance of powers between the sexes."[10]

Admitting that fighting and fortifications have occupied our way of life since the bronze age (3200 to 600 BCE) Gimbutas writes "there are no depictions of arms in Paleolithic cave paintings, nor are there remains of weapons used by man against man during the Neolithic of Old Europe. From some hundred and fifty paintings that survived at Çatal Hüyük, there is not one depicting a scene of conflict or fighting, or of war or torture."[11]

And, she states,"The primordial deity for our Paleolithic and Neolithic ancestors was female, reflecting the sovereignty of motherhood. In fact, there are no images that have been found of a Father God throughout the prehistoric record."[12]

No matter how comforting it might be to hear that our Paleolithic and Neolithic ancestors lived free of wars or conflict, there will continue to be critics who disagree or have other ideas. My reading suggests that archeologists are conservative investigators; they prefer the already established over the surprising new clue. Caution in science is definitely called for because error can always sneak in. I confess I laughed reading this line from Angela Saini who notes the shock that ensued "after a high-status warrior grave in the Viking Age town of Birka, Sweden, dating from the middle of the tenth century CE, was found to be a woman."[13]

Archeology offers valuable scholarship about our ancestors while reminding us that cultures and societies developed slowly, through uncounted millennia. Climate, plagues, and wars all played a role, and so did individuals. It's unlikely that our understanding of any prehistoric culture can be fully realized because each was a product of unique humans living in groups of varied status, with all the needs, wants, confusion, misunderstandings, and mishaps that have always afflicted us. There's no doubt though, that when patriarchy rears its head it has tended to succeed, leaving women relegated to subordinate roles, including various forms of slavery.

Theories about the origins of patriarchy—and there are many—will come later. Though it's impossible to say definitely, let's assume gender bias was unknown in the hunter-gatherer period, which wasn't completely replaced in Western Eurasia until approximately 4000 BCE.

In her book *Who Cooked the Last Supper?* Rosalind Miles writes that hunting "was a whole group activity" and that *"the only regular, un-*

*avoidable call on man's aggression was as protector: infant caring and group protection are the only sexual divisions of labor that invariably obtain in primate or primitive groups.*"[14] (Emphasis Miles.)

Here's a description of prehistoric women by historian Will Durant: "The differences in strength which now divide the sexes hardly existed in those days, and are now environmental rather than innate: woman, apart from her biological disabilities, was almost the equal of man in nature, endurance, resourcefulness and courage; she was not yet an ornament, a thing of beauty, or a sexual toy, she was a robust animal, able to perform arduous work for long hours, and if necessary to fight to the death for her children or her clan."[15]

How does that description fit women today? Ignore "ornaments-and-sex" and consider today's women in the armed forces fighting alongside men, female athletes who continually break records, and any woman holding a family together under the pressure of poverty, war, or environmental disaster. Do you not see endurance, resourcefulness and courage? Such qualities may not surface in our day-to-day lives, but they still exist to be called on when needed, just as they do for men.

As for "arduous work for long hours," that has always described ordinary women's lives. I immediately think of the women who took part in our country's western migration, living for months in covered wagons, walking for miles, cooking over campfires, nursing the sick or injured, doing whatever needed to be done, and eventually helping to build a new home. Or my grandmother Alice, bearing and raising eight children on a farm without benefit of electricity or running water. Many women today work physically hard jobs and/or long hours to support their families or themselves. There is not and never has been a dearth of women doing "arduous work." The idea is laughable.

I'm assuming that women, being limited by babies and their care, did most of the gathering. It seems only natural that over several millennia of seeking, finding, tasting, and collecting all kinds of plants, women would be experts. With every new find they tasted a tiny bit to determine, was it safe to eat or dangerous? Was it tasty? Would it dissuade hunger, or flavor other foods? Followed later by: Did it help bring down a fever? Did it speed the healing of a cut or sore? Did it ease an upset stomach? Did it bring on visions?

It would be silly to deny that women were knowledgeable about plants, and that knowing was passed from one generation to the next, each adding to the collective store of knowledge and wise use. This is why women, not men, ruled the ancient rituals—about which more later—and concocted the potions that brought ecstatic visions. And why, centuries later, such knowledge would brand them as witches.

Witch is also a term used by some for the Goddess, but slander hasn't made her disappear. Her worship was once deeply ingrained throughout the Mediterranean and beyond. She was known by many names: Ashtoreth, Artemis, Isis, Ishtar, Cybele, Demeter, Hera. The list is endless and complex, as different names were often given to the same deity in different locations. Beloved from the ancient past, the goddess moved with humanity from the fertile crescent, north to Turkey and Greece and eventually across the known world.

Statues of the goddess have been found across Neolithic and Paleolithic Europe. The Willendorf Goddess was carved of limestone about 25,000 years ago. An earlier version, the Acheulian Goddess, was shaped from an existing rock, and is said to be as much as 200,000 years old. Both statues are distinctly female and resemble those found at Çatalhöyük, with large breasts and hips and featureless faces.

I've long been familiar with the goddess, meeting her frequently in books, art, a few movies, and during our visits to Turkey—a country awash in goddesses. During our travels I was drawn to the many examples of goddess art and today my small collection sits on a nearby shelf. With one exception these are copies sold to gullible tourists. Typical is one of pale, roughly carved stone, about three inches high, bought from a young boy among the ruins of Hierapolis. She is shown naked, clasping her breasts while standing on tiny feet, which cause her to fall over frequently. Another of stone is also three inches tall, but this artist has done a better job. She's rather elegant, wearing a decorated cap and holding a bowl.

One of my favorites is carved in relief on stone. She wears a tall headdress and a small child stands each side of her; I bought her from a carver plying his skill on the streets of Antalya. He gave her a name which I no longer remember, but in fact names seldom attach to these small carvings; they are not always recognizable in the classic sense, though they were surely known by their owners. They are representative of the ancient goddess statues found across the region. I imagine people carried them, perhaps as good luck, or placed them in an honored spot in their home.

The details of goddess ritual varied from place to place, but its basic elements were surprisingly consistent. She was worshipped as the creator of the world, the bringer of all life. She was known as the Queen of Heaven and adored as the wisest of all counselors. She is often seen in relation to a son/brother/lover, who dies, is mourned, and is brought back to life.

The most ancient were honored for their life-giving qualities, but over the centuries various goddesses were claimed for other jurisdictions. Hera, for example, played many roles. She was He Era, the Earth, then Rhea, the pre-Hellenic Great Mother and the mother of the Greeks' Hera. As the primordial feminine trinity, Hera appears as Hebe, Hera, and Hecate— new moon, full moon, old moon; or virgin, mother, crone.[16]

Isis is a more familiar name. She was worshipped in Egypt and throughout the Greco Roman world as the Oldest of the Old, the Giver of Life and the One Who is All. Her cult moved across the known world, as far as the British Isles.[17]

"Cleopatra followed the precedent of Egyptian rulers in general and turned herself into a divinity. At an Alexandrian festival she 'assumed the robe of Isis and was addressed as the New Isis.'"[18] The cult of Isis arrived in Rome about 80 BCE and became the dominant religion. That dominance lasted about 400 years, fading with the growing strength of Christianity, though Isis herself took on traits of the Virgin Mary—or more likely it was the other way round.

**Sophia**

One name transcends the boundaries of Hellenistic philosophy, Platonism, Gnosticism and Christian theology. She is Sophia, or Wisdom.

Sophia may have been worshipped as a goddess, but her name and her mythology are deeply embedded in Gnostic writings, dating from around the first century CE. These portray not a single belief, but rather variations on a theme. She is usually identified with the *anima mundi,* or world soul. One source declares she was God's mother, or God's female soul, and the source of His power. The *Trattato Gnostico* also said she was God's mother and "the great revered Virgin in whom the Father was concealed from the beginning before He had created anything." She's also been held responsible for darkness and confusion in the heavenly realms.[19]

Another myth has her giving birth to a male spirit, Christ, and a female spirit called Achamoth. It was Achamoth who gave birth to the terrestrial world and sent "her own spirit in the form of the serpent Ophis" (the serpent was also called Christ) to teach men to eat the fruit of knowledge, despite Jehovah's prohibition.[20]

Still another says Sophia was Jesus's mother, "for she was the virgin of Light whose spirit entered into the body of Mary to conceive him." She was also identified with the goddess Isis-Hathor. And that's just a start.[21]

There are more myths about Sophia than there are letters in her name. What is known is that to the Greeks, Sophia represented female wisdom. In the 6th century CE Justinian I built a shrine in Constantinople to honor her: the Church of Holy Sophia (Hagia Sophia).[22] According to *The Penguin Book of Saints,* Catholic scholars deny Sophia was ever the Great Mother, or even a saint: "The church's name, they say—which means 'Holy Female Wisdom' in plain Greek— really meant 'Christ, the Word of God.'"[23]

No matter how you define Sophia, or which myth you choose to believe or not, note that in every instance she is a powerful female, possibly the mother of God himself. If Catholic scholars denied her that should come as no surprise. It is simply one more example of how religion and patriarchy unite to sever humanity's belief in a feminine force equal to that of the masculine.

"As soon as humans forged an agricultural society and began to build structured communities," writes historian Beth Allison Barr, "they also began to build hierarchies of power, designating some people as more worthy to rule than others."[24]

There is no single event or individual to blame for denying women the rights and humanity of males (though Eve's mythology proves useful). It is, probably, a loss built on the infinitely slow accretion of actions over eons; a change here, a denial there, an insignificant word choice in a minor rule that somehow altered perceptions. And inevitably, a law. Such things varied from place to place, but it's fair to say that as I write today, authoritarian patriarchy has been normalized across the globe.

# 3
# THE GODDESS DENIED

The world's ancient history, as we've seen, is obscure and subject to re-evaluation. We can point to the known writings of the ancients but they're a mere sliver of what has been lost. Too often they are fragments. Stephen Greenblatt writes in *The Swerve* that "At the end of the fifth century CE an ambitious literary editor known as Stobaeus compiled an anthology of prose and poetry by the ancient world's best authors: out of 1,430 quotations, 1,115 are from works that are now lost."[1]

Nothing is more obscure while declaring its truth than the book of Genesis. Scholars disagree over when Genesis was written, with some parts emerging around the year 1000 BCE, and others dated in the 6th and 5th centuries BCE. Little is sure, and for my purposes exactness is unnecessary. I'm here for the story.

Genesis is generally agreed to be a compilation of ancient tales and myths, drawn from the oral traditions of untold generations and possibly written sources. Who wrote it is also disputed, though Merlin Stone, in her book *When God Was a Woman* suggests it was the work of Levite priests attempting to maintain the legitimacy of their religion and society in an area of the world which had, for many thousands of years, worshipped the Great Mother Goddess.[2]

Certainly the goddess was the antithesis of early traditional Jewish belief, which held rigidly patriarchal and paternalistic views. The Old Testament reverberates with anti-woman diatribes. Women were considered only slightly better than slaves, and fierce punishment was decreed for those who failed to abide by the harsh demands of Jewish law.

The lines between the ancient, woman-centered goddess religion and the virulently male-dominated religion of the Old Testament were cleanly drawn in ancient Israel. Moses may have preached fidelity to a single god, but long after the Jews entered the promised land worship of the female deity maintained a powerful hold on the people of Israel and Judah. In I Kings 11:5 we see King Solomon turning away from the Jewish god to worship the goddess Ashtoreth. So did King Ahab, influenced, we are told, by his wife Jezebel, who followed the ancient religion of her parents and was brutally murdered for doing so.[3]

These lapses of devotion surely angered the priests, for the Old Testament is full of repeated exhortations to forsake the old idolatries and worship the single male deity.

It was because the priests were fighting this uphill battle, claims Stone, that the portrayal of Eve's role in the creation story became one of vengeful wrath, "betray[ing] the political intentions of those who first invented the myth." Stone writes that "in each sentence of the biblical myth, the original tenets of the goddess religion were attacked" and suggests that references to the sacred tree and serpent were allusions to the goddess that would clearly be understood by the people of that time. [4]

It's a tempting explanation. Certainly politics is almost as old as religion and if the men who compiled Genesis thought those tales could be manipulated to strengthen their position, they surely would not have hesitated.

One of the best-known goddess sects is that of a triple goddess, Demeter (virgin, mother, crone; or creator, preserver, destroyer) and her daughter Kore, later called Persephone. Demeter is thought to have originated in Crete, and as the Wise One and the Barley-Mother she played many roles over the centuries. In Greece she governed the sacred laws and the cycle of life and death. As the maiden Persephone, who myth says was abducted by Pluto (or Hades) to reign as Queen of the Underworld, she returned to earth each spring. This idea, however, is said to be "a late, artificial myth." [5]

The famous temple at Eleusis honored both Demeter and Persephone (and her son Dionysus) and held elaborate annual rites where initiates, guided by priestesses, were said to learn the secrets of life after death. Traces of the famous mystery school traditions have been found in southern Italy, and as far west as Spain.[6]

Some of Greece's most famous writers and thinkers were initiates who praised the Eleusis experience, with its promise of an afterlife. Those who underwent the experience were sworn to secrecy under penalty of death. Plato used cryptic language to describe the "blessed sight and vision" he had witnessed.[7] For Sophocles, "Thrice blessed are those among men who, after beholding these rites, go down to Hades. Only for Them is there life; all the rest will suffer an evil lot."[8]

Author Brian Muraresku, in *The Immortality Key,* takes a well-documented journey across Europe, searching out the source of the mystery in the "mystery religions" of the ancient past. Like every good detective story there are clues lost and clues found as the author's search carries him into new territory. It's a fascinating read that begins with the hunter-gatherers and the earliest beers, maybe tainted with ergot—a natural occurring fungus that grows on certain grains. "It contains a number of highly poisonous and psychoactive alkaloids, including lysergic acid (LSD), which was synthesized from the ergot fungus in 1938 by chemist, Albert Hoffmann."[9]

Muraresku suggests that ergot and other psychoactive plants may have been used in the Eleusian mysteries, and by other, older cults, to produce ecstatic and life-after-death experiences. It was the women of Eleusis who created the *kukeon*, the doctored beer or wine used in their famous ritual. For nearly 2000 years they offered the secrets of life after death to initiates, a process that meant two annual visits to the temple at Eleusis, fasting for several days, a 13-mile trek, and more. It was a major commitment of time and energy so I can only assume it offered great benefit to those who chose to partake.[10]

It's no surprise to learn that psychedelic drugs are suspected of playing a role, and new methods of analysis are suggesting truth in that idea. After all, Theocritus, a poet born c. 300 BCE, referred to Demeter as the poppy goddess, "Bearing sheaves and poppies in both hands. (Idyll vii.157) [11]

Muraresku spoke with archaeochemists and archaeobotanists who are now using their skills to test the dregs of ancient goblets, trying to learn what exactly it was that the goddess's women were giving the initiates. With the increasing cultivation of grapes, the favorite beverage shifted from beer to wine, and Dionysus, ruler of the grape harvest, vegetation, fertility, and festivities quickly became a favorite. "He was a prototype of Christ" writes Barbara Walker, "with a cult center at Jerusalem as well as nearly every other major city in the middle east." [12]

His worship took varied forms but wine was always the focus. Like the potions of Eleusis, the wines of Dionysus were doctored by his *maenads,* or female followers, with herbs said to induce trances and visions of the afterlife, for he also represented a link between the living and the dead. The Romans called him Bacchus and thought his festivals subversive due their mixing of genders and classes, among other issues. The popularity of these rites involving food and wine overlapped with the earliest Christians, and some suggest they were simply absorbed as the early Christian Eucharist.[13] More on this later.

Like all conquering nations the Romans made a habit of imposing their beliefs on conquered lands. A valley in southwest France was named by them for the goddess Diana in her persona as the huntress, for there was bountiful game. They raised a temple in her honor on a low hill near the center of the valley where all could see it. The remains of her temple have since been replaced by a small chapel. My husband and I spent several years in that valley and often visited the site. According to local gossip some residents still honored Diana—or the idea of Diana—and occasionally paid homage to her there.

"That," said a local, "is why they built the chapel."

To the Romans Diana was the Queen of Heaven; the Greeks called her Artemis. Her temple at Ephesus dates from the 4th century BCE. The Artemis/Diana cult was widespread and early Christians thought her their greatest rival. Even as late as the 15th century Tomas de Torquemada, Dominican friar and the first Grand Inquisitor, declared that Diana was the devil.[14] I could say the same about him.

How is it that the goddess, so long ensconced across the Mediterranean and into northern Europe, was replaced? There is no single theory. Gimbutus's research (see chapter 2) suggests that migrations from patriarchal cultures in the east and north, beginning as early as 3000 to 6000 BCE, or earlier, brought various herding tribes and powerful warriors into Europe, deeply changing existing societies.

Another view suggests that until the beginning of the Iron Age, about 3500 BCE, the male's role in conception was not understood. But once that knowledge was common currency, long-held belief in a goddess was inevitably diminished. Men could, for the first time, claim their own children—a first step in the concept of ownership. When property became the father's to use and bequeath, "The patriarchal family, with the oldest male at its head, became the economic, legal, political and moral unit of society. The gods, who had been mostly feminine, became great bearded patriarchs." This change, says Will Durant, was fatal to women, who became the property of their father or older brother to be sold in marriage "Marriage began as a form of the law of property, as a part of the institution of slavery."[15]

In c. 1750 BCE the famous law code of Babylonian King Hammurabi gave women many of the same advantages as men, setting examples other cultures would later imitate, allowing upper class women certain rights concerning property and business while "overall, women's sexual rights and freedom were sharply restricted. Eunuch chaperones and veiling became commonplace."[16] Further, an "adulterous wife and her paramour . . . were drowned, unless the husband, in his mercy, preferred to let his wife off by turning her almost naked into the streets."[17]

Leonard Shlain offers yet another point of view in *The Alphabet Versus the Goddess,* suggesting that the introduction of writing encouraged more linear, left brain, "masculine" thinking, which gradually subsumed the right brain's oral and visual dominance. This rewiring of our brains, he says, created an imbalance that continues to this day.

The Sumerians, one of the oldest known cultures, had a cuneiform system of writing that was used in Mesopotamia for about 2000 years, beginning as early as the fourth millennium BCE. They also had gods and goddesses, and cultures that look suspiciously patriarchal. But it was left to the early Hebrews to write the story of their invisible god, who revealed himself through the Word and forbade all images. It was those written laws and stories, suggests Shlain, that deliberately challenged the goddess and her images, and demeaned the power of women.[18]

Greek culture also embraced writing, though their use of images did not immediately diminish. Over time, however, we see the goddess's role dwindle to one of shared power with male gods, who increasingly became more powerful and odious. Zeus, greatest of all, was in the end nothing but a serial rapist.

And it was Zeus who gave us Pandora. She was to be the wife (not her choice of course) of a "slow-witted Titan, Epimetheus," whom Zeus entrusted with a lidded jar containing all the evils of the world. You know how it ends. Curious Pandora disobeyed the god's instructions and opened the jar. As punishment Zeus cursed Pandora and all her daughters forever with painful childbirth, and demanded subservience forthwith to fathers and husbands.[19]

This tale was related by the Greek poet Hesiod (c. 750–650 BCE), and is believed to be a retelling of an even older myth in which Pandora is the first woman created.[20] Could Pandora have inspired the biblical Eve? And why blame innocent young females for such world-destroying calamities?

As a child I learned a slightly different version of this tale. I found it again in volume 13–14 of *The Book of Knowledge*, adapted from Nathaniel Hawthorne's *Wonder Book*. I must have read it frequently because when I searched for the story in this now-ancient volume it fell open to the page. In this version Pandora was sent to live with a lonesome orphan, Epimetheus. On her arrival she saw a great box and asked what was in it. ". . . that is a secret," Epimetheus said, "the box was left here to be kept safely, and I do not myself know what it contains."

Curious, Pandora opens the box. Out fly "a crowd of ugly little shapes, with bats' wings, looking abominably spiteful, and armed with terribly long stings in their tails." Both versions conclude with one tiny creature exiting last. This was "a sunny, happy little creature" who begged to be let out. Its name was Hope.[21]

Pandora's story may be older than Eve's, but Eve had better publicists, and it is she who has been endlessly referenced by men wishing to blame women.

# 4

# MEETING EVE

I suppose I learned the story of Eve from a Sunday school teacher. Probably I doubted it, for I was a doubting child, curious and questioning. When I was young my mother and I attended the local Methodist church fairly regularly. She wasn't overtly religious but she believed in God and thought I should too; thus Sunday school. My father, growing up in a strict Quaker family, said he'd had enough religion to last a lifetime and except on special occasions was never seen in church.

Eventually I learned there were two versions of Eve's creation. The first says simply "in the image of God he created him, male and female he created them."[1] That's a perfectly adequate account and it's too bad it wasn't left that way. But 25 verses later we find a second version, the one most of us are taught:

"And the Lord God . . . took one of his ribs and closed up the flesh instead thereof; and the rib, which the Lord God had taken from man, he made into a woman, and brought her unto the man."[2]

As the tale continues Adam and Eve enter Eden, the paradise created for them by their maker. Here, encouraged by a talking serpent,

Eve eats fruit from the tree of knowledge, forbidden them by God. Now awakened—though what that means exactly we are left to surmise—she urges Adam to do the same. An angry God appears, curses the serpent, chastises his two creations, and tells Eve she will henceforth bear children in pain and sorrow, and that Adam must labor. They are then summarily tossed out of Eden to make their way on mortal Earth.

Though Adam participated in eating the forbidden fruit and is chastised by God, it's Eve alone who becomes the putative cause of humanity's expulsion from Paradise. And with a female as the scapegoat for all humanity, perhaps it's no wonder we are where we are.

I have no idea how this fable affected me. I can guess, but I have no proof. Knowledge does not always come to us in a recognizable form. Sometimes it stabs us obliquely; a comment that on one day might not affect us, on another will mark a critical turning point. Or it may slide silently into our subconscious leaving us to discover, if we're lucky, a lesson we can use. If Eve's story was a broadside meant to leave me trembling with guilt, I failed to recognize it. But that doesn't mean I wasn't influenced.

I don't know if my mother would have reaffirmed the Bible's content regarding Eve. We certainly never talked about it. Born in 1910 she remained, in many ways, a 19th-century woman living a 20th-century life, and the "second wave" feminist revolution that arrived when she was in her sixties felt uncomfortable and strange. It felt a little strange to me too. I was born in 1941, and I remember the post war years as full of promise.

I was not aware that Black people in the south, including servicemen who had fought in World War II, were not allowed to vote. Or that U.S. citizens of Japanese descent were locked away in internment camps for the duration of the war. Nor was I aware that women who had worked in factories or offices during the war, supporting themselves and perhaps their families for the first time, were told they were no longer needed—their jobs belonged to men. I neither knew nor was I taught that many women resisted that idea. Women who had spent the last four or five years building planes and working at other war-related jobs returned, often reluctantly, to the home.

They were encouraged in this by government propaganda and advertising; by the growing influence of radio shows—including daily soap operas—and movies, and by the endless articles pumped out by women's magazines. When television entered our homes in the early 50s, there was increasing pressure to conform to the housewifely role. *Father Knows Best* a weekly sitcom, aired on radio beginning in 1949. In 1954 it moved to television where it ran for six seasons—and many years in reruns—and became one of America's most popular shows. The father of this ideal family was portrayed as gentle and wise. Mother was the reasonable and patient housewife, played by Jane Wyatt, who always wore dresses and looked beautiful.[3]

During television's early years only three broadcast network channels were available, and viewing them depended on where one lived and the kind of reception available, typically a rooftop antenna. As a result of those limited choices, popular shows like *Father Knows Best* were familiar to most Americans. They set the standards—deliberately or not—for all of us. The network's nightly news shows served the same purpose and were governed by the FCC fairness doctrine, adopted in 1949 and abolished in 1987.

Eve would not have been surprised by this push into housewifely adoration. As the great transgressor she too was confined to a nonspeaking role, one that directed her to follow Adam's lead, make no decisions, and never venture into the wider world. Her walk-on part kept her at home, but she still contributed to the '50s zeitgeist, emerging in uncounted ways throughout my youth, always affirming the role I was expected to play.

And I listened. I was a shy only child living in a small, conservative town, and when as a young teenager I received a copy of *Betty Cornell's Teenage Popularity Guide,* I read it from cover to cover. It held every 1950s motif and meme, including how to set a table and be a good hostess. Wanting to fit in I absorbed it without question.[4]

Somewhat surprisingly though, I was not convinced that only marriage would make my life worthwhile. I was curious about the world (maps had always decorated my rooms) and I wanted "more," though what that might be I had no idea. In my teens I declared that I would not marry until 25, an idea that was considered extreme by most of my high school classmates, many of whom married soon after graduation. A few of us, though, resisted the push into matrimony and refused to think of ourselves as old maids when not married by 21.

# 5
## UNREST DISTURBS THE FORCE

The words of the ancient Hebrew texts were certainly detrimental to the cause of women, and that was not about to improve. Perhaps a thousand years after they borrowed or invented the story of Eve and wrote the history of their people, Jesus of Nazareth was born in Bethlehem, to become the heart of a new and powerful religion.

With the birth and death of Jesus and the spread of his teachings, the whole of Judaic history and mythology, along with its patriarchal structure, arose wherever Christianity was preached. Despite that, many, maybe even most of the early adopters were well-to-do women who turned their homes to "house churches," sharing Jesus's message of love and compassion. Female influence grew in sects pursuing a more egalitarian, even feminist version of the new church.

Karen Jo Torjesen, in *When Women Were Priests* tells us "the earliest Christian communities, which—inspired by Jesus's radical teaching and example—were much more egalitarian than the society at large." So these Christians, "familiar with the authority and leadership role of the [Roman] female head of household, would have perceived women's leadership within the church as not only acceptable but natural. The early church's specific leadership functions posed no barriers to women."[1]

Between the first and fifth centuries CE the new religion struggled for dominance over the long-ingrained influence of the goddess, as it continued to spread across the known world. In 250 the Roman Emperor Decius, in an attempt to restore the polytheism of the ancient world, instituted the first persecution of Christians by issuing an edict requiring everyone in the empire to sacrifice to him. This was an attempt to ensure loyalty, and wasn't aimed particularly at Christians, though some refused to comply "to such a 'demon'" and thus were punished. The edict lasted only a year.[2]

A "Great Persecution" beginning in CE 303, lasted ten years and is considered the worst of such periods, as churches were destroyed, scriptures burned, and Christians tortured and executed. About half of all Christian martyrdoms occurred during this period.[3] However, the belief that thousands of Christians were martyred has been proven by history to be an exaggeration. As Catherine Nixey reports in *The Darkening Age*, "We know of no government-led persecution for the first 250 years of Christianity with the exception of Nero's—and Nero . . . persecuted everyone."[4]

I have to admit that reading this surprised me. I suspect my ideas about persecution were encouraged not by our Methodist minister or my Sunday School teachers, but by the movies I saw growing up in the '50s. Blockbuster movies like *Quo Vadis, Ben Hur,* and *The Greatest Story Ever Told,* wowed Americans around the country with technicolor scenes of the early Roman Empire. Brave Christians and strong Roman gladiators shared winning roles, and at least one handsome gladiator would convert to the new religion before the movie ended.[5]

During the first 300 years of Christianity Church leaders and followers continued to argue over ritual and the divinity of Christ—a disagreement the Nicean Council in 325 CE failed to end, though it affirmed Jesus was a divine being. Other arguments came and went, far too numerous and complex to dwell on here. But slowly, irretrievably, a single, "authorized" Christianity came to dominate, and belief in the goddess weakened. So did the influence of women, which succumbed to both the fierce patriarchal society of Rome's empire, and the growing bureaucracy of the established Catholic Church.

In 330 CE, Constantine the Great, the first Christian emperor, established "new Rome" in Constantinople, and gave Christianity the blessing of governmental authority. Polytheism, however, continued to resist. The famous temple at Eleusis was finally destroyed in 396 CE though, writes Durant, schools in Athens continued for awhile to teach the old knowledge: "Plato, Aristotle, Zeno. (Epicurus was outlawed, and became a synonym for atheist.)"[6]

Author Brian Muraresku suggests that the millennia-long practice of adding herbs and other plant additives to the wine used in important rituals to provoke mystical insight, like those at Eleusis, might have also been used by the women who opened their homes to the new religion. During the first few hundred years after Jesus's death the new religion and the ancient ones could not help but interact. It would be no surprise if the effective rituals of the gods and goddess worshipers were adopted by the earliest Christians. Muraresku asks, "Was it their [women's] ability to manufacture a mind-altering Eucharist that kept the ecstasy alive in the house churches and underground catacombs of the new faith?"[7]

I don't know if early Christian women adopted such rituals but they certainly would have had the capability. It had been passed on from one generation to the next for centuries, each adding to the store of knowledge. The promise of "instant immortality" had been used by the women at Eleusis and the followers of Dionysus for centuries.

Which brings us to the pagan continuity hypothesis which suggests that the early Christians deliberately integrated their new stories with already popular ones. For example, the Church set about condoning or transforming popular pagan rites by conflating them with Christian traditions, in order to attract new worshipers. In this way saints replaced gods; Isis and Horus became Mary and Jesus; the feast of the purification of Isis became the Feast of the Nativity. The Saturnalia became Christmas celebrations; the Floralia (after the Roman goddess of spring) was now the Pentecost, and the ancient festival of the dead became All Souls Day. The resurrection of Attis became the resurrection of Christ. And pagan altars were rededicated.[8]

Attis deserves our attention because his myth, like several others, closely resembles that of Jesus. Attis was originally attached to Cybele, the Great Mother of the Gods, brought to Rome from Phrygia in 204 BCE. The god Attis was "tolerated" by the Romans and was typical of many gods born to virgins. His mother was Nana, the Great Mother's earthly incarnation, who birthed him on December 25th. He was crucified on a pine tree and was resurrected three days later as the Most High God, bringing salvation to mankind. His body was eaten by his worshippers in the form of bread.[9]

While the goddess was being absorbed into new, Christianized versions of older pagan rituals and traditions, her temples and statues were being destroyed, along with much of the classical world, including the works of ancient philosophers, poets and writers. These "demons" and their "disgusting monuments and statues," declared various church leaders, must be completely abolished. In fact, writes Catherine Nixey, during the fourth and fifth centuries "the Christian Church demolished, vandalized and melted down a simply staggering quantity of art . . . A temple widely considered to be the most magnificent in the entire empire was leveled. . . faces were mutilated, hands and limbs were hacked off, gods were decapitated."[10]

The Christian destruction of ancient temples and knowledge, and the killing of those who refused to convert to the new single-god religion, must have confounded those to whom the worship of multiple gods and goddesses had been common practice and a way of life for millennia. The idea that "my god or goddess is better than yours," did not appear to exist.

"Augustine later marveled at the fact that the pagans were able to worship many different gods without discord," writes Nixey, "while the Christians, who worshipped only one, splintered into countless warring factions."[11]

The persecution of early Christians by Rome and its soldiers and rioters mirrors the later murdering and destruction of polytheists and their monuments by Christian "thugs." Thus do disagreements over ideas and questions no one can answer, become motivation for anger, resentment and murder.

One well-documented example can stand for all: Hypatia of Alexandria (c. 350-415 CE) taught philosophy and astronomy, was a brilliant mathematician and one of the most respected figures in Alexandria. Unfortunately her strange symbols and astrolabes were thought by some to be tools of the devil. And despite being known and esteemed for years throughout the city and beyond, she was waylaid on her way home, and blocked by "a multitude of believers in God." She was pulled from her chariot, and after being dragged into a nearby church she was brutally murdered, her body flayed, then torn apart and burned on a pyre.[12]

The long dead have no need of our sympathy, but we may weep for the lost knowledge and insights that might now be ours, had they not been destroyed in the magnificent museum and library of Alexandria, said to house hundreds of thousands of volumes, as well as uncounted other libraries and private collections. Earthquakes and wars took some of the remaining temples and the art and documents they contained. More might remain for us to walk through, admire, and learn from, had they not been pounded into dust because they honored a hated Other.

Meanwhile, the story of Eve as the "first sinner" was being diligently spread throughout the Mediterranean and beyond. Eve would become the capstone of the new church's increasingly misogynist views.

When Emperor Constantine died in 337 he left his empire divided between three sons and two nephews. Naturally, civil war resulted. Thirty years later, in 361, the new Roman Emperor Julian (a nephew of Constantine the Great) backed away from the Christianity of his childhood and turned in his '20s toward a neoplatonic philosophy. While studying in Athens he was initiated into the Eleusinian mysteries and as Emperor he attempted to revive polytheism, issuing an edict stating that all religions were equal before the law. Julian avoided executing Christians during his reign, but tightened restrictions on the Church. He died three years later in 363 when pierced by a spear, a victim of continuous war.[13] The new Emperor Jovian reestablished Christianity throughout the empire.

The official Roman Church, which was firmly established by 400 AD, had already made it clear that women were not welcome to officiate, or play any important role in the church hierarchy. This despite the fact that it was women who had been the major force in developing and maintaining the house churches, and who, supported by Paul through his many letters, extended the reach of Jesus's teaching.

The clashes and confusion that worried this early period continued through the fourth, fifth, and sixth centuries, as the Roman Empire, which had supplied structure and unity to much of the known world for 400 years, was overtaken by numerous plagues (killing 5–10 thousand daily at one point), famines, invasions, erratic leadership and weakened and failing governments. The western Roman Empire, founded in Rome by Augustus in 27 BCE., officially ended in 476 CE when the emperor Romulus Augustus was deposed. The eastern empire, led by Zeno in Constantinople, held on a little longer. [14]

Rome's new weakness naturally encouraged its enemies, and Europe entered a centuries-long struggle between various barbarian tribes including Goths, Visigoths, Ostrogoths, Huns, and the Vandals who sacked Rome in 455.[15] "Pope Gelasius (c. 480 CE) described great regions of northern Italy as almost denuded of the human species."[16] Rome itself went from 1,500,000 souls to 300,000 in a hundred years.

But let us return to women, who shared in the struggles and perilousness of this period. Unless they had power or wealth, and few did, their lives must have been in a fairly continual state of upheaval, or worse. The failure of crops and resulting starvation, the disintegrating social and governmental structures, along with plague and constant warring, would have made life hell for the average person, male or female. And with the rooting out and annihilation of the goddess and the strengthening of a patriarchal church, women lost an emotional and spiritual ally at a time they needed her most.

# 6

# THE EARLY CHURCH

What women need, said the early Church fathers, is to obey their husbands. This old dictum veils both fear of the goddess and of woman herself, her misunderstood bodily functions, her ability to give birth, and her facility in seducing a man away from worship and toward marriage and family. (The early church stressed virginity for both sexes.)

Yet St. Thomas Aquinas called Mary Magdalen the "apostle of the apostles" and modern scholars speculate that she was Jesus's most valued disciple; some posit they were married. Experts on Jewish traditions declare it almost unheard of for a man of that period not to be married, and some gnostic texts quote Jesus referring to Mary as his wife. Clearly, he was more sympathetic to women than Old Testament writers; he treated them as equals. That perceived equity is no doubt why women were among his earliest followers.

Whether Jesus believed in women's equality or not, that idea failed to impress the men who came after him. It was Paul, writing to Timothy (2:11) who said, "Let a woman learn in silence with all submissiveness. I permit no woman to teach or to have authority over men; she is to keep silent. For Adam was formed first, then Eve."[1]

And it was Paul, preaching to the Corinthians, who said "let the women keep silence in the churches . . . they are commanded to be under obedience." Historian Beth Allison Barr, in her book *The Making of Biblical Womanhood,* defends Paul's words, writing that he was attempting to placate the patriarchal Romans in order to protect early Christians.

Barr is clear in her belief that Paul was supportive of women, and in fact he did work with ministries that included many women, some even as deacons. Paul was addressing the people of Corinth, who lived under Roman law, as did the Christians of the city. It would be astonishing if Corinthian men did not assume women's subservience and include it as part of the budding church's doctrine. Barr and others believe Paul was attempting to correct this idea." Paul is not limiting women's leadership . . . he supports their ministries."[2]

If that was the case, his words were not enough. Roman patriarchy was too strong and too punishing to be demolished by activist women, earnest leaders, and a struggling new, anti-polytheism religion. And it was Peter—the rock upon whom the Catholic Church is built—who said "Likewise, you wives, be submissive to your husbands."[3]

Given what follows that's pretty mild. Speaking with all the authority of the growing church the early Fathers, men like St. Jerome and Tertullian, firmly established the defectiveness, incompetence and innate evil of women. And it's all Eve's fault.

"Do you not know that you are Eve?" wrote the influential Tertullian (CE 155–c. 220)."You are the Devil's gateway. . . How easily you destroyed man, the image of God. Because of the death which you brought upon us, even the Son of God had to die."[4]

Not only should women feel guilty for the sin of Eve; women should feel guilty for being women. Only by not being women, that is, by never marrying, never having children, always remaining a virgin, could women hope to attain unity with the Lord.

"As long as woman is for birth and children," wrote St. Jerome (342–347 CE),"she is different from man as body is from soul. But when she wishes to serve Christ more than the world, then she will cease to be a woman and will be called man."[5]

So hateful were women that they must give up their identity to be saved: "She who does not believe is a woman and should be designated by the name of her sex, whereas she who believes progresses to perfect manhood, to the measure of the adulthood of Christ. She then dispenses with the name of her sex, the seductiveness of youth, the garrulousness of old age."[6]

There is the recurrent theme," writes Mary Daly in *The Church and the Second Sex*, "that by faith a woman transcends the limitations imposed by her sex. It would never occur to the Fathers to say the same of a man. . . there is an assumption that all that is of dignity and value in human nature is proper to the male sex. There is an identification of 'male' and 'human.'"[7]

The mental and physical inadequacies the Fathers so deplored was in fact female reality. But it was a reality produced by the conditions of a woman's life, not the other way round. Roman law stated that "Wives legally had to submit to the authority of their husbands; unmarried women had to submit to the authority of their fathers or nearest male relatives; women could not own property or run businesses in their own right; women could not conduct legal or financial transactions without a man acting on their behalf."[8]

Women were isolated from society, uneducated, and trained only in the duties of the household. Married young at the command of their father (who undoubtedly profited if he could), they had no legal rights, could not divorce, and in fact were little better than slaves to their husbands. This life of enforced mindlessness surely lent support to the early Fathers' idea of female incompetence and insignificance. But let us not be too eager to forgive.

There is not just disdain in these writings, there is an element of real hatred and an almost pathological fear of females. It is one thing to deplore woman's part in the original sin, it is quite another to portray her as the most harmful among all savage beasts, as St. John Chrysostom did (347– 407 CE).[9]

What irritated these men beyond all rational understanding was female sexuality. The whole biological role of women was considered frightening and somehow unfortunate—women were unclean creatures whose own enjoyment of carnal pleasure seduced men away from the celibate road to salvation. Marriage was a salve to those without the willpower to resist. Feminine beauty was a snare to be concealed, for it led to wantonness. Women were despised, ignoble creatures; "how vile, how shameful" were their caresses.

These ideas, expressed so uncompromisingly by men who had great authority in the early church, became intricately entwined with the Christian religion, and their hold on the minds of women and men remained intact through the following tumultuous centuries. While empires waned and collapsed, borders changed hands or disappeared, invaders invaded and residents fled, the church endured, and so did its negative and paternalistic view of women.

Historian Rosalind Miles tells us that despite the major religions preaching love for all, including women, "the five major belief systems of Judaism, Buddhism, Confucianism, Christianity, and Islam by their very nature insisted on the inferiority of women and demanded their subjection to values and imperatives devised to promote the supremacy of men."[10]

And what this supremacy offers is power. And apparently power, once attained, is very difficult to relinquish, especially to a creature considered inferior. Adam, despite taking part in the wicked act, suffers no censure and always comes first.

# 7

## THE MIDDLE AGES

Historians generally divide the years between the 5th and the 17th century into two parts. The earliest, after Rome's fall, is considered the Dark Ages, so named by Petrarch. It was a period when the Catholic church dominated throughout Europe, a church often corrupted by ambitious popes and avaricious priests. Resistance to the strictures of the church encouraged heresies, magic, and sorcery because the miserable, the hungry, and the ill seek whatever remedies they can find to end their misery. At first the church responded to such antics with fines and general leniency, but as we shall see, that didn't last.

No matter what you call these years, they represent a confusing, jumbled time cursed with war, plague, and famine; with multiple characters creating a good deal of havoc having little to do with this narrative.

Two events, however, are worth noting. The first is the advent of Charlemagne (768–814 CE), who together with his predecessor Pepin II, managed to weld disparate regions of Gaul into the single state of France. He then enlarged his kingdom by subduing invading Saxons and Slavs and conquering part of Italy. He was crowned as Charles the Augustus, Roman Emperor by Pope Leo in 800, an unexpected honor that he did not welcome. But Charlemagne managed to bring order out of chaos, at least temporarily, for a large portion of western Europe.[1]

Also crucial to this period was the growing influence of the Moors, who emerged as a force during Muhammad's life (c. 520–632 CE). From Islam's beginnings in Mecca, on the Arabian Peninsula, the Moors proselytized and fought to instill Islamic beliefs across the Mediterranean world. In 711 they invaded the Iberian Peninsula and by the end of the 8th century the Umayyad Caliphate extended from Iberia in the west to the Indus River in (now) Pakistan. The Moors ruled Spain for about 400 years, much of the time in conflict with the Christians, until only a part of southern Spain was held. The fall of Granada in 1492 ended their rule.[2]

Muslim women in this early period were granted rights most other women at that time lacked, including the right to choose her own spouse, retain her family name, divorce, hold property, and inherit. Indeed, Mohammad's first wife was a successful businesswoman. The Qur'an is said to promote spiritual and moral equality between men and women. While living in Turkey I read most of the Qur'an (an English translation) and found nothing unusual or outrageous (although at iv 34, "The wife should recognize the superior intelligence and therefore superior authority of the male; she must obey her husband . . .") [3]

It is a religious text like others, setting out guidelines on how to live according to God's wishes, as told to Muhammed. The Qur'an does ask women to dress modestly and not display their bodies, but it says nothing about needing to wear black from head to toe, with only a slit for eyes. In fact "we find Muslim women moving about freely and unveiled in the Islam of [Mohammed's] time, and a century thereafter."[4]

However, in 649 CE, seventeen years after Muhammad's death, Islam recognized the authority of the Sharia, a complex legal system that, among other things, required women to remain veiled and segregated, and prescribes covering the body in public: specifically, from the neck to the ankles, and above the elbow. This decision is still haunting women in multiple countries, about which more later.[5]

Women across the Middle East and southern Europe had for centuries covered their heads when outside their homes. There were reasons to do so, including protecting oneself from the sun and ever-present dirt and dust. I suspect it was a habit that became a tradition that became a rule set by men. "The earliest known recorded reference to veiling, the act of covering one's hair with cloth, comes from a 13th-century BCE Assyrian text that describes the practice as reserved for aristocratic women and forbidden for prostitutes and those of lower social status, who were punished if they were caught in head coverings." [6]

As time passes, habits and culture often override religion, even when it's practiced religiously. Early Islam, like early Christianity, was inconsistent in many areas of life, including head covering, and disagreements persist to this day, especially between Shia and Sunni. In the West at least, most Islamic women today are free to choose whether to wear the hijab, and Catholic women no longer need to cover their heads for mass.

The origin of why head coverings became an issue will probably always be a mystery, but even western women, into the 19th and early 20th centuries, seldom left home without a stylish hat, bonnet, or scarf on their heads.

Islam and Christianity share many beliefs and honor many of the same people, but Islamic women appear to have escaped Christianity's depiction of Eve. The two miscreants are said by Islam to have repented of their deed and been forgiven. Unfortunately some Islamic leaders fail to recognize that fact, or do so but choose to ignore it (see Chapter 25). Another reminder that holding power is a potent motivator for continuing to hold power.

Islamic culture flourished from the 8th to the 13th century, developing in both sexes a high degree of scientific, mathematic, and artistic skill that far surpassed most of Europe at the time. The library at Cairo is said to have contained over 100,000 volumes.

## The Late Middle Ages

The 11th through the 17th centuries in Europe are commonly referred to as the High or Late Middle Ages. It was a period of gradual improvement for most, as both secular and ecclesiastic rule solidified, providing dependable structures for the population. But it was also a time of strife and sadness that was surely hardest on women who suffered the heavy weight of care giving. The Great Famine (1315–1317) is estimated to have killed 30 to 60 percent of Europe's population. This was followed by the Bubonic Plague, which struck north Africa and Eurasia in 1346 and was carried into Europe the following year. The terror eased in 1351, but outbreaks continued into the 19th century. During the worst of the pandemic it's estimated that 70 to 300 million people died.[7]

The decimated population lived predominantly on the land or in small villages, usually part of a fief overseen by a lord or other noble. Agriculture was the main source of income, though home-based industries like spinning and beer making contributed to the general economy. Guilds, associations of craftsmen of all kinds, developed as a way of protecting workers interests. Over time long-standing guilds often morphed into aspects of city government, essentially controlling local economies.

Barbara Tuchman in *A Distant Mirror* writes that the 12th and 13th centuries were "stimulated by commerce" and "great bursts of development" that included the compass, the mechanical clock, the spinning wheel and treadle loom, the windmill and the watermill."[8]

During this period the Catholic church remained dominant, touching every aspect of people's lives. "Christianity," she writes "was a matrix of medieval life. . . It governed birth, marriage, and death, sex, and eating, made the rules for law and medicine, gave philosophy and scholarship their subject matter. Membership in the church was not a matter of choice; it was compulsory and without alternative, which gave it a hold not easy to dislodge."[9]

Pope Clement V had settled in Avignon in Provence to live in luxury. Tuchman quotes Petrarch, writing in the 1340s: "I am living in the 'Babylon of the West,' where prelates feast at 'licentious banquets' and ride on 'snow white horses 'decked in gold, fed on gold, soon to be shod in gold if the Lord does not check this slavish luxury.'"[10]

It was during this period that the cult of Mary emerged and slowly began to spread. She had previously been little noticed by the Church, though veneration was sanctioned in 431 when she was officially acknowledged as the Mother of God. But it wasn't until the 12th and 13th centuries that Mary became the focus of religious fervor, and an intercessor against plague and other troubles. "Women were considered the snare of the Devil, while at the same time the cult of the Virgin made one woman the central object of love and adoration."[11] Her growing honor soon reflected on noble and upper-class women who became objects of (fictional) honor, devotion, and courtly love.

Chivalrous knights and roaming troubadours traveled the roads composing and reciting love poems to wealthy damsels who were frequently left alone by their rightful lords and no doubt found the attention flattering. Marriage, especially among the nobility, was a financial arrangement and love almost never entered the picture. Romance was a new idea, and this courtly devotion from afar, with heroic deeds of valor designed to win hearts, and with its overlay of piety and honor it was no doubt an exciting and welcome change.

It was encouraged by powerful women like Eleanor of Aquitaine; Marie, Countess of Champagne, and Ermengard, Viscountess of Narbonne, all of whom frequently entertained and encouraged troubadours at their courts, most in southern France. The earliest stories and myths about King Arthur and the Holy Grail appeared during this period and lent popularity and credence to the ideas of chivalry. So did writers such as Dante, Malory, Chrétien de Troyes, and Marie de France.

It may have been a relief after living with the fierce strictures of the Roman Church for women to suddenly find themselves the objects of "courtly love," with its principles of honor, devotion, and protecting the ladies. But again, the benefit—if benefit it be—accrued only to upper-class and noble women. This emanation of feminism may have been welcomed, but it couldn't last, and didn't.

A 13th or 14th century woman has been stuck in a back closet of my brain for some time. She isn't real, she has no name, but I see her clearly in my mind's eye. Since I can't seem to banish her I'll tell what little I know of her story.

She is seated in a small stone room. The only wall my imagination will conjure is curved so perhaps it is a tower room, the kind of room where romantic prisoners or beautiful girls like Rapunzel were held. But this woman is neither beautiful nor ugly. She is a woman of pleasant visage who had the advantage—or misfortune—to be born into a wealthy and titled family.

The clothes she wears are finely loomed and trimmed with touches of velvet and silk. On her head she wears a gold circlet from which hang triple layers of silk cloth. Her sleeves are full and long and because she is alone she has pinned them back to prevent their tangling in the silk thread that travels through the needle she holds. In front of her is a large embroidery frame on a stand.

This work is her life, for she is indeed captive to a husband who married her only for the wealth and title she brought to their union. She has no children. The marriage was arranged by her father who benefited financially and socially. Her husband, an unexceptional noble with powerful connections, had and has other women. He allows her morning rides when weather permits and plays his husbandly role when presenting her to prominent guests on the rare occasions they visit or dine. Otherwise, her life is confined to this room and the bed that awaits her sleepless nights. Her chief happiness arrives in early morning when she feeds and names the crows and other birds who arrive with the sun at her window ledge.

She has a servant who brings her meals, a younger woman who gave up curtsying a few years ago and who seldom speaks. My lady would like to converse, to know about this other life, but the servant has been ordered to repel such advances.

Like so many whose lives are cramped and bordered by the strict rules of a society in which women play a minor role, she has accepted her fate. She survives by drawing strength from the birds, her religion, and rare visits from a bishop who hears her confession and accepts her finely embroidered altar cloths and vestments to distribute among his churches.

# 8

# WOMEN'S VOICES BEGIN TO RISE

In the introduction to her book *The Fourth Estate,* Shulamith Shahar tells us that "from the eleventh century onward, contemporary writers repeatedly describe society as made up of three classes: Worshippers, Warriors and Workers." This society is said to be "horizontal, purposeful, and harmonious," a society that reflects divine will. But by the 12th century that society had become vertical, composed of "regular and secular clergy" from the pope to the lowest priest. "Warriors" were dukes, counts, knights and sergeants, and the Worker class was made up "of free peasants, serfs, merchants, notaries, physicians, various artisans, beggars and thieves."

Women, when classified at all, were defined by their socio-economic and marital status (maiden, wife, widow). Shahar quotes Etienne Fougeres' *Livre de Manieres* [*Book of Manners*] written in the second half of the 12th century, describing the faults and sins of women as "vanity, pride, greed, promiscuity, gluttony, drunkenness, bad temper, fickleness, and more." Women, said Fougeres, may not take part in assemblies, public office, councils, etc., and must devote themselves to their domestic functions.[1]

Two hundred years later, writes Tuchman, women in the 14th century, both noble and peasants, found "equality of function, if not of status, thrust on them by circumstance." It wasn't unusual for a woman whose husband was away to take charge of his fief, his business, his farm, or his hovel. She did what was needed: managed any workers, kept accounts, and ran the household whether large or small. Some women maintained positions as artisans and held monopolies in areas like textiles and other home-related businesses, and might have been members of women's guilds. Some of these skills included hat and wig making, weaving wool and flax, jewelry making, and other delicate work.[2]

But women in the Middle Ages were not exempt from heavy work and heavy loads, and thinking of that I was reminded of the women I saw in eastern Turkey during our year-long stay in the late 1990s.

"I watched them guiltily from the comfort of our rented car, bending low to pick cotton, squatting with a plastic tub doing laundry, guiding a horse or donkey with a plow, scattering seed, cutting grapes, beating raw wool clean in a stream, herding cows and goats, stooping with loaded backs, overseeing flocks of sheep. . . . Rarely do they waste time or exhibit idle hands. Two girls tending sheep beside the road were typically doing double duty; one knitted as she walked, the other spun wool onto a traditional spindle."[3]

Such scenes would surely have been seen across Europe during the Middle Ages. Women's work supported families, villages, and regions, without which economies and societies would collapse. This is almost never acknowledged; women's strength, discipline, and determination have always been overlooked and undervalued.

Though Christianity officially regarded both sexes as equals in the face of God, there's no question reality painted a different portrait. A 12th century ecclesiastical author, Abbot Hugh of the Flavigny monastery, described the metaphysical hierarchy this way: "Peter and Paul, the other Apostles, the saintly hermits, the perfect monks living in communities, good bishops, good laymen, women."[4]

"Woman was the Church's rival," writes Tuchman, "the temptress, the distraction, the obstacle to holiness, the Devil's decoy. Theology being the work of males, original sin was traced to [Eve] the female." Preachers in general "denounced women on the one hand for being the slaves of vanity and fashion, for monstrous headdresses and the 'lascivious and carnal provocation' of their garments, and on the other hand for being over-industrious, too occupied with children and housekeeping, too earthbound to give due thought to divine things."[5] In other words, you can't win for losing.

As the Church established monasteries for Christian men and later, nunneries for women, it opened up avenues for even the poorest male peasant to learn to read and, if fortunate to become a priest or even, though rarely, bishop. This was not an option for women in convents; in almost every case women who took the veil were high born, and the only upward mobility was to become a mother superior or reverend mother, though a few of those held considerable power. Outside the convents noble women could acquire power and wealth, if they were lucky, through inheritance. And more than a few became mystics, poets, or writers, finding ways to express themselves by closely aligning with the church, which gave them credence they were otherwise denied. Their identities, in most cases, have not come down to us, but a few made names for themselves and left records.

I've always been drawn to biographies and autobiographies of independent female travelers, especially when that travel involves breaking barriers. I don't remember when or how I came across the English Christian mystic, Margery Kemp (c. 1373–c. 1438) and her spiritual autobiography *The Book of Margery Kempe.* But her persistence in traversing what were then vast distances with rough or nonexistent accommodations was irresistible.

She was born Margery Burnham in Norfolk, where her father was a merchant, mayor, and Member of Parliament. She married John Kempe and they had at least 14 children. Kemp was of course, an orthodox Catholic. After the birth of her first child she suffered a health crisis that lasted almost eight months. During that time she reported being harassed by devils and demons and had visitations and conversations with Jesus, Mary, God, and other religious figures. She was known for constantly weeping, which increased during her pilgrimage to Jerusalem when "she had such great compassion and such great pain at seeing the place of Our Lord's pain." Her crying, moaning, and falling to the ground "continued for many years, once a month or a week, sometimes daily or many times a day, sometimes in church or in the street or in her chamber or in the fields."[6]

Apparently anything could set her off though she tried to contain it, and her visions frightened others, including the clergy. "Margery Kemp," writes Tuchman in *A Distant Mirror*, "was obviously an uncomfortable neighbor to have, like all those who cannot cancel the painfulness of life."[7]

Kemp was intensely devoted to Christ, prayed often, and wore a hair shirt. In 1413, soon after her father's death, she left her husband to make a pilgrimage to the Holy Land. She traveled with other pilgrims, walking most of the way to Venice (about 950 miles on today's roads). After staying 13 weeks in that city, splendid and rich at the time, she joined a voyage to Jerusalem and visited sites in the Holy land, sometimes with others, sometimes on her own. Returning to Italy, she traveled to Assisi and Rome before returning to England in 1415. Two years later she made the long pilgrimage to Santiago de Compostela in Spain.

As she journeyed Kemp sometimes stayed with local and often well-known clerics, while at the same time she irritated many with her crying outbursts and was frequently accused of heresy. On her return from Spain the mayor of Leicester, for instance, accused her of being a "cheap whore, a lying Lollard,"[8] and threatened her with prison. She was eventually brought to trial in Leicester and imprisoned for three weeks.

After her husband died in 1431 she continued her travels. Marjory Kemp may have been ignorant and uneducated, but no one can say she wasn't dedicated, brave and determined. Nearly everything known about Kemp comes from her dictated book. Lost for centuries, it may be the first English autobiography. A manuscript found in a private library in 1934 is the only surviving copy; it's now in the British Library. In 2020 a statue in her honor was erected on the entrance to a medieval bridge in Oroso, Spain, on the pilgrimage trail she walked to Santiago de Compostela.

During her travels Kemp sought out the important Christian mystic and writer Julian of Norwich, England (1343–c.1416). Almost nothing is known of Julian's life, not her real name, nor her birth date, nor how old she was when she became an anchoress—a religious recluse—in a cell attached to St. Julian's Church in Norwich. Anchorites had to follow strict rules set by the church, and a ceremony marking the beginning of her seclusion would have been held in the presence of the Bishop of Norwich. An anchorite served as an ideal of devout holiness, and was supported by donations. Julian's name appears in several wills of the period, the earliest dated 1394, the last in 1429.

As for her writing, she produced two manuscripts, a "short text" and a "long text." The short text was written after an illness that produced visions of Jesus. The long text became *Revelations of Divine Love.* Its 86 chapters were written over several years and underwent many revisions. It was completed in the early 1400s. Julian's theology was optimistic; she believed in the certainty of God's love. "Prayer" she wrote, "is not overcoming God's reluctance. It is laying hold of His willingness."[9]

Though she wrote anonymously and lived in seclusion, she was influential during her lifetime. Her book, however, waited more than 200 years to be printed, in 1670. A 1901 edition edited by Grace Warrack introduced her writing to 20th century readers and she's now recognized as one of England's most important mystics.

And Julian is far from forgotten. In 2013 the University of East Anglia named its new study center after her, and the city of Norwich hosts an annual celebration, Julian Week, with events including concerts, lectures, and workshops held around the city. I was lucky to attend one of these events a few years ago during a visit to East Anglian friends.

Of the many thousands of women who, over centuries, dedicated their lives to God and Church, perhaps the best known is Hildegard of Bingen (1098–1179). Hildegard was sent to the local Benedictine community when she was eight. She was educated there, learned Latin, and had access to philosophical and religious books of the period. In 1136 she was elected Abbess. A prolific composer, mystic, and visionary, and some say an early feminist.[10]

Hildegard later moved the convent to Rupertsberg, Germany, permitting her considerable freedom from the Church's male hierarchy. She was recognized by Pope Eugenius III and the leaders of the period, and corresponded with Henry II and Eleanor of Aquitaine. She continued to travel frequently, write prolifically, and denounce the Church's corruption. Unfortunately, much of her work was lost during WWII. Her most precious manuscripts were sent to Dresden for safety, but the city was destroyed by Allied bombs and her remaining works were pillaged, leaving only one volume extant.

Dresden fell into Soviet hands and her writings would probably have been destroyed but for the work of two brave women. Margarete Kuhn, a medievalist, accessed that priceless volume by proving a need for it in her work. She then passed it onto her American friend Caroline Walsh, who smuggled it out of Soviet control and into safe hands. Hildegard's music is still played today. The Church granted her sainthood in 2012.[11]

Those devoted women and others like them were often dismissed as overly sentimental, hysteric, and even narcissistic, and women who threatened the Church or patriarchy could be severely punished. Marguerite Porete, for instance, an educated French mystic, wrote *Le Mirouer des Simples Ames [The Mirror of Simple Souls]* in the 1290s. Her book, written in French instead of the Latin the church demanded, described seven levels of grace that bring the soul into communion with God, and she wrote that the soul no longer "has need of sermons or sacraments or the Church as such." Porete refused to halt publication and was burned at the stake.[12]

As for their non-mystical sisters, not everyone was happy with the power and politics of the Catholic Church. The emotion most associated with women in the Middle Ages was anger. Even Thomas Aquinas, a noted philosopher and one of the few early Church leaders I've felt some esteem for, claimed that woman "was by nature subject to man, in whom reason predominates." Also," it is clear that man is much nobler than woman and of greater virtue."[13]

Clear to whom I wonder? Certainly not women. I suppose those words can be blamed on the culture in which he was immersed, but it's difficult to accept from a man who was clearly capable of knowing better. If women were angry about their low status and the ongoing criticism and belittlement of their sex, I can't say I blame them. "If the lay view of medieval woman was a scold and a shrew," writes Tuchman, "it may be because scolding was her only recourse against subjection to man, a condition codified, like everything else, by Thomas Aquinas."[14]

Such words and condescension encouraged heresies like the Cathars, where women could become respected leaders, even Perfects who could administer sacraments. The Cathar influence, which honored Mary Magdalene "as perhaps even more important than Saint Peter," predominated across southern France (then Occitania) and included many of the region's leaders. Its growing popularity and the equality it granted women, were threats to the Catholic Church which in turn made an intense and almost successful effort to eliminate it.[15]

For 32 years various popes attempted, through papal legate missions and efforts at conversion, to halt the spread of the Cathar heresy. Their efforts repeatedly failed and in 1209, Pope Innocent III called for a crusade, saying, "Anyone who attempts to construe a personal view of God which conflicts with Church dogma must be burned without pity."[16]

The resulting war, known as the Albigensian Crusade (after the city of Albi where Catharism flourished) lasted twenty years, killed thousands of innocents, and is perhaps best known for a papal legate's apocryphal instructions to his abbot-commander in Béziers, who asked how to tell Cathars from Catholics. "Kill them all," he replied. "The Lord will recognize his own." The result was a slaughter that took 20,000 men, women, and children and essentially wiped out the city of Béziers.[17]

There is plenty of evidence that this war was brutal, and that it dramatically changed life in the south, especially for women. The crusade led inevitably to the Inquisition, founded in an effort to capture the last of the heretics. It also opened the door for Phillip II of France to unite much of the Southwest with his northern Kingdom, resulting in a French map much like that today. History proclaims that the last known Cathar, Guillaume Bélibaste, was burned at the stake in 1321.

Having lived in Languedoc for several years I can confirm that both the religion and the crusade that took so many lives still live in the memories of the natives. When I erroneously identified the cross on the regional flag as Cathar I was quickly and firmly corrected by our local vintner, whose shop we were in.

"No crosses for Cathars, no. Cathars don't like crosses." When asked, he confirmed that yes, there were still Cathars in the region. He had been passionate in his response and I longed to know more, but not wanting to pry, I moved on.

Our years in France proved again how powerful history is, and how potent and long-lasting its influence. In many ways there is no escaping; one can be touched by history without knowing its details or even that it exists. History ties each generation to the next in ways impossible to characterize. It's not about famous people, or dates to memorize. It represents the countless individuals who lived out their lives in the places we visit or live; walking where they walked, seeing what they saw.

Much of my love for travel lies in the comfort I've found surrounded by centuries of both visible and invisible history—even when that history is dark— and knowing that uncounted humans have been in this place before me. It's a validation that while all things change, the gift of life continues.

# 9
# THE CHURCH ATTACKS AND DEFENDS

The Cathar heresy was one among many, and in the eyes of Pope Gregory IX there were far, far too many heretics. To deal with them he established the Inquisition—an ecclesiastical court of discovery and punishment of heresy— in 1232, assigning this duty to the Dominican and Franciscan Orders. Its scope and power grew in response to the Protestant Reformation and the Catholic Counter-Reformation. In 1323 Pope John issued the bull *Cum inter nonnullos*, which defined the belief in the poverty of Christ and the Apostles as heretical. The following year he issued *Quia quorundam* that provided for the torture and killing of "heretics." For the next 500 years the leaders of the Inquisition in France, Italy, Spain, Portugal, and their colonies, sought out and destroyed anyone professing beliefs contrary to Church doctrine. No one was exempt: civil authorities, noblemen, peasants, children, or witches.[1]

It was inevitable that the Inquisition would turn its evil eye toward witches, and in 1484 Pope Innocent VIII added his own encouragement in a Papal Bull, *Summis desiderates affectibus,* directed at witches and heretics in Germany's Rhine River valley. Three years later he appointed the infamous Tomás de Torquemada Grand Inquisitor of Spain, spreading the evil.[2] But it was the moralists of the Reformation who appear to have done at least as much, if not most of the damage.

Witchcraft was part of an ancient tradition that spawned magicians, wizards, necromancers, soothsayers, and sorcerers. Witches were feared for their supernatural abilities; they were said to use spells and charms, and were often accompanied by evil spirits or "familiars" who assisted them in their work. From the earliest times there were male as well as female witches, and while the practice was discouraged by the early Church, penalties for such "addiction" usually consisted only of fines and doing penance.

Sorcerers were generally male whose abilities included working magic and curing disease. Charles VI of France was thought to have been made insane by such magic. Unfortunately the two sorcerers hired to restore his wits failed, and were beheaded (1397). In the 13th century the image of witches took a subtle but predictable shift when, for the first time, a witch was defined as a "woman in collusion voluntarily or enforced with a demon."[3] Thereafter, witchcraft became predominantly a woman's crime.

Once defined as female, a witch also got uglier. By the time of the Reformation, when witches were said to have made pacts with the devil and celebrated unholy Sabbaths, they were described by one writer as: "commonly old, lame, bleare-eyed, pale, fowl and full of wrinkles; poor, sullen, superstitious; in whose drowse minds the devil hath gotten a fine seat. They are lean and deformed, showing melancholy in their faces to the horror of all that see them. They are doting, scolds, mad, devilish."[4]

Pity the poor, the old, the lame, the wrinkled, the unhappy. Indeed, pity them, for in the next few centuries, too many of these women would fall victim to the strangest and most dire obsession ever to be embraced by the Christian religion.

The Reformation is usually defined by historians as 1400 to 1700, though such definitions are necessarily fuzzy. It wasn't until 1517 that the German priest known as Martin Luther published his Ninety-five Theses. Luther taught that the Bible is the only source of divinely revealed knowledge, and he translated that book into the German vernacular, making it widely accessible, as opposed to its Catholic counterpart in Latin.

John Calvin, born Jehan Cauvin in Noyon, France in 1509, grew up intending to be a priest but at the urging of his father turned to the study of law. A speech by his close friend Nicolas Cop led to Cop being denounced as a heretic. He escaped to Switzerland; two years later Calvin, who was implicated in Cop's declaration, also fled. Calvin differed with Luther regarding some aspects of dogma, but both were firm in their support of the Protestant movement.[5]

Luther had directly challenged the Catholic Church and conflicts erupted as Catholic governments tried to stop the spread of Protestantism. Inspired by the words of Luther, Calvin, and others, evangelists from a growing variety of sects traveled across Europe preaching the need to live sin-free lives. "He retained the medieval notion that copulation is sinful even in marriage, but 'God covers the sin.'"[6]

Such challenges to the Church that had once controlled nearly every aspect of people's lives was not surprising, especially given the intolerance of the Papal Inquisition, which had slowly spread dread and/or horror across every region of Europe. England managed to escape, but used some of the same techniques on Catholics during the first Elizabeth's Protestant reign.

"Intolerance," wrote Durant in *The Age of Faith,* "is the natural concomitant of strong faith; tolerance grows only when faith loses certainty; certainty is murderous."[7]

The growth of Protestantism and its multiplying sects of committed devotees brought immense and long-lasting challenges to the Catholic Church, to leaders, and to ordinary people. Faith was, in a sense, at war with itself. It was the beginning of a never-ending struggle that divides us even today.

Referring to the post-Reformation world, Beth Allison Barr writes, "Historically, women have always been subordinated to men, but now their subordination became embedded in the heart of evangelical faith. To be a Christian woman was to be under the authority of men."[8]

As the hand of the Catholic Church grew weaker and the social order deteriorated, the pushers of the new morality began to connect the concept of sin to sexuality, an unoriginal idea.

And women, who were said even by doctors of the time to have insatiable lust (and wandering uteruses) were the obvious source of evil in the eyes of religious zealots. Somehow the female created by God to be man's partner, has become instead man's enemy, and a willing partner to the devil. Once more Eve's role in the Fall became an excuse for misogyny—reflected this time in the debasement and torture of women. The new take on witches was essentially the same as the Catholic Inquisition's—they were associates of Satan.

"Everywhere," writes Joseph Klaits in *Servants of Satan*, "witchcraft was a woman's crime. Those who advocated witch trials saw nothing remarkable in this sexual imbalance. It conformed perfectly with the dominant notions of female inferiority, while it confirmed the legitimacy of woman-hatred with each new case."[9]

And there were many new cases. According to current estimates, about 40,000 people were executed as witches in Europe between 1450 and 1750. Klaits cites evidence from 7,500 witch trials throughout Europe and North America during the 16th and 17th centuries—over 80 percent of the victims were women. In some places their number rose to nine in every ten.

These women were accused of horrendous crimes, but the primary evil in the minds of the persecutors was their supposed pact with the devil and all it signified. Just as Eve had consorted with Satan disguised as the serpent, so these women were seen as his "sexual servants." They flew on broomsticks or dogs or any other handy device to an unholy Sabbat meeting where human babies were eaten and sexual orgies celebrated. Sabbats were said to be attended by hundreds of witches who flew great distances to attend, usually accompanied by the hated Goddess Diana, who joined them in worship and revelry.

"Nearly every continental demonologist of the era of the witch craze," says Klaits, "laid great stress on the Sabbat as the occasion for witches to express their perverse sexuality."[10] Since about 80 percent of witches were female this naturally included copulating with the devil, who was meticulously described by one author as having a huge penis and scaly testicles.

The women accused of this obscenity had often been denounced by their neighbors; they were said to have caused some unfortunate or perhaps mysterious occurrence: a bad fall, the death of a farm animal, the loss of a valued item. Sometimes the accused had a talent for herbs and balms, or a gift for healing that made them appear suspicious. Often they were eccentric, reclusive or ugly. Almost always they were either old, poor, widowed, or otherwise unattached; they did not conform to "normal" social patterns. Once denounced they were delivered into the hands of the reformers, who cared little about the neighbor's accusations, but a great deal about the alleged witch's communion with the devil.

Witches were said to carry a stigmatizing mark hidden on their bodies as a sign of their secret pact. It was the search for this "devil's mark" that offers the clearest proof of the sadomasochistic tendencies of the prosecutors. Women, no matter their age, were stripped in front of their male judges. Their shaved bodies were then poked and pried for the mark that would indicate their evil pact. This mark, said to be insensitive to pain, could be anything; a mole, a wart, a birthmark. Experts warned that such marks were often found on the "shameful parts"of a woman, and judges were urged to search diligently for such evidence. Indeed, some men made a career of finding these devil's marks.[11]

If that were the limit of the women's debasement it would surely be enough, but after the prodding and probing the victims became the subjects of hideous torture. The *Malleus Maleficarum,* written in 1486 by a Catholic clergyman, was the primary document in advising judges and clerics how to discover and prosecute witches. "Torture is not to be neglected," said the author, and it certainly wasn't. The rack, boiling water, seats of spikes, all the inhuman devices then known were used on these unfortunate women. If by some miracle they failed to confess and their guilt could not be determined, they were often branded and/or banished.[12]

But few escaped punishment. Before the era of the witch hunts ended, many thousands of innocent women (and some men) were murdered, pressed by stones or tied to a stake and burned.

As the fanaticism and hysteria faded in Europe it was lit briefly in the colonies, when more than 200 people in Massachusetts were accused between February 1692 and 1693. Thirty were found guilty and hanged (including five men), five died in jail, and one died under torture.[13] The guilt these victims carried to their graves was not their own, but the projected guilt of their many prosecutors.

The accusations leveled at the mythical Eve echo clearly in the accusations of witchcraft leveled at real women in the 14th, 15th, 16th and 17th centuries. Fear and hatred of women is a refrain that begins in Genesis, swells in the writings of the early Fathers, repeats in the medieval church and is heard again in the words of the reforming new Protestants. If John Calvin pulled on a bell-rope, the bell would ring in Eve's ear.

# 10

## THE RENAISSANCE

Putting witches and their craft aside, let us take a deep breath and grant temporary relief to the Church and the Protestants, and look for other reasons why men continued to demean the female sex, frequently beat them, and handicapped their efforts to live as they wish and speak their own truth.

Misogyny has never needed an excuse to stick its ugly snout into women's business, and some human attributes play easily into its grasping hands. The physical strength of male bodies versus the biological role of women creates a dichotomy that males have used for centuries to intimidate and dominate females. But male strength can be a blessing, as it was during the dark years of the early Middle Ages when it was needed to harvest essential crops, fight battles, and build homes.

Women, the child bearers, were the only means by which mankind could perpetuate itself, and when only one out of two or three infants survived, continual pregnancies were expected and encouraged. Childbearing and child rearing was painful, hard, and usually a constant occupation for wives of this period. Add cooking, sewing, brewing, or otherwise adding to the family income and you easily have a full day. And while women were home raising the next generation, their husbands were out in the world, working at a craft perhaps, or using that strength wherever it was needed. Some of the more enterprising were also harvesting status and political power for themselves. And it is in that word power again, that the secret lies. Men had it; women didn't.

There are clear reasons why women of the Middle Ages did not speak out, did not write, did not involve themselves in the growing civic life around them. But this is about to change, for we have reached the Italian Renaissance when the rekindled cultures of ancient Greece and Rome began to percolate in the minds of the learned, and when increasing wealth and a reasonable stability made room for new ideas.

While the Reformation continued its tortuous work, Italy was becoming known as the world's center of artistic beauty, feeding and inspiring the emergence of the Renaissance. Might it be that Italy's early acceptance of women's education played a role in that Renaissance? As early as 1237 Bettisia Gozzadini, a woman, earned a law degree at the University of Bologna, established in 1088. Two years later she was teaching law at the same university.[1] Italy continued to lead the education world until the 1500s when Spain began allowing women to study at universities.

In contrast, it wasn't until 1803 that Bradford Academy in Massachusetts became the first higher education institution to admit women in the United States. The first public high schools for girls opened in 1826, in New York and Boston. In 1850 Lucy Stanton earned a literary degree from Oberlin College (founded in 1833), becoming the first Black woman in the U.S. to earn a college degree.[2]

Great Britain's deeply rooted patriarchy and misogyny held women back until 1849, when Bedford College in London opened its doors to women. This was more than 100 years after Lady Mary Wortley Montagu (whom you'll soon meet) decried the lack of education for women, and a mere 650 years after the founding of the men-only Universities of Oxford (1200–1214) and Cambridge (1209–1226).

Will Durant dedicates an entire volume of his *Story of Civilization* to the Italian Renaissance and its incredible explosion of arts and letters, along with the political machinations of various popes, the Borgias and the Medici family.

This is a history thick with military adventures, sexual peccadillos, religious obtuseness and an urge to return to the "pagan" ideas of classical Greece. Durant begins his book with Petrarch (1304–74), who studied to be a lawyer in Bologna, but hated the law. Instead, "he read all that he could find of Virgil, Cicero, and Seneca," and spent much of his life searching for and reading whatever he could find from the classical period.[3]

These cherished documents "opened to him a new world, both of philosophy and of literary art."[4] Petrarch frequently traveled, searching out lost fragments of classical writing. He transcribed many with his own hand, hiring copyists to help. He urged the establishment of public libraries, and is called by many the first humanist and Father of the Renaissance.

A hundred years after Petrarch, inspired Italian book hunters were still searching for ancient documents. It was Poggio Bracciolini who discovered Lucretius's poem *On The Nature of Things,* a document that with its "deeply subversive" ideas helped to reshape modern consciousness.[5]

Bracciolini was one of a swarm of Italians who were captivated by the beauty, knowledge, and rhetoric of ancient Greece and Rome. These men, who called themselves humanists, were driven to seek out every ancient document—and scraps of documents—buried in monasteries and churches across Europe. Their efforts to retrieve, copy, translate and spread the words and ideas of lost philosophers and scientists opened long-hidden doors and strengthened the reform movement.

"Country after country," writes Durant, "was inoculated with the new culture, and passed from medievalism to modernity. . . the literary and philosophical transformation had a far profounder result for the human spirit than the circumnavigation and exploration of the globe. For it was the humanists, not the navigators who liberated man from dogma, taught him to love life rather than brood about death, and made the European mind free."[6]

I have, over the years, found a good deal of pleasure reading from Will Durant's 11-volume *Story of Civilization* (the final five volumes also credit his wife Ariel). I like his gentleness, his humor, and often the beauty of his sentences. He is exact and endlessly patient and sympathetic to human follies, without turning away from the evil inflicted on others. Famous names and critical battles are given equal footing with the lives of ordinary people, as well as the arts, religion, and philosophy. He and his wife Ariel, were, in the best sense of the word, humanists and over the years I've become quite fond of them.

Durant was also a man of his time (1885–1981) and history is not static. Every decade offers new looks at old documents, new historians with fresh eyes, new techniques for analysis and understanding. The past as a place is often as fallible as a fun house mirror, and while serious historians strive for accuracy, misinformation and misunderstanding are always at hand.

Thus, when Will Durant writes of women he sometimes falls prey to the influences engulfing men of his period. He likes and admires women and generally treats them fairly but, I regret to say, he can be patronizing at times.

For instance in *The Renaissance* he gives us five and a half pages about Isabelle, Marchioness of Mantua, "the First Lady of the World," an intellectual prodigy "who made diplomats gape" by the age of six. Married at sixteen she became a well-known collector of art and books and later "could rule Mantua with the tact and good sense alien to her husband; and in the debility of his later years she held his little state together despite his blunders, his wanderings, and his syphilis." About this paragon Durant still thought it appropriate to write that "she had a wide and varied culture without being an 'intellectual' or ceasing to be an attractive woman."[7]

In every volume of the Durant's extensive history readers will find, amid the copious listings of the index, the word women, followed by appropriate page numbers. (Interestingly, the word *men* never found an independent listing in any book I'd come across—until I scanned the index of *The Second Sex*—brava Simone!)

I turned to the index in *The Renaissance* to see how many references we women had earned. Sadly only two, though one link led to the five pages referenced above. On the other hand, Raphael was referenced 111 times, Michelangelo 130, da Vinci 72, Pope Julius II 70 and Bracciolini 16. But let us not quibble. Here's some of what Durant tells us about Renaissance woman:

"The emergence of woman was one of the brightest phases of the period." He continues with a long paragraph about the idealization of upper-class women and concludes with what we surely already know, that "We must not imagine that this was the pleasant role of the average woman in the Renaissance; it fell to a fortunate few, while the far greater number put off their bridal robes to carry domestic burdens and family headaches to their graves."[8]

He gives us several paragraphs about hair, makeup and clothing styles, love of jewelry and scents, and the popularity of bare bosoms "that invited the male eye." He describes this woman of the upper class as one who "raised her sex out of medieval bondage and monastic contempt to be almost the equal of man." She conversed on equal terms with him about literature and philosophy; she governed states with wisdom, like Bianco Maria Visconti who governed Milan in her husband's absence, while also known for her piety, compassion, charity and beauty; or with "all-too-masculine force," like Caterina Sforza (who sometimes followed her husband into battle wearing armor). This imaginary female, he continues "refused to leave the room when rough stories came up; she had a good stomach, and could hear realistic language without losing her modesty or her charm."[9]

He then offers a few paragraphs about various women who were intelligent: one had the confidence of her husband, one was the mother of a famous man, another was the daughter of a famous man, another loved her husband and was faithful to him after his death at an early age; and Caterina Cornaro, "who made Asolo a school for poets, artists, and gentlemen." He then gives us a paean to Vittoria Colonna, "the untouched goddess of Michelangelo" who had "all the quiet virtue of a Roman heroine of the Republic, and combined with it the noblest features of Christianity."[10] She had distinguished parents and a loving husband who composed a book of sonnets dedicated to his wife.

I admit I've not given full credit to Durant's descriptions of those women, I'm sure they were all accomplished and virtuous, and raising a Lorenzo the Magnificent (Lucrezia Tornabuoni) might certainly have been a trial, but it's hard to forgive Durant for giving only a few sentences to these interesting women. In almost all cases though, history is silent when it comes to ordinary—and these were not ordinary—women, even when historians give it a try. He ends the section with this:

"The educated women of the Renaissance emancipated themselves without any propaganda of emancipation, purely by their intelligence, character, and tact, and by the heightened sensitivity of men to their tangible and intangible charms. [W]omen moved into every sphere of life; men ceased to be coarse and crude, and were molded to finer manners and speech, and civilization, with all its laxity and violence, took on a grace and refinement such as it had not known in Europe for a thousand years."[11]

I find it revealing but not surprising that the successes of these Renaissance women are always made in relation to men. I recognize that it was near impossible for a woman to live an "acceptable" life as an independent female, so I suppose we should be happy that women succeeded in making men less coarse and crude. Remembering that Durant wrote this volume in 1953, perhaps we can forgive his obvious sexism.

Before leaving Renaissance Italy let us remember the words of Saint Bernardo of Siena (1380–1444): "And I say to you men, never beat your wives while they are great with child, for therein would lie great peril. I say not that you should never beat them, but choose your time "[12]

So where is Eve during this period of change? She is certainly not forgotten. Eve has no voice of course, but she is frequently mentioned in sermons, diatribes, and articles throughout history—a constant reminder to women that it's all their fault. She was a favorite subject of Renaissance artists who often portrayed her alone, naked, and vulnerable (what could be more titillating?). But Titian, in a famous work, shows her reaching for the infamous apple while Adam hesitantly extends an arm as though, maybe, to stop her. This too was a common theme, but although Adam never halts the wicked act, and indeed he partakes, he is never chastised except by his maker, and no one seems to blame him for succumbing to temptation. Why not?

This has always puzzled me. The first man appears weak-minded, bewildered by Eve's boldness, and hesitant to act. Not much of a hero. Was Eve so tempting he couldn't refuse her? That's a lame excuse. Nevertheless he didn't resist temptation and he didn't obey God's law. Yes, he was cast out of Eden, both were guilty; both were punished. But only Eve remains accountable.

Back on Earth the ideas blossoming across Italy made their slow way across Europe, encouraging, thanks to Petrarch and men like Bracciolini, a reconsideration of the classics and a growing emphasis on education, writing, and the arts. Those more refined manners and a new emphasis on fashion may be credited, one assumes, to women.

And thanks in part to the growing number of convents, more women had access to learning, and they quickly grasped that the art of letters offered freedom that was denied them elsewhere. Christine de Pisan (1364–c. 1430) of France surely benefited from the early Renaissance influence. Indeed, the Italian Petrarch, who was only a generation ahead of her, lived most of his life in France.

De Pisan was a poet and writer who gained fame across Europe. Born in Venice, Italy, she moved with her father to Paris in 1368 where he was astrologer to Charles V. He taught his daughter Latin, philosophy and a bit of science. In 1379, at 15, she married Etienne du Castle, a notary and royal secretary. She had three children before her husband died of the plague in 1389. When her father also died she was left to support her mother and children. Using her wits she wrote poems and ballads that pleased members of the royal court. With their encouragement and support she became a prolific writer, not only of poetry but of political and moral subjects that included defending the rights of women. She was also a clever user of patronage and succeeded in part by writing and lecturing on topics of importance to those who ruled. De Pisan is considered by some to be the first female professional writer and the first notable feminist.

In her history of the middle ages Shulamith Shahar writes that "Christine de Pisan defined certain qualities as feminine: tenderness, mercy and compassion, and these qualities are regarded as positive. This emphasis on the desirability of such feminine traits was not only a protest against feudal society and the ethos of the warrior but also opened up the way for liberating men from obsessive masculinity, false heroics and all they implied." She goes on to remind us that "hers was an isolated and unique voice."[13]

*The Book of the City of Ladies* (1405) was de Pisan's most famous work and the first to speak of women's contributions to society, and to defend and promote the importance of women's lives. It is still in print and I stumbled across it many years ago. It felt tame compared to the feminist tomes released in the seventies and eighties, but it remains impressive considering the constraints binding women of that period. Perhaps more indicative of her outspoken bravery was her public disdain of the popular book *Roman de la Rose* (*The Tale of the Rose*) written in 1402 by male author Jean de Meun, a satire that described women as seducers and blamed them for "humanity's departure from the ideal," among other sins. De Pisan denounced the author for his "extremely vicious and vitriolic" portrayal of women.[14]

I came across this de Pisan quote in Beth Allison Barr's book, *The Making of Biblical Womanhood.* Like many early women writers de Pisan uses irony to make her point:

"If women's language had been so blameworthy and of such small authority as some men argue, our Lord Jesus Christ would never have deigned to wish that so worthy a mystery as His most gracious resurrection be first announced by a woman . . . ."[15]

# 11

## WAR, ROSES, SPIES AND ARTISTS

Of course it was a woman who made the difference. Elizabeth I's long reign marks the beginning of the end of the late Middle Ages and the birth of what is sometimes called the Enlightenment. She ruled England for 45 eventful years (1558 to 1603). The daughter of Henry VIII and the disgraced Anne Boleyn, she was called a bastard, imprisoned for conspiracy against her half-sister Queen Mary, and sentenced to the Tower. Mary later released her to house arrest. An act of parliament in 1553 restored Elizabeth's right to the throne, and on Mary's death she became Queen at the age of 25.[1] Her problems had just begun.

The country she inherited was broke, divided, and confused after a series of short reigns, changing laws, and several beheadings. Her father had declared England a Protestant country, an enactment more violent than the statement assumes. His daughter Mary, a devout Catholic, had been consumed with returning England to its former religion and had neglected nearly everything else. The economy was plagued with false coinage, and trade had collapsed. Defense too was near collapse: the army ill-paid, the navy unfit, fortresses forgotten. Poverty was the rule rather than the exception.

Foreign relations were muddy and opaque, with France and Spain struggling for European dominance and the Pope threatening Elizabeth with excommunication unless she returned to Catholic rule. This she refused to do. Her decision produced outcries and violence, as more than half the population of England were devoted to the Catholic religion.

"She was saved," writes Will Durant, "by the disunion of her enemies, the wisdom of her counselors, and the courage of her soul. . . . Europe had not expected to find the spirit of an emperor behind the smiles of a girl."[2]

Elizabeth was intelligent and well educated for the age. Her first governess taught her French, Dutch, Italian, and Spanish and her second added Latin and some Greek. She was tutored daily in religion though she seems to have been somewhat skeptical. She chose her advisors well and kept them even when they disagreed. She read consistently throughout her reign, but also delighted in being entertained: dancing, masques, theater, music were all applauded. Her enthusiasm for entertainment lent a positive charge to the efforts of Shakespeare, Marlowe, Bacon, and no doubt hundreds of others.[3] We're also told she was a great flirt, which no doubt provided a different kind of entertainment.

Elizabeth had her faults, of course. She did not take well to criticism or opposition. Though she had a parliament she rarely summoned it and held to the divine right of kings and queens, with all that right assumes. She didn't hesitate to punish nobles who crossed her and free speech was not favored. She could be quick to anger but doesn't appear to have held grudges, and she often forgave her antagonists. She was notably parsimonious, but thought nothing of spending on beautiful clothes and jewels (she died owning 2000 dresses).[4]

Because she was Queen of England (and young, fair, and shapely) she immediately became the object of marriage by other reigning monarchs, either for themselves or their sons. Although she declared that she planned to remain a virgin, she managed the many offers of marriage with signal strength: holding off, postponing, changing her mind, threatening to marry another—for years in the case of the Spanish king, Phillip—until she had what she wanted. And what she wanted was the reduction or removal of threats to England, including any place offering a point from which foreigners might invade, especially Ireland, Scotland and the Netherlands. Her years of marital indecision played out as a strategy for keeping her enemies at bay until England's defenses were stronger.

After more than 20 years Philip of Spain (a Catholic) had had enough of her dallying and in 1586 the two countries prepared for war. Spain was by far the superior power, with hundreds of colonies in the Americas contributing trade and gold. England had none. When the Protestant English government ordered the death of the Catholic Queen Mary of Scotland, Spain had its excuse and prepared to attack.

But Phillip had waited too long. England now had a decent navy with several good officers, including Sir Francis Drake, who had circumnavigated the globe in the Golden Hind, returning home in 1580 with booty for the queen and years of experience as a privateer. The Spanish Armada had 130 vessels, 8,050 sailors and 19,000 soldiers, all on a mission to dethrone the "heretical" Elizabeth. Drake, now a vice admiral, had just 82 ships gathered at Plymouth. But where the Spanish galleons were tall and bulky, the English were smaller, fleeter, and quicker to maneuver. The shot from Spanish cannons passed over the smaller English ships. In their first encounter the Spanish lost 4,000 men, and their remaining vessels were crippled. When the English returned to Plymouth they had lost just 60 men and not one ship. The war continued until 1598, but the famous armada's defeat, says Durant "changed almost everything in modern European culture."[5]

As for the "average"women living under Elizabeth's rule, they were as they had long been, mothers, homemakers and artisans. But now nearly every home was a small factory, turning out woven and spun wool and flax, liquors, herbal medicines, embroidery and sewn garments (the queen's love of fashion deemed fashionable clothing necessary). The popularity of lace and embroidery undoubtedly helped fill many coffers.

In the field of education though, there were still few to no opportunities for women, though girls of noble families were sometimes taught Latin or other languages, and were expected to excel in some form of music or other arts. Institutions for boys and young men continued to grow. Women were barred from such schools, which was, again, a deliberate retaining of male power. Even as late as 1813 Jane Austin portrays the upperclass women in *Pride and Prejudice* as exemplifying the attitude that women did not need to be formally taught.[6]

But women did not unite in rebellion when society deprived them of education, or the right to keep and spend their own money, or to choose their own husbands or divorce them. Women loved men or didn't, but bore their children and raised those children to respect the laws and customs of the time. And if that meant a daughter might fail to develop a talent, or another must live unhappily with a man who beat her—so be it. Women have willingly, sometimes fervently, helped create and maintain paternalistic societies. If we say that women were coerced, we must add that women often did the coercing.

Despite these attitudes Elizabeth's 45-year reign was a period of growth and change that over the next few centuries affected almost every aspect of European life, including a flourishing of the arts and literature. Colonization by Spain, Portugal, France, and England—though late to the game—brought wealth and new products to Europe (often to the detriment of the colonized). And since colonies needed labor the hideous but widespread use of slavery was encouraged. In 1563 Elizabeth declared that "If any African were carried away without his free consent it would be detestable and call down the vengeance of Heaven upon the undertaking." But a year later she took shares in John Hawkin's slave-running venture to Guinea, even loaning one of her ships. There was money to be made.[7]

### Aphra Behn

A generation after the death of Elizabeth I and 200 years after Christine de Pisan, a woman in England named Aphra Behn (1640–1689) picked up a pen and began to write poetry.

"All women together," writes Virginia Woolf in *A Room of One's Own*, "ought to let flowers fall upon the tomb of Aphra Behn which is, most scandalously but rather appropriately, in Westminster Abbey, for it was she who earned them the right to speak their minds."[8]

Unfortunately little can definitively be said about the early life of

Aphra Behn. She was married, her husband died, and she was forced to support herself. It's said by some that she was a spy for King Charles II. It's known that she traveled to the West Indies—a perilous voyage in those days—and that she became involved in a slave rebellion. She was once imprisoned for debt. She was an outspoken feminist, a sexual pioneer declaring men and women should love freely and equally, and she vigorously supported women's right to an education.

Aphra Behn wrote 17 plays, performed in 17 years. She wrote 13 novels of which *Oroonoke* is the best known. It was the first popular depiction of the horrors of slavery.

Author Dale Spender describes Behn as "a political activist who argued the Royalist point of view at Will's Coffee House and from the stage of the Drury Lane Theatre."[9]

Despite the success of her plays and poetry it was said by (male) critics that the writing wasn't hers, that it was her lover's, "or else if it was hers, then it was of no value and her popular success could not be taken as a measure of her artistic or aesthetic ability."[10]

Perhaps what made the critics so angry were her frequent descriptions of men from a woman's point of view. She was witty and mocking in print, which no doubt fed the flames of male criticism. She "exposed some of the male myths," says Spender. "Her poem 'The Disappointment' is about impotence, and most definitely not from a male perspective: it does not, therefore, offer the same explanations or portray the experience in the same way as a male might do."[11]

Two hundred years later, after a limited edition of Behn's works was reprinted, an article in the 1862 *Saturday Review* described it as "Literary Garbage."[12]

The ideas Behn was writing about were considered radical in her time, but her fearless defense of those ideas and her paid literary output meant that, in Woolf's words, "writing became not merely a sign of folly and a distracted mind but was of practical importance."[13]

Behn was writing during a period of incredible creativity, not only in England and Italy but across Europe. This is the century of Cervantes and Shakespeare (both died in 1616); Ben Johnson, Madam Sévigné, famous for her letters; Samuel Pepys, a diarist, and in science Galileo and Kepler; and so many others. Artists picked up their brushes: El Greco and Velazquez in Spain, and the Flemish painters Rubens, Van Dyck, Hals, and Rembrandt, to name only a few of the most famous.

Referring to the Holland of this period Descartes said, "There is no country, in which freedom is more complete, security greater, crime rarer, the simplicity of ancient manners more perfect than here."[14] An unnamed Frenchman is quoted in 1660, writing "There is not today a province in the world that enjoys so much liberty as Holland."[15] Perhaps that's why Durant can show us two Dutch women of note. The first is Maria Schuurmans, "who read eleven languages, spoke and wrote seven, practiced painting and sculpture well, and was adept in mathematics and philosophy." (Her Wikipedia page says she was proficient in 14 languages.) Schuurmans was also one of the first women to attend university, though she was an unofficial student and sat behind a screen so male students couldn't see her.[16]

The second, Maria Tesselschade (1594–1649), wrote poetry, painted, carved, etched, and played the harp. Wikipedia tells us that "she and her sister Anna Visscher were the only female members of the Muiderkring, a group of Dutch Golden Age intellectuals who met at Muiden Castle."[17] A goblet engraved by Maria is in the Rijksmuseum in Amsterdam. Happenstance led me to view it during a visit there a few years ago, when I had no idea I'd be writing this.

# 12

## JOURNEY TO TURKEY

Lady Mary was not on my mind in July, 1996, as Ray and I were madly preparing to live in Turkey for a year. But when I came across a book by Dervla Murphy called *Embassy to Constantinople: The Travels of Lady Mary Wortley Montagu* I shoved it into my already bulging suitcase and found it a perfect companion to a year spent observing and learning about Turkish women.

She was born the year Aphra Behn died; 1689. I had first learned of Lady Mary in Spender's book, *Women of Ideas,* where I read that she was "a staunch advocate for feminism, a 'friend' of literary figures, a patron of young writers, a prolific letter-writer and the person who introduced smallpox inoculation in England."[1] In 1737 and 1738 she published a political periodical called *Nonsense of Common Sense,* in reference to an opposition journal entitled *Common Sense,* and she was one of the first women to be called a political journalist.

*Woman not Inferior to Man,* written under the pseudonym Sophia, is a satirical feminist book about patriarchy, assumed now to have been written by Lady Mary, though she never claimed it. Spender quotes extensively from this "sustained, systematic and satirical thesis, a comprehensive overview of patriarchy."[2] There is much to like here, including Mary's famous wit.

Referring to male opinions of women's education she asks "Why is learning useless to us? Because we have no share in public offices. And why have we no share in public offices? Because we have no learning." And if "the Men had been so little envious and so very impartial to do justice to our talents, by admitting us to our right of sharing with them in public action; they would have been as accustomed to see us filling public offices, as we are to see them disgrace them."[3]

She was born Mary Pierrepont. Her father was Lord Kingston (later the Marquess of Dorchester). Her mother, Elizabeth, died when Mary was about 10. The family was wealthy and she spent most of her youth in a Palladian house with a 65-acre park, but her favorite place was her father's well-stocked library. Her father disapproved of schooling for girls but he hired a governess—whom she disliked. As a result she was mostly self-taught, including the Latin she easily conversed in by age 13.[4]

As a young woman she was known for her beauty, intelligence, and wit. In 1712, after a five-year on-again, off-again courtship, and the inability of her father and attorneys to reach a settlement, she eloped, despite her father's wishes, with Edward Wortley, grandson of the first Earl of Sandwich and an aspiring politician.[5] In April 1716 he was named Ambassador to Turkey and charged with negotiating a peace treaty between Turkey and Venice.

During their stay in Turkey Lady Mary wrote letters home detailing her experiences. She immediately fell in love with the country, worked at learning the language, and even adopted the Turkish style of dress. Her husband's position in Constantinople gave her access to Topkapi, the sultan's palace, where she quickly made friends with the Sultana and women of the harems.

Her writing is often humorous, sometimes biting, and full of details few foreigners would have access to. Wearing the beautiful and elaborate Turkish dress favored by the upper classes she was fully covered when in public, including her face, and she moved easily about the city while enjoying total freedom. Her explorations took her into the public baths (hamams) and other places only women could attend, and her letters corrected many of the misunderstandings and misstatements previously made by Western males.

I suspect though, that she viewed the apparent freedom of women in Constantinople's harems, bath houses, and upper classes through rose-colored glasses; she was after all the wife of an important diplomat and not subject to the whims and rules of Turkey's autocratic rulers. But for an adventurous woman such opportunities were surely a welcome change from life in uptight, straight-laced, patriarchal London.

It was Mary's curiosity and her willingness to try just about anything that made her a welcome guest. It was from women that she learned about the annual practice of *variolation*, a process for inoculation against smallpox. She had her small son inoculated, and on her return to England tried to convince British doctors to take up the procedure. In response to the public's fear she wrote a piece (anonymously) describing and advocating for the process. She failed to win over the doctors but her campaign played a positive role in the later development and acceptance of vaccines.[6]

Unfortunately, her husband's mission to Turkey failed in less than a year and the couple  returned to England. Mary and her husband later separated and she spent the next few years in Italy, having fallen in love with a much younger Francesco Algarotti. They planned to live together in Venice but that failed to occur. She then traveled and lived in Avignon until her husband's death in 1761, when she finally returned to England. She died August 21, 1762. Lady Mary's letters home were published to great success after her death.[7]

Turkey was a very different place when the two of us arrived almost 300 years later for our third and longest stay. Kemal Atatürk, the post WWI leader of the new republic, had introduced massive reforms in order to bring Turkey into the modern world. These included: excluding Islam from any official role in government, closing religious schools, adopting a constitution, encouraging Western clothing for men and women, discouraged veiling of women, and adopting a new alphabet. He introduced a new civil code that ended polygamy and divorce by renunciation, and gave women the right to vote and hold office.[8]

The village we landed in, on the Mediterranean coast, was tourist oriented and modern enough that most things worked most of the time. I met and grew fond of many Turkish women during our year there, finding them strong, intelligent, and determined. Special to both of us was Mîna Urgan, a retired professor-doctor of literature at the University of Istanbul, and a writer of numerous books including an award-winning biography of Virginia Woolf.

We first met Mîna during our first visit to Bodrum in 1987, introduced by one of her former students, who was also our landlord. She lived there during the summer months, "until the sea is too cool to swim in," and spent winters in Istanbul.

Mîna's stepfather had been a close friend of Atatürk's and she told us that as a child she had danced with the great man. She was in her 70s then, a fierce feminist and anti-authoritarian worried about her country's future (a prescient concern). She once took us to meet a friend who lived in a Yali, one of the few remaining wooden mansions that once lined the Bosphorus in Istanbul—a great treat. Mîna was still writing and swimming when we last saw her in 1998. "Writing is my life," she said then. Sadly, she died in 2000 at the age of 85, after publishing two volumes of her best-selling autobiography. It pleased me to read that her funeral was attended by renowned authors and artists, and the "Internationale" was played.[9]

In the same month and year of Lady Mary Wortley's death (1762) far to the east, across the English Channel, across Holland and Germany and various parts of the Prussian empire, in far away Russia, Tsar Peter III had just been deposed and murdered.

Russia was a country stifled by centuries of isolation, bound to its serfdom, its conservative religious orthodoxy, and its rule-bound monarchy. It was ready though, and in some ways anxious, to join the changes spreading across Europe. Tsar Peter III was succeeded by his 33-year-old widow Sophia-Augusta of Anhalt Zerbst (1729–96), better known as Catherine the Great, an "enlightened despot" according to Voltaire, with whom she corresponded. She loved the arts, theatre, and intellectual stimulation. Catherine II is also famous for taking numerous lovers, but whether she was enlightened or a despot in that cause only they could say.

An admirer of Peter the Great, Catherine embraced Western taste and ideas, and encouraged European immigrants. She also encouraged speaking French, and it soon became a second language among the educated. By the time Tolstoy was writing, in the mid-1800s, most of the upper classes had trouble speaking Russian. She was serious about governing, working ten, sometimes fifteen hours a day. She pored over state papers and wrote not only her own laws but the arguments in their favor and philosophical commentaries on them.[10]

Catherine and her armies were successful expansionists of Russian territory, and diplomacy opened the doors to more. After the Russo-Turkish War she gained long-sought access to the Black Sea and immediately ordered cities to be built, among them Odessa and Kherson (now being fought over in Ukraine). Even distant Alaska was claimed by Russian settlers beginning in 1784.[11]

While these changes were celebrated by the fledgling world power, the country beyond the major cities continued to be its hidebound Russian self. The serfs were still owned and the peasants still poor. Tsar Peter the Great had finally released royal women from seclusion in the terem (the Russian equivalent of harem, a bad idea borrowed from Byzantium). But the power of the omnipresent, conservative Orthodox Church meant that women remained second-class citizens.

Tsar Peter, however, resisted. For instance, "in April 1702, to the immense joy of young people, Peter decreed that all marriage decisions should be voluntary, that the prospective partners should meet at least six weeks before their engagement, that each should be entirely free to reject the other and that the bridegroom's symbolic wielding of the whip at wedding ceremonies be replaced with a kiss."[12] The priests must have been livid.

Catherine had a mixed relationship with religion and the Orthodox Church. Its lands were expropriated for her wars and its budgets cut; 569 monasteries were closed. She took various stands with Catholics, Islam and Judaism during her reign, sometimes trying assimilation, particularly with Islam, and sometimes retreating. She wanted the nomadic Muslims in the south of the huge country to settle in one place.

The status of Jews also underwent several changes during her rule. They were a small population until the partition of Poland, then treated as a separate people, defined by their religion and heavily taxed unless they converted. In 1782 she attempted to assimilate them; in 1785 she declared them officially foreigners, and in 1794 she declared that Jews bore no relation to Russians.[13]

Because Eve was (and still is) fully present in Russia, Catherine gets extra credit for opening the Smolny Institute of Noble Maidens in 1764, the first state-sponsored higher education establishment for women in Europe. That education was said by some to be excellent and by others mediocre but at least young maidens were recognized as deserving of such things. The following year she opened a school for girls, the Novodevichii Institute, and in 1786 she opened free public primary and high-school education to girls. Brava Catherine!

Catherine's reign has been documented in numerous books and films and there is little I can add that hasn't already been said. She was, perhaps, unique among rulers, certainly of that era, and her influence—good and bad—was extensive and long-lasting.

Here I must confess my sympathy for historical Russia, a country that has long held a fascination for me. As a teenager I read an abridged translation of *War and Peace* and fell in love with the Rostof family. But I was also intrigued by the habits and customs of the Russian people, so beautifully described by Tolstoy. I quickly turned to *The Brothers Karamazov* and then to Dostoevsky's *Crime and Punishment.* But our small Carnegie Library had its limits and this was the Cold War era; few books about Russia were readily available except those considered classics, or in relation to WWII or Communism. But in a round-about way my continued fascination with that country led in 1977 to a six-week trip through the USSR in a VW camper. You never know where a book might lead you.

# 13
## WOMEN AND REVOLUTION

We now reach a period when women's voices become less obscure and more openly in favor of—if not yet full rights—wanting at least to be appreciated for their skills and talents. Early in the 18th century women began to appreciate the power that putting pen to paper gave them. Having an alternative to an arranged marriage, or one guaranteed to bring unhappiness, meant that women whose minds were bent toward learning and independence could turn to the pen for sustenance. True, it provided only a meager living, but it was an alternative to the less acceptable but always available options.

Since society presumed that only men could be capable thinkers and writers, women frequently wrote anonymously. But not always. One of the braver souls was Delariviere Manley (c.1670–1724) who wrote plays, satire, and novels. One of her novels, a roman à clef in 1709 titled *New Atlantis,* went through seven editions, which made her famous and got her arrested for libel (the charges were dropped). But despite its success, or probably because of it, satirist Jonathan Swift declared it "fine words packed up in a bag and that she pulled them out by handfuls, and strewed them on her paper, where about once in five hundred times they happened to be right."[1]

A few years later a group of English women who wrote and engaged in intellectual pursuits began to meet frequently to share ideas. They were led by Elizabeth Montagu and included Harriet Bowdler, Elizabeth Vesey, Sarah Fielding, Frances Pulteney and others. Members of this "Blue Stockings Society" were married and did not write for income but rather for the pleasure of creating. Men were not excluded and for awhile Samuel Johnson and Edmund Burke attended their informal meetings.

One of the best known, a younger member of the original group, was Fanny Burney (1752–1840), called by Virginia Woolf the mother of the English novel. Her books include *Evelina* (first published anonymously), *Cecilia, Camilla,* and *The Wanderer or Female Difficulties.*

As you might guess, these women and others like them were frequently belittled, and the term used to describe them became a scornful label, bandied about by people too narrow-minded to know better. For years after, every intelligent woman who voiced an opinion—especially about the status of women—risked being labeled a "bluestocking." William Hazlitt (1778–1830), a well-known essayist and literary critic is credited with this insightful definition: "The bluestocking is the most odious character in society . . . she sinks wherever she is placed, like the yolk of an egg, to the bottom, and carries the filth with her."[2]

Lack of praise or recognition did not, however, stop these women and others from writing plays or novels, working at scientific pursuits, or documenting their lives. And while the frequently controversial author "Anonymous" continued in the 18th century to be the subject of gossip and guessing games, by the 19th she had almost disappeared.

In 1792 Mary Wollstonecraft wrote under her own name when she published *Vindication of the Rights of Woman* at age 33, a work that inspired generations of feminists and has far outlived its critics, and the criticism of its author's personal life. *Vindication* justified women's right to equal access to education. "The faults of women, Mary believed, were nearly all due to the denial of educational opportunities, and to the male's success in getting women to think of themselves as sex toys before marriage, and as decorative ornaments, obedient servants, and maternity machines afterward."[3]

Wollstonecraft had an unhappy childhood, with a father who beat his wife during drunken rages. She left home in 1778 and took a job as a lady's companion, then as a governess; but unhappy with her limited choices she decided to make a career as an author in London and found work with publisher Joseph Johnson. She learned French and German and translated texts and wrote reviews for Johnson's periodical, the *Analytical Review.* It was during this time that she met Thomas Paine and William Godwin, as well as members of the Blue Stockings Society.

Like many during this period Wollstonecraft was captivated by the ideals represented by the revolution in France, and she moved to Paris after the publication of *Vindication.* There she fell in love with Captain Gilbert Imlay, who served for short time with the U.S. Embassy in Paris. They lived together and he arranged for her to register with the embassy as his wife, making her a U.S. citizen, though they never married, and she had his child, Fanny. But Imlay left her with the child and returned to England, promising to reunite with her there. Desperate for funds she left Paris and moved to Le Havre to save money. Her letters to Imlay asking for help went unanswered.

While in Le Havre she wrote *An Historical and Moral View of the French Revolution,* published in 1794. She returned to England in 1795 hoping to find Imlay, who rejected her but offered annual support which she refused. Desperate, she twice tried to commit suicide.

During this period her friendship with William Godwin revived and she became his common-law wife. She was pregnant again and they agreed to marry. The attempt, however, revealed that she had not been married to Imlay—a disgrace that lost them friends. Their relationship, however, appeared strong and loving, and on August 30, 1797 she gave birth to a daughter. Ten days later Wollstonecraft died.[4] Her daughter, Mary Shelley, inherited her skill as a writer and in 1818 published *Frankenstein or the Modern Prometheus* and at least six other novels before her death in 1851.

Interestingly, William Godwin wrote a memoir in 1798 titled *Memoirs of the Author of A Vindication of the Rights of Woman.* Though he believed he wrote it out of love, he was reviled by many for revealing her illegitimate children and suicide attempts, which shocked readers.[5]

The book's negative influence prejudiced her memory for years. Outspoken and fervent in her beliefs, Wollstonecraft's words on the rights of women continued to inspire others long after her death. I don't remember where I came across her words but *Vindication* was among the first feminist prose I read in the early 1970s, when the new rights movement was beginning to percolate.

## French Revolution 1789–99

It's a cliché to say the French Revolution marked a turning point in history, but in fact it did offer a beacon of light in an age of overwhelming disparity and poverty. Its ten-year history is one of high confusion, swift and stunning developments, rising hopefulness, crushing disappointment, and too much needless bloodshed. Volumes of history and novels have carried its stories to readers far beyond France and the 18th century. It's an event that deserves far more than this summary provides; but I'm writing about women, not revolutions.

King Louis XVI's years of weak and failing rule, high debt, and widespread poverty among the general populace led to the Estates General attempting and failing to control a deteriorating situation. The EG was an assembly of representatives from the three "estates" recognized in France: the clergy, the nobility, and the commoners. (That the clergy was deemed equal to the other two makes clear the power of the Church at the time, though it would not last.)

The failure of the Estates General to establish order led to the creation of a more representative National Constituent Assembly on July 9, 1789. This was quickly followed on July 14 by the Storming of the Bastille (now celebrated as France's "independence day"). That famous event led to massive uprisings and protests across the country.

On August 5, the new Assembly took the major step of abolishing feudalism, along with the tithes and fees collected by the Catholic Church, and extending the right to vote, with changes in taxation and freedom of worship, which culminated in a Declaration of the Rights of Man and of the Citizen. The unrest, however, continued to grow. Peasant revolts, attacks on the nobility and their estates, and scenes of near anarchy brought much of the country to a halt. Factions, counter factions, and various leaders were raised up only to crash down; the long confusion led inevitably to inflation, a poor harvest, and a starving public.

In 1790 a new French Constitution was ratified by King Louis XVI. It was a short-lived constitutional monarchy that permitted men over 25 who paid a poll tax to vote. Women were not afforded that right, nor were children, domestic servants, Protestants, Jews, actors, hangmen, slaves, and probably others.

In June, 1791 the royal family fled Paris in disguise but the king was recognized and they were forcibly returned to the city. The king held his position, though imprisoned, until January 21, 1793 when he was executed "for conspiracy against public liberty and general safety."[6]

That act initiated threats and outrage from the crowned heads of Europe and resulted in France declaring war on Britain and the Dutch Republic. They were joined by Austria and Prussia, then Spain, Portugal, Naples and Tuscany in the War of the First Coalition.

Queen Marie Antoinette bore much of the public's blame for the regime's failures. Yes, she had been extravagant when young; she had tried with her husband to escape, and she urged help from foreign governments to reinstate the monarchy. She had, however, played little role in governing and remained loyal to France. (Wollstonecraft thought her manipulative and evil.) The Queen was also the mother of four children, and when offered a second chance to escape in March 1793 she refused because it meant leaving her children behind. Durant tells the story of her finals days:

"On October 12 the Queen submitted to a long preliminary examination; and on October 14 and 15 she was tried before the Revolutionary Tribunal . . . questioned from 8 a.m. to 4 p.m. and from 5 to 11 p.m. on the first day and 9 a.m. to 3 p.m. on the next. . . . now white-haired at 38, clad in mourning for her husband, fighting for her life with courage and dignity against men who were apparently resolved to break her spirit."[7]

On the morning of October 16, 1793 she was taken in a cart to the Place de la Révolution. Her severed head was held up to the cheering of the multitude.

The French revolution played out in real time, but its drama was revealed to the world by slow and often unreliable sources. Still, the shocking news touched men and women across Europe and the globe. Many saw it as a chance to end feudalism in their own countries; women found sustenance in the brave acts of French women fighting in the streets alongside men. Indeed, women played a major role in the revolution, though not necessarily a united one.

One of those women was Olympe de Gouges (1748–93), a playwright and activist born Marie Gouze. At 17 she was forced to marry a man she did not love—a statement that could be applied to many, if not most of the women mentioned to this point. They had a son, Pierre Aubry. After her husband's early death Marie changed her name and never remarried. In 1768 she moved to Paris after an affair with a wealthy businessman, who continued to provide her an income.

De Gouges was an advocate for human rights and denounced slavery, which made her a target of slave and slave-ship owners. She favored a constitutional monarchy and criticized violence, which made her an enemy of hard-line republicans. She wrote numerous pamphlets supporting the working class and rights for women and was castigated for her opposition to the "natural order." She is best known for her *Declaration of the Rights of Woman and of the Female Citizen*, which she wrote in 1791 and dedicated to the Queen.

In her "Postambule" to her *Declaration* she writes "Women, when will you stop being blind? What advantages have you gained from the revolution? A greater scorn, a more pronounced disdain. . . . Reclaim your heritage, founded on the wise decrees of nature. . . . Whatever barriers are placed in your way, it is in your power to break them down; you simply have to want to."[8]

After De Gouges called for an end to the bloodshed and published her Declaration, she was arrested and spent three months in jail. She was executed on November 3, 1793 for seditious behavior and trying to restore the monarchy.

Six years later, in 1799, the revolutionary war ended with the formation of the French Consulate, a coup d'étate that brought Napoleon Bonaparte to power as First Consul of France. His Napoleonic Code confirmed and established women's secondhand status, which was no great surprise.

One of my favorite sources for on-the-ground views of the revolution is a book I picked up at a used book sale 20 years ago. *Travels in France and Italy During the Years 1787, 1788 and 1789* was written by Arthur Young, a prominent British agronomist planning to study the agricultural methods in those countries. In fact, he found himself observing a revolution as he criss-crossed France and eventually made his way into Italy.

Young, who never hesitates to offer his opinion, traveled in upper-class circles and had letters of introduction to agricultural functionaries and titled persons, but he also shared inns and dining tables with all kinds of travelers and encountered a variety of viewpoints daily. One of his frequent complaints was the difficulty of finding accurate news.

"In the streets," he wrote, "one is stunned by the hawkers of seditious pamphlets and descriptions of pretended events, that all tend to keep the people equally ignorant and alarmed."[9] Confirmation, if needed, that some things never change.

Newly arrived in Paris in 1789, after a day spent "in much company" he writes: "I find a general ignorance of the principles of government; a strange and unaccountable appeal, on one side, to ideal and visionary rights of nature; and, on the other, no settled plan that shall give security to the people . . . . But the nobility . . . are most disgustingly tenacious of all old rights however hard they may bear on the people. The popular party, on the other hand, seem to consider all liberty as depending on the privileged classes being lost."[10]

Young traveled by carriage when he could, but on one trip spent several months riding a blind horse. He came close to being arrested several times, once for not honoring the revolution because he wasn't wearing a cockade, and was told he deserved to be hanged. "If I had not declared myself an Englishman, and ignorant of the ordinance, I had not escaped very well. I immediately bought a cockade."[11]

In a final chapter he offers this summation: "The true judgment to be formed of the French Revolution must surely be gained from an attentive consideration of the evils of the old government: when these are well understood—and when the extent and universality of the oppression under which the people groaned, oppression which bore upon them from every quarter—it will scarcely be attempted to be urged that a revolution was not absolutely necessary to the welfare of the kingdom."[12]

Before we leave France, I must acknowledge a puzzling, fascinating woman named George Sand. In 1975, browsing a local bookstore, I came across a new biography and bought it on a whim. I had known her name as a writer but nothing else, and I found her tangled life, her early status as a popular female author—with almost instant fame—and her disdain of conventional habits both oddly out of step and compelling.

Aurore Lucille Dupin (1804–1876), better known as George Sand, was born the year Napoleon came to power. Her father was a minor French noble who married a commoner. This did not suit the noble grandmother; the two women never got along. The conflict disrupted Aurore's childhood, for she loved them both. Her father, as an aide-de-camp, was often away from home and he died in an accident when Aurore was four. After his death she spent most of her childhood at her grandmother's house, in the French province of Berry. At 18 she married Casimir Dudevant and they had two children, Solange and Maurice.

Like many women of the period Sand was unhappy in her marriage; she craved romance and it wasn't long before she had an affair with Jules Sandeau after meeting him in Paris. The two collaborated and published several stories and a novel under the name Jules Sand.[13] A few years later she left her husband and, after a court battle, took custody of their daughter Solange. (Maurice remained with his father.) A romantic idealist, she had a series of affairs. The longest, with Frederic Chopin, lasted more than ten years.

She wrote her first independent novel, *Indiana* (1832) under her new pen name, George Sand, at the age of 27. Almost instantly she was one of the most popular and famous novelists in France and England, and she remained popular throughout her life and after her death.[14]

A leader of the new Romantic style, her books are seldom read today; even her biographer, Curtis Cate, seemed somewhat mystified by her popularity and admits that today they are difficult to read. Yet the Russian author Dostoevsky could write, "Even Dickens, who began appearing in our country at about the same time, came after her in the admiration of the public."And her "glory was so high and the faith in her genius so great that we, her contemporaries, all expected of her in the near future something immense and unheard of, not to say definitive solutions."[15]

Because she was "something of a spendthrift"[16] and always in need of money Sand wrote constantly, filling the pages of 70 novels and numerous articles, pamphlets, plays, and stories. Her biographer includes an anecdote that has her sitting down to write at 10 p.m., finishing the novel she was working on at 1 a.m. and immediately beginning another. She often wrote all night and slept only a few hours before beginning again. She enjoyed entertaining guests for dinner, but would leave them soon after to write.

A political idealist and a champion of women's rights, she maintained her belief that marriage "between equals" was the best hope for happiness. During most of her life Sand split her time between Paris and her grandmother's home in the village of Nohant, where she loved to entertain. She occasionally wore men's clothes and smoked in public. Neither habit was considered acceptable for a female at the time; nor was Sand deterred. In fact, very little deterred her.

She was appreciated as a kind, helpful neighbor in Nohant, and she often gave money to friends in need, despite desperately needing it herself. Cate's book is filled with tales of her borrowing money from her publisher so she could keep writing and support her family, along with whoever her current lover was—usually a destitute artist.

Though Sand is seldom referenced today, she was loved by her numerous readers and friends and hosted in Nohant most of that period's most famous writers and artists: Honoré de Balzac, Eugène Delacroix, Alexandre Dumas *pére* and *fils*; Gustave Flaubert, Victor Hugo, Franz Liszt, Ivan Turgenev and others. Elizabeth Barrett, writing to her future husband, said ". . . that wonderful woman George Sand; who has something monstrous in combination with her genius, there is no denying at moments . . . but whom, in her good and evil together, I regard with infinitely more admiration than all other women of genius who are or have been."[17]

The post-Napoleonic years were also the beginning of a fruitful period for a number of English authors who gave us novels that are still read and loved today: Jane Austin (1775–1817), Charlotte Brontë (1816–55), Emily Brontë (1818–48), and George Eliot (Mary Ann Evans 1819–80). Of these talented women only Eliot lived what might be called an "unacceptable" life. For 24 years she lived with George Lewes, who had previously had an open marriage with Agnes Jervis. Eliot changed her last name to Lewes and they considered themselves married.[18]

Women like Wollstonecraft, Sand, Eliot, de Gouges, and others, who lived by their own rules and expressed life in ways that were outside convention, are of great value to us as women. Because with every cracked and broken rule, and every outside-the-margins action, new space is revealed for those who come after.

It's not the broken glass ceiling that most women crave; not all of us are called to be the highest example of success. Some of us just want more space in our lives, to walk whatever road in whichever direction it takes us. And to do that without fear of being suspect, or having our motives questioned, our bodies controlled, or our ideas defamed.

Like the mythical Eve, women share the universal need to understand the world we woke up in, what it is, why it is, and how it works. Eve broke the rules and paid the price, a price that still casts a shadow too dark for many of us to see through. But those cracked and disregarded rules, like broken windows let in unfiltered light. When we can step into that shadowless space, the world changes.

(End of Part One)

# 14
## ALL MEN WOULD BE TYRANTS IF THEY COULD

Among those inspired by the words of Mary Wollstonecraft were Lucretia Coffin Mott and Elizabeth Cady Stanton who met for the first time in 1840 at a World Anti-Slavery Convention in London. Because they were females they were not allowed to speak or even sit on the main floor, so they sat in the balcony and became friends. The two found they shared a common appreciation of Wollstonecraft's ideas. Eight years later their joint effort became the first women's rights conference, the Seneca Falls Convention in July, 1848. It lasted two days and issued a daring Declaration of Sentiments that sparked numerous other women's rights meetings.[1] When the first annual National Women's Rights Convention was held two years later, the right to vote was central. Those meetings continued annually until the Civil War began in 1861.

The crucial partnership of Elizabeth Cady Stanton and Susan B. Anthony began in May, 1851, when they were introduced by a friend, Amelia Bloomer, whose shorter skirt over pantaloons was setting a new style. She was also the first woman to own and edit a newspaper for women.[2] Stanton and Anthony, along with Mott, were the primary movers in the early fight for the vote. Like many friends, they didn't always agree; Anthony was single-minded in her work for the vote; Stanton had a wider lens that included other rights. But the two women worked together for many years, including on the creation of six impressive volumes of *The History of Woman Suffrage,* by Elizabeth Cady Stanton, Harriet Blatch, Ida Harper, Matilda Gage, and Susan B. Anthony ("collector of material," researcher and business manager).

As we have seen, protecting and increasing all women's rights—not just voting—was no new idea. It was in fact an old contest, as Abigail Adams surely knew when in March 1776 she wrote the famous letter to her husband and the Continental Congress, urging them to

> ". . . remember the ladies and be more generous and favorable to them than your ancestors. Do not put such unlimited power into the hands of the Husbands. Remember all Men would be tyrants if they could. If particular care and attention is not paid to the Ladies we are determined to foment a Rebellion, and will not hold ourselves bound by any Laws in which we have no voice, or Representation."

That's the most remembered part of her letter, but there's more:

> "That your Sex are Naturally Tyrannical is a Truth so thoroughly established as to admit of no dispute, but such of you as wish to be happy willingly give up the harsh title of Master for the more tender and endearing one of Friend. Why then, not put it out of the power of the vicious and the Lawless to use us with cruelty and indignity with impunity."[3]

Quite a statement coming from the wife of a future president. Her prediction of a rebellion never came to fruition, as she probably foresaw, but a century later women began working together to guarantee their voices would finally be heard. It would take them almost 150 years.

It's unlikely that Abigail Adams heard stories growing up about a woman called "the great Mary," though Massachusetts was still a small colony and anything is possible. They didn't overlap; Mary died on Nantucket Island in 1717 and Abigail was born 27 years later in Weymouth, Massachusetts. Abigail's father was a Congregational minister and a leader in Yankee society. Mary brought the Friends Church (Quakers) to Nantucket. But they had two things in common—both were responsible for the family's finances, and apparently quite good at it, and both believed women deserved a voice.

I was aware of Mary Starbuck from reading about her over the years in various family histories; she is my 8th great-grandmother. But I was surprised when I stumbled across a short piece about her in a publication called *Our Paper,* published by the Massachusetts Reformatory, and dated August 26, 1911. It's titled "Our First Suffragette." Here's the lede:

> "While the earnest efforts of Mrs. O.H.P Belmont, Mrs. Clarence Mackay, and other women of prominence for woman's suffrage are engaging the public mind of the present day, it is interesting to note that nearly two hundred and fifty years ago the same movement was started in [sic] the island of Nantucket by a daughter of Tristram Coffyn (as he always signed his name) and Dionis Stevenson, Brixton, England."[4]

Mary was born in Haverhill, Massachusetts Bay Colony, on February 20, 1645. Her parents emigrated to America in 1642 with Tristram's widowed mother, five small children, and two unmarried sisters. He was "of the landed gentry in England" and there are only guesses as to why he chose to move his family to the colonies. They lived in several places in the Massachusetts colony before moving to Nantucket in 1660 when Mary was 15. Coffyn was one of the original proprietors of the settlement and the island's first chief magistrate.

At age 17 she married Nathaniel Starbuck and soon became widely known for her intelligence, wisdom, and guidance. That respect grew quickly when as a young woman, "she supported her husband's efforts to run the island's first trading post, which grew into a large mercantile business with the advent of the whaling trade."[5] Since Nathaniel could not read or write, the accounting fell to his wife, at least in the beginning.

Mary raised ten children while "esteemed as a judge among the islanders." Apparently little of consequence was done without her input. "She was a most extraordinary woman, participating in the practical duties and responsibilities of public gatherings" and "she was consulted upon all matters of public importance, because her judgment was superior, and she was universally acknowledged to be a great woman."[6]

In her early fifties she brought Quakerism to the island, holding the first meeting of the Society of Friends in 1701. The Society, with its concept of spiritual equality for men and women, and trust in the Inner Light, eventually grew to several hundred. That religion remained influential on and off the island through many generations; in my case as far as my paternal grandparents, who always spoke to me using "thee."

That a female in the 17th century could be considered the island's mediator and problem solver is worth acknowledging. That her husband and the other men on the island accepted her wisdom and guidance is rather surprising. Mary died in 1717, but her influence continued to be felt.

The women living on Nantucket at that time were treated as equals by their faith and in other ways, especially after whaling became the chief employer. Husbands, brothers, and sons were gone for months, sometimes years, leaving the wives to manage whatever came up, including what became international businesses. Those women surely grew to appreciate their mutual accomplishments and their personal freedom, as well as passing those ideas onto their children. I like to think Eve's shadow faded almost to invisibility at that place and time.

*Our Paper* confirms its "Suffragette" title with this line: "The genius of whatever attaches to the Equal Rights for Woman movement of the present day, in every true and proper sense, [Mary] anticipated by two centuries, and reduced them to practice without neglecting her domestic relations. . . . [This] should convince those who may doubt that the home need not necessarily be neglected by women whose interest and brains seem to warrant their taking part in the public welfare."[7]

And in Elizabeth Cady Stanton's memorial eulogy for Lucretia Mott, she began with Mary, calling her "a woman of remarkable breadth of intellect as well as great executive ability, [who] converted the colony to Quakerism, and vindicated women's right to interest herself in the commerce of the world . . . . from these distinguished ancestors, Lucretia Mott received her inheritance."[8]

Lucretia Mott was born on Nantucket on January 3, 1793, and her childhood was influenced by the independence and self-confidence exuded by the women of the island. In 1804, aged 11, she moved with her parents to Boston. She attended Boston schools for two years, then at 13 was sent to the Friends Boarding Schooling in Dutchess County, New York, where she attended three years—the last year as an assistant teacher.

In 1811 at the age of 18 she married James Mott, with whom she had six children, raising five. By all representations it was a happy marriage. The couple's home "was the castle of safety for runaway slaves, and the paradise of the unfortunate." Mott was active in the women's movement from its beginning, often as presiding officer of the early conventions. To no one's surprise those efforts and debates "were stigmatized as 'the maudlin sentimentalisms of unsexed men and women.'"[9]

Mott wrote in her diary that "The unequal condition of woman in society . . . early impressed my mind. Learning while at school that the charge for the education of girls was the same as that for boys, and that when they became teachers women received but half as much as men for their services, the injustice of this was so apparent, that I really resolved to claim for my sex all that an impartial Creator has bestowed."[10]

Stanton and Mott were present when their anti-slavery delegation in London was presented to the Duchess of Sutherland and Lord Morpeth, who were curious about the movement. Stanton describes Lucretia as "oblivious to all distinctions of rank, she talked freely and wisely on many topics, and proved herself in manner and conversation the peer of the first woman in England. . . .Nothing was too sacred for her to question, as to its rightfulness in principled practice."[11]

Although Mott is frequently portrayed as "the quiet Quaker" her public life put her at the center of the 19th century advocacy of women's rights and the anti-slavery movement. As Carol Faulkner writes in the introduction to *Lucretia Mott's Heresy,* "most Americans believed racial equality was impossible . . . . and viewed marriage and motherhood as women's highest and only calling." Mott's speeches and public statements did prompt public derision and vilification as a heretic. But that never stopped her.[12]

Indeed, Mott was in many ways a fierce radical who urged her followers to be "obnoxious" but peaceful. Her demure Quaker dress hid an exceptionally brave woman who stood for her beliefs, including the Quaker "heresy" and, more important, full rights for slaves and women to equality and freedom. As Stanton wrote in Mott's obituary, "It was not possible that a woman like Lucretia Mott should keep silence in the churches, no matter what [St.] Paul might say to the contrary, because that great brain was created to think . . . ."[13]

One more suffragette deserves to be mentioned here: Matilda Joslyn Gage. She first made her name at the Syracuse National Convention in 1852, at the age of 26, by giving a speech wherein she outlined women's past achievements: Joanna Baillie, called the female Shakespeare; Caroline Herschell and Margaret Mitchell astronomers; journalist and feminist Margaret Fuller; Jenny Lind, a highly regarded singer; and Mary Somerville, mathematician. "Gage's documentation came as a revelation. . . . and raised the question of why didn't they know about these women and their impressive achievements?"[14]

I was seven years old when I told my mother I wanted to be an astronomer. I don't know when the idea originated, but the Milky Way was clearly visible in the skies over our small rural town and being curious, I wanted to know more. I remember long evenings with friends, staring into those skies from blankets spread out on the roof of our garage; we were awed by the mystery and beauty suspended above us.

Reluctantly, mother told me that I could not be an astronomer. When asked why she replied, "because only men can do that." When asked why only men, she said, "that's just the way it is."

One of the great consequences of centuries of unending misogyny and patriarchy is the loss of women's history and women's stories. My mother did not know about the astronomer Maria Mitchell, for example, even though Mitchell died just 21 years before mom was born. Mitchell was the first woman admitted to the American Academy of Arts and Sciences, a member of the Association for the Advancement of Science, and president of the Association for the Advancement of Women (1874).

She taught at Vassar College, lectured around the country on astronomy and women's rights, "and demonstrated that it was a fallacy for women to believe that things would gradually improve: because men's attitudes about women's 'inferiority' had not changed . . ."[15]

I doubt my mother would have answered as she did had she known about Maria Mitchell.

Matilda Gage worked closely with Anthony and Stanton on the writing of the *History of Woman Suffrage*, and wrote the first two chapters and the final chapter of volume one. But Gage's ideas of women's rights and women's history were considered radical by many, especially the men of the day. A few of her reports have been questioned, particularly in regard to Sojourner Truth's famous "Ain't I a Woman" speech. Given that her words were presumably edited by the other women producing the *History* (and who were often present at events she describes), I've elected to include some of her work.

If Lucretia Mott was a radical of quiet voice and modest gray, Matilda Gage was an outspoken reformist in flashing red, ready to take on the world. Her densely written book *Woman, Church, and State*, published in 1873, presents what she called the patriarchate as closely linked to Christianity:

> "The most stupendous system of organized robbery known has been that of the church towards woman, a robbery that has not only taken her self-respect but all rights of person; the fruits of her own industry; her opportunities of education; the exercise of her own judgement, her conscience, her own will."[16]

Since my own research reveals similar ideas put forward over the centuries, it's hard to disagree with her opinion without acknowledging that such ideas were considered shocking, almost anathema, to most 19th century readers. It isn't a surprise that she has been ignored by many. I leave it to you to decide whether that ignoring was simply carelessness, the result of spite, or fear of the truth. You will meet her again in the next chapter.

The outbreak of the Civil War in America affected everyone, including those whose entire focus had been achieving rights for women. Now those same people suspended that work to refocus on the abolition of slavery. Anthony and Stanton formed the Women's Loyal National League in 1863 to campaign for an amendment to the Constitution that would end slavery. At the founding convention Stanton gave the opening address:

"There is great fear expressed on all sides lest this shall be made a war for the negro. I am willing that it shall be. It is a war which was begun to found an empire upon slavery, and shame on us if we do not make it one to establish the freedom of the negro."[17]

The League collected 400,000 signatures in the largest petition drive in America up to that time—work that made a consequential difference in gaining approval of the Thirteenth Amendment.

After the war ended, the 14th Amendment extended the Constitution's protection to all citizens defined as "male." The 15th Amendment gave Black men the right to vote, but not women. This action ignoring women led in 1879 to a new group, founded by Stanton and Anthony—the National Woman Suffrage Association. This in turn led to a split in the movement, one of several setbacks. Some felt the new push for women's suffrage would minimize the work being done for Black rights. But the activism shown by women across the country had an effect, and it encouraged a new generation of women, willing to fight for both Black rights and women's rights.

### Great Britain

The struggle for women's suffrage in the United States was being equaled in Great Britain, though success took a bit longer there, and the fight was more violent. The very few women who owned property had voted in some elections before the 1832 Great Reform Act, which excluded women from the electorate. Twenty years later the Sheffield Female Political Association was founded and immediately submitted a petition to the House of Lords calling for women's suffrage. Thus began a long and tedious battle, with numerous women's leagues founded, many votes taken, and many women arrested.

As in America, supportive men were active as well. John Stewart Mill was a philosopher, politician, and author of an early feminist work, *The Subjection of Women,* published in 1869, with ideas developed jointly with his wife Harriet Taylor Mill. As he wrote in his autobiography, "All that is most striking and profound in what was written by me belongs to my wife . . ."[18]

Mill's essay opposed the then-common attitude that women must be protected from doing things outside their archetypical duties as wife, mother, homemaker. Society was saying men don't want women to do those things, so we'll all agree that they are incapable. Echoing Lady Wortley Montague, Mill is saying, how can we know what women are capable of if we never let them try?

I first read Mill's essay in the early 1970s. He wasn't the first to recognize that dubious lack of sense and its obvious remedy, but he may have been the first male to forcefully explain it to other males.

Laurence Housman was an artist who contributed his support through art as propaganda. He and his sister Clemence opened a studio called the Suffrage Atelier. He encouraged other men to participate and formed the Men's League for Women's Suffrage along with Israel Zangwill, a British author; Henry Nevinson, war correspondent and political commentator; and Henry Brailsford, journalist and writer who resigned from *The Daily News* when it supported forced feeding of jailed women.

Outspoken Emmeline Pankhurst and her two daughters founded the Women's Social and Political Union (WSPU) in 1903.[19] Her husband, Richard Pankhurst, had authored the first British Women's Suffrage bill and the Married Women's Property Acts in 1870 and 1882. After his death Emmeline and her daughters, Christabel and Sylvia, became militant activists, encouraging large parades and sometimes destructive behavior designed to encourage supporters. One notable example occurred in 1914 when Mary Richardson slashed a Diego Velázquez painting, *Venus*, with an axe.

The Pankhursts' ideas were a sharp change from the step-by-slow-step actions and attitudes that had begun in the late 1870s. And they had mixed results, increasing on one hand the numbers of supporters who were actively involved, and on the other hand, leading to a predictable backlash. Women were jailed; some were force-fed, and a few died as a result. (The *Venus* slashing was in response to Emmeline Parkhurst's forced feeding.)[20] But the WSPU's activity encouraged movements worldwide, including the United States. Women in Britain finally received full suffrage equal to men in 1928, with the passing of the Representation of the People Act.

After Abigail Adams wrote that famous letter to her husband I expect she waited anxiously for his reply. It wasn't what she hoped. He said her proposed "code" would subject men to "the despotism of the petticoat."

Abigail knew her husband well; I doubt she was surprised. But I was, the first time I read it. Just what did Mr. Adams think "petticoat despotism" might do that would be so horrible? Would wives suddenly refuse their conjugal and household duties? Was he afraid women might wish to control their own money? Ask for a divorce? Go to college? Run for office? Or was it simply because it meant—oh no!—men lost power?

So much despotism; so many questions.

# 15

## BLACK WOMEN RISING

While studying a map during our 1999 cross-country road trip on U.S. highway 20, I was excited to find along our route the Women's Rights National Historical Park in Seneca Falls, NY. It's a small site, but inspiring for any who identify with the fight for women's rights, or are simply curious.

Ray and I spent several hours exploring and learning more about this brave group of women and men who weren't afraid to speak out in the face of ridicule and disrespect. I was surprised to learn that Lucretia Mott had resisted including the right to vote in the final Declaration of Sentiments, fearing it would put other goals at risk. Frederick Douglass made an impassioned speech defending that right and convinced the group to include it.

He published this statement in his paper the *North Star* soon after:

> "In respect to political rights, we hold woman to be justly entitled to all we claim for man. We go farther, and express our conviction that all political rights which it is expedient for man to exercise, it is equally so for women. All that distinguishes man as an intelligent and accountable being, is equally true of

> woman; and if that government is only just which governs by the free consent of the governed, there can be no reason in the world for denying to woman the exercise of the elective franchise, or a hand in making and administering the laws of the land. Our doctrine is, that 'Right is of no sex.'"[1]

Douglass remained involved and influential in both women's rights and African-American rights until his death in 1895.

Everyone who signed the Declaration of Sentiments joined a crowd of invisible women marching through history. We know the leaders, of course, but they would be the first to admit that gaining freedom and rights was a group venture, and that they couldn't have done the work without the thousands of unknowns who supported their efforts. Many of those unknowns were free Black women, like Sojourner Truth, Harriet Tubman, and unnamed others.

Mott's sister, Martha Coffin Wright, who also participated in the Seneca Falls meeting, was an abolitionist, as were many of the others. Her home, like Lucretia's, was actively involved with the underground railroad. The Park's website displayed a portion of a letter Martha wrote to her daughter Ellen on December 30, 1860. It's worth including here.

> "We have been expending our sympathies, as well as congratulations, on seven newly arrived slaves that Harriet Tubman has just pioneered safely from the Southern Part of Maryland.—One woman carried a baby all the way and bro't two other chld'n that Harriet and the men helped along. They bro't a piece of old comfort and a blanket, in a basket with a little kindling, a little bread for the baby with some laudanum to keep it from crying during the day. They walked all night carrying the little ones, and spread the old comfort on the frozen ground, in some dense thicket where they all hid, while Harriet went out foraging, and sometimes cd not get back till dark, fearing she wd be followed. Then, if they had crept further in, and she couldn't find them, she wd whistle, or sing certain hymns and they wd answer."[2]

If White women have been discriminated against throughout history, and they have; if their writings, their science, their research, their capabilities have too often been ignored, debased, and deleted, and they have; how much worse has this been for Black and brown women? How much of their work, their abilities, their contributions, their brilliance, has been deleted, ignored, criticized, and forgotten?

In this effort to understand the negative treatment of women through history I do not want to join the debasers, forgetters, and ignorers when it comes to Black women. Yet I feel hampered—I personally know no Black women. While growing up my small town had only two or three Black families; I knew that a Black girl was several years ahead of me in school, but I never met her. A Black girl from Los Angeles did join my 6th grade class for a few months in 1953. We had nothing in common but we were slowly becoming friends, until she left at semester's end to return home.

At some point during the late '50s or early '60s civil rights protests, I thought about hopping on a bus and going south to help with voter registration. I wanted to do that, but I knew in my heart that I didn't have the courage or the financial wherewithal to do it. And of course when I broached it my father immediately said "no way!"

I have lived most of my adult life in Oregon, a state with a terrible civil rights history, and one with very few Blacks or African Americans. The 2020 census ranks that population as two percent to 3.2 percent depending on how the two categories are sorted.

Through many jobs in California's Bay Area and in Oregon, I've had only one Black co-worker, a young woman who worked at the front desk three rooms away, and quit after only a few months.

But fortunately for me, I did have a dear Black friend in France. I met her shortly after Ray and I had purchased a house in her village. Her name was Haydee (pronounced Idey). She was from the island of Mauritius, in the Indian Ocean, and had been a midwife before becoming a mail-order bride. Idey spoke excellent English and helped me with my French—always needed—and I looked forward to seeing her after we'd been away. She lived just down the street and we visited several times a week; she was curious and funny, and helped ease our way into the village, which had very few foreigners. I loved hearing about her life on Mauritius, and her family.

After Ray and I retired it was our habit to spend six months a year in the village, and while we were in the States Heidi and I corresponded. That was how I learned she had cancer. At first "it was nothing," but she died before we could get back. The village never felt the same. She was loved and greatly missed by all who knew her.

Before America's Civil War, African Americans in the south, almost all held as slaves, could not attend school. Even if they managed somehow to learn to read and write, they would have had little-to-no leisure to do either, let alone regular access to pen or paper. But those who escaped slavery didn't hesitate to speak publicly against it, and against the laws that kept all women from voting.

Finally, in 1920 the 19th Amendment granted women the vote, though a few states had previously legalized it.[3] That amendment, however, did not eliminate the exclusionary state laws in effect across the former Confederacy, including literacy tests and poll taxes. In fact, Black women and men continued that fight for 44 more years, until the Civil Rights Act of 1964 and the Voting Rights Act in 1965 outlawed discrimination based on race,. color, religion, sex, and national origin. The latter Act was severely diminished in 2018 by the Supreme Court. More changes are under review as I write.

Despite terrible conditions and few opportunities, Black women made powerful contributions in the fight for the vote and an end to slavery. Two of the most famous, Harriet Tubman and Sojourner Truth, demand our attention.

Tubman combined her intellect, bravery, compassion, and common sense with a deep devotion to freedom, liberty, and God. She was called Moses by those she led out of slavery via the underground railway, and Thief by slaveholders who longed to eliminate her. During the Civil War she successfully spied for the north while nursing injured soldiers, and she fought as well.

Author Catherine Clinton says "Tubman's skills as a root doctor were formidable at a time when disease was the army's number one enemy. Three out of five Civil War soldiers who died during the war were killed by disease unrelated to wounds."[4] After dysentery had troops "dying off like sheep . . . Tubman journeyed south to give her time and energy to the soldiers as well as to contrabands, seeing them through this severe outbreak. She also tended men with smallpox and other 'malignant fevers,' without being felled herself. Once again, miraculous powers were ascribed to her, as her healing powers became legendary among her Union comrades."[5]

On June 2, 1863 she commanded an action along the Combahee River in South Carolina. The carefully planned attack used three Union gunboats to liberate more than 750 Blacks—who had been previously alerted to the plan—while Rebel soldiers scrambled to halt the action. "More than 750 slaves were spirited onto Union gunboats that night, shepherded by 150 Black soldiers. The estates of the Heywards, the Middletons, the Lowndes and other Carolina dynasties were left bereft and humiliated. Tubman's plan was triumphant."[6]

After the war ended Tubman fought for years to obtain the government pension she had earned, and finally received in 1899 by an Act of Congress. She was almost 80.

Born into slavery in March, 1822, in Maryland, she was Araminta Ross before her brief marriage to John Tubman in 1844. In 1849 she escaped to Philadelphia, then risked her life to return to Maryland and bring members of her family north to freedom. Soon she was making regular, dangerous trips back and forth, from slavery to freedom, like the one reported above by Martha Wright.

As a child Araminta was repeatedly "hired out." The first hiring came at age five when she was given the responsibility to care for a newborn White baby. In Catherine Clinton's compelling biography, *Harriet Tubman: The Road to Freedom,* she writes of this episode:

> "Once installed in a new master's household, she was given a full load of domestic tasks, as well as caring for the infant. . . . she remained on duty at night, instructed to rock the cradle constantly

to prevent the baby from disturbing the master or mistress." If her efforts failed and the parents were awakened, mother did not go to the wailing baby but instead "lifted her hand to grab a small whip from its shelf . . ." Tubman remembered one day being whipped five times before breakfast.[7]

Harriet Tubman has been the subject of many children's books and films, but the details of her complicated life—first as a slave, and then a rescuer of slaves, then a nurse, a spy, and a fighter in the Civil War—is one that deserves far more attention and recognition.

Her life-long goal was to establish a charity home for Blacks. She finally achieved that in Auburn, New York, long after the war, when she bought property adjoining her home, then coaxed donors to help her make the down payment. And she fought for women's rights as long as she was able. For example, in 1905 she made a trip to Rochester, NY for a meeting the next day, and sat up all night in the train station—"knowing, perhaps by experience, that there would be 'no lodgings which would take in a woman of color.'"[8]

She died at about 90 years of age in March 10, 1913, surrounded by friends. Calling her a remarkable woman is an understatement. Scholars debate whether she actually said the words most attributed to her, but given her long years of fight and struggle the words, if not exact, surely reflect her attitude: "If you are tired, keep going; if you are scared, keep going; if you are hungry, keep going; if you want to taste freedom, keep going."

Sojourner Truth was born into slavery c.1797 and given the name Isabella Baumfree. She grew to the age of nine on a Dutch farm in Swartekill, New York. When her owner, Colonel Johannes Hardenbergh, died she was sold at auction to John Neely. She spoke only Dutch and was beaten daily for not understanding English. She was sold again, and then again to John Dumont who raped her repeatedly and fathered a child, Diana, in 1815. Around that time she fell in love with a slave named Robert, but his master forbade a marriage. She eventually married an enslaved man named Thomas with whom she had four more children.[9]

In 1826, after her master refused to honor his promise to free her, she escaped, taking her infant daughter. "I did not run away, I walked away by daylight . . ."[10] Isabella became a wandering preacher, following her conviction that God wished her to "testify to the hope that was in her." She wandered up and down the eastern seaboard, speaking her truth. In 1843 she changed her name to Sojourner Truth, and by the 1850s she was involved with the antislavery movement, then with the effort for women's rights.

Sojourner spoke often at various meetings, withstanding the hisses and catcalls from those determined to mock any woman who stood for voting rights, especially a Black woman. But she continued, unfazed.

She is most famous for her extemporaneous speech "Ain't I a Woman?" given in 1851 at the Ohio Women's Rights Convention. There are varying reports of this event, and different versions of the speech. One, appearing in the *Anti-Slavery Bugle* by Rev Marius Robinson, omits the repetition of "Ain't I a woman?" and disputes the Black dialect (she was raised speaking Dutch) given her in Matilda Gage's report of the event in 1863.[11] I'm including part of Gage's report as included in the *History of Woman Suffrage* because it offers a sense of the moment.

On day one of the convention:

> "The leaders of the movement trembled on seeing a tall, gaunt Black woman in a gray dress and white turban, surmounted with an uncouth sun-bonnet, march deliberately into the church, walk with the air of a queen up the aisle, and take her seat upon the pulpit steps."

On day two, five ministers representing their denominations rose to speak about the resolutions being discussed:

> "One claimed superior rights and privileges for man, on the ground of 'superior intellect' . . . Another gave us a theological view of the 'sin of our first mother' . . . The atmosphere betokened a storm. When slowly from her seat in the corner rose Sojourner Truth. . . . There was a hissing sound of disapprobation above and below. I rose and announced 'Sojourner Truth' and begged the audience to keep silence for a few moments.

> "The tumult subsided at once, and every eye was fixed on this almost Amazon form, which stood nearly six feet high, head erect, and eyes piercing the upper air like in a dream. At her first word there was a profound hush. She spoke in deep tones, which though not loud, reached every ear in the house and away through the throng at the doors and windows."

As Truth's speech ended, Gage writes:

> "Amid roars of applause, she returned to her corner. . . . I have never in my life seen anything like the magical influence that subdued the mobbish spirit of the day, and turned the sneers and cheers of an excited crowd into notes of respect and admiration."[12]

During the Civil War Sojourner Truth helped recruit Black troops to fight for the Union cause and then fought against the U.S government for land grants for the formerly enslaved—a hopeless endeavor after Lincoln's death.

In 1867, at the annual meeting of the American Equal Rights Association in New York, Truth was greeted again with cheers after her introduction by Lucretia Mott. Her speech is recorded in *The History.* It includes these lines:

> "I come from another field—the country of the slave. . . . There is a great stir about colored men getting their rights, but not a word about the colored women: and if colored men get their rights, and not colored women theirs, you see the colored men will be masters over the women, and it will be just as bad as it was before."[13]

Frances Gage, in her "Reminiscences" wrote: "Sojourner combined in herself, as an individual, the two most hated elements of humanity. She was Black, and she was a woman, and all the insults that could be cast on color and sex were together hurled at her, but there she stood, calm and dignified, a grand wise woman, who could neither read nor write, and yet with deep insight could penetrate the very soul of the universe about her."[14]

Sojourner never stopped working for reforms, and to better the lives of others, traveling as far as Kansas in 1879–80 to help feed and clothe refugees. She made many such trips. She also worked for the U.S.

Government's Freedmen's Bureau, charged with "promoting a successful transition to free labor" in the South, a challenging effort.

Just as there are alternative versions of what Truth said, there are discrepancies regarding her age at death. She said in 1867 that she was over 80. Vol III of *History of Woman Suffrage* refers to proof that she was over 100 years old, and "closed her eventful life in Battle Creek in 1883 . . . having reached the great age of one hundred and ten."[15]

Sojourner Truth was the first African American woman to have a statue in the U.S. Capitol building.

Ida B. Wells was born in Mississippi in 1862, less than a year before Emancipation. She grew up to become a journalist and a civil rights icon. According to a *New York Times* obituary by Caitlin Dickerson, "Wells is considered by historians to have been the most famous Black woman in the United States during her lifetime, even as she was dogged by prejudice, a disease infecting Americans from coast to coast."[16]

Both her parents and a brother died during a yellow fever epidemic, leaving her to care for her remaining family with help from her grandmother. She found work as a teacher in a rural Black elementary school. After her grandmother died she moved with her two youngest sisters to Memphis, Tennessee to live with an aunt and again found work as a teacher. During the summer she attended Fisk University, and in 1889 began writing for the *Free Speech and Headlight*, a Black-owned newspaper, which she co-owned.

Racial segregation and inequality were her primary subjects but in 1892, after a mob dragged three Black men (who were friends of Wells's) from a jail and shot them, she began investigating and documenting lynching in the Unites States through articles and pamphlets, naming the victims. After the murder of her friends, she published a piece urging Blacks to leave Memphis: "There is, therefore, only one thing left to do; save our money and leave a town which will neither protect our lives and property, nor give us a fair trial in the courts, but takes us out and murders us in cold blood when accused by white persons."[17]

Despite constant threats and harassment she continued this work for many years, as "her fiery pen condemned lynching and violent and legal efforts by white Southerners to deny newly freed Black Americans the vote, writing 'The reproach and disgrace of the twentieth century, is that the whole of the American people have permitted a part, to nullify this glorious achievement, and make the fourteenth and fifteenth amendments to the Constitution playthings, a mockery and a byword; an absolute dead letter in the Constitution of the United States."[18]

As the White press continued to proclaim African Americans "villains" and Whites as innocent victims, Wells was a respected voice in the South and was listened to. She organized an anti-lynching campaign and wrote openly about it in ways Whites did not approve. Her life was frequently threatened. After a White mob destroyed her newspaper office she continued to write for national Black-owned papers. She moved to Chicago and married in 1895, and bought *The Conservator* newspaper, becoming its editor, publisher, and business manager. She continued organizing for civil rights and women's rights, and writing until the end of her life. She died in 1931, aged 68.

Chicago was also the home of another ground-breaking female Black writer. Ethel Lois Payne (1911–91) was called the "First Lady of the Black Press."[19] She was born in Chicago to parents who were the children of former slaves. Her father was a Pullman porter, her mother a former Latin teacher. She attended Lindblom Technical High School where a writing teacher inspired her, then the City Colleges of Chicago and night school at Medill School of Journalism at Northwestern University. Not surprisingly perhaps, there were few jobs available for Black journalists, so she took a job as a library assistant at the public library, and joined the NAACP, working to promote equal-employment opportunities for African Americans. She went on to break barriers.

After a 1948 detour in Japan, where she worked as a service club hostess at the Army Special Service Club (and eventually became the director), she returned to Chicago to work full-time for the publisher of *The Chicago Defender*, a paper with national reader ship. Her journal writing while in Japan had captivated a visiting

*Defender* reporter who shared it with his publisher, who began publishing her pieces. She stayed with that paper, and its owner, Sengtacke Newspapers, for 25 years, 1951 to 1978. In 1953 she moved to Washington D.C. to become the company's only national correspondent and one of only three accredited African Americans in the White House Press Corps.

She focused not just on national stories, but international as well, the first African American to do so. It should be no surprise to learn that she covered some of the most important stories of the era, including the Montgomery bus boycott, the 1963 March on Washington, and desegregation at the University of Alabama.[20]

When President Johnson signed the Civil Rights Act of 1964 Payne was present, and was honored with one of the pens used to sign the legislation.[21] Two years later she was in Vietnam to cover African-American troops, followed by the International Women's Year Conference in Mexico City, and travel with Secretary of State Henry Kissinger on a six-nation tour of Africa.

In 2002 Payne, an "aggressive journalist who asked tough questions" was one of four journalists honored by the U.S. Post Office in a set of four stamps celebrating "Women in Journalism." She won multiple awards, including being the first recipient of Fisk University's Ida B. Wells Distinguished Journalism Chair, and a National Association of Black Journalists Lifetime Achievement Award in 1988.[22]

We live in an era when the voices of Black Americans speak to us from every field of endeavor. We see them on our multiple screens, we are informed by their expertise as doctors, professors, lawyers, reporters, researchers, entertainers, activists and so much more.

Two Black writers, Nikole Hannah-Jones and Isabel Wilkerson, deserve endless thanks for their work in bringing to light the true origin story of Blacks in America. Wilkerson is the author of *Caste: The Origins of Our Discontents,* published in 2020, and winner of a Pulitzer Prize. She is also the author of *The Warmth of Other Suns,* which won the National Book Critics Circle Award for Nonfiction, and is on the *New York Times's* list of the Best Nonfiction of All Time. *Caste* opened my eyes in many ways, as she linked our country's underlying but hidden caste system with that of India and the Third Reich. It should not surprise you to learn that it's all about power. I found it beautiful and enlightening, and I highly recommend it.

Nikole Hannah-Jones is a Pulitzer Prize-winning reporter covering racial injustice for the *New York Times Magazine*, and the Knight Chair in Race and Journalism at Howard University. She has won too many awards to count, beginning maybe in 2007 with the Society of Professional Journalists Pacific Northwest Excellence in Journalism Award (also received in 2008 and 2010).

In 2016 she co-founded the Ida B. Wells Society for Investigative Reporting, an organization dedicated to training and mentorship for reporters of color. But it was her *1619 Project* for the *New York Times* that brought her wide attention. The *Project* is a collection of writings, essays, and poems created to honor the 400th anniversary of the arrival of the first African slaves on our shores. A book with the same title followed in 2021, with contributions by a variety of writers. The two efforts made her name familiar across all 50 states. They also left her despised by those who could not or would not accept the truth that she and others had written.

It is emotionally rending to read some of those words. In a piece called "Justice," Hannah-Jones quotes Frederick Douglass in 1881:

> "When the Hebrews were emancipated, they were told to take spoil from the Egyptians. When the serfs of Russia were emancipated, they were given three acres of ground upon which they could live and make a living. But not so when our slaves were emancipated. They were sent away empty-handed, without money, without friends and without a foot of land to stand upon. Old and young, sick and well, were turned loose to the open sky, naked to their enemies."[23]

Both these women make it clear that we have failed to live up to our ideals as a country, and that we have miles to go before this country will finally accept its duty. As Hannah-Jones writes in *The 1619 Project:*

"A truly great country does not ignore or excuse its sins. It confronts them, and then works to make them right. If we are to be redeemed, we must do what is just: we must, finally, live up to the magnificent ideals upon which we were founded."[24]

# 16

## THE 20TH CENTURY ARRIVES

On December 31, 1899 people around the world were happily anticipating the coming new century. The industrial revolution was well underway, the telegraph brought instant news from afar, automobiles would soon be affordable to the masses, and fast, luxurious steam ships brought goods and people swiftly across the seas. Though occasional fighting had occurred in places like Crimea and the Balkans—places with strange-sounding names that few who scanned the daily news sheets cared about— no one was worried. After all, it will soon be the 20th century! A telephone in every house! Airplanes carrying passengers across the ocean! Imagine!

Yes, the 20th century brought amazing progress. It also brought the unimaginable, the deadliest war in history. Known today as World War I, its causes were several, including a weakening of the once powerful Ottoman Empire that stretched from central Europe across the Middle East into parts of Africa.

It was an assassination in Sarajevo that lit the match. Archduke Franz Ferdinand, heir to the Austro-Hungarian throne, was shot and killed by a Bosnian Serb on June 28, 1914. The monarchy blamed Serbia and a month later declared war. That brought Russia to Serbia's defense and within days Germany, Russia, France, and the UK were at war.

The Ottomans joined later that year and by 1915 there was fighting in Italy, Bulgaria, Romania, and Greece. Discontent in Russia gave revolutionaries the break they needed. They took advantage of the chaos, and in 1917 a revolution ended the Russian Empire forever. Finland and Ukraine, previously ruled by the Tsar, quickly declared their independence, which sparked still more fighting. In April 1917 the U.S. entered the war.

It was the War to End All Wars, or the Great War, or the World War. No matter its name, it was a catastrophic event that redrew borders across Europe and beyond. Historian and diplomat George Kennan (1904–2005) called it "the great seminal catastrophe" of the 20th century.[1] Thanks to the film industry, trench warfare and poison gas are perhaps that war's most remembered features, but submarines, a relatively new development, did great damage to transatlantic shipping, and of course brought the sinking of the Lusitania—a passenger ship—in 1915 (the Titanic sank before the war, in 1912). Every weapon seemed to grow more efficient, while old reliables like horses and wagons, were shoved aside. By the end of the war in November, 1918, armies were using the latest technology: wireless communication, the telephone, aircraft, armored cars, and tanks.[2]

An Armistice was signed and famously took effect at the 11th hour, of the 11th day, of the 11th month, 1918. It demanded an immediate end to hostilities, repatriation of prisoners of war, Germany's immediate withdrawal from occupied lands, and the creation of a neutral zone. Fighting continued on the edges, and in Russia's civil war, into the 1920s.[3]

I'm not going to dwell on the battles and political machinations that played themselves out over those four horrendous years. I'm more interested in what came after—significant changes in attitudes, in styles, and in expectations. The staid, relatively settled 19th century world seemed to explode into a whirlwind of energetic change. And a lot of it affected women.

In the U.S. Vice President Calvin Coolidge served as president after Warren Harding's death in 1923. Harding's administration had been tainted by numerous scandals but Coolidge was a quiet man who restored confidence in government, and the economy grew. He supported racial equality and signed into law the Indian Citizenship Act of 1924, which finally made U.S. citizens of all Native Americans.

As the economy grew stronger, women—who finally won the vote in 1920—were beginning to more visibly work outside the home, as secretaries and typewriters (yes, that's what they were called) and in similar jobs. Of course they'd always worked in homes and hotels as maids and cooks; and many worked in the clothing factories that had sprung up.

Liquor was outlawed, but speakeasies (illicit nightclubs) made it relatively easy to get. It was the Roaring Twenties and everything was in flux.

Clothing styles changed dramatically. Skirts were lifted from the floor, first to ankles and then to knees. Waistlines dropped to high hip or lower, and breasts were minimized. Long hair, once considered a standard of beauty, became a chin-length bob, frequently worn under a cloche hat. Makeup grew more acceptable and was used to shape features like cupid's bow lips (after actress Clara Bow) and kohl-rimmed eyes.

Dresses remained *de rigueur.* There were morning dresses, afternoon or tea dresses, and the new cocktail dresses. Long gowns were only for formal dinners. Sporting clothes for men were suddenly in fashion, and women too wore pants on "sporting" occasions. The rigid, Victorian dresses and confining laced corsets were left to fill trash receptacles. Everywhere it seemed, women were stepping out, happy to be free of binding clothes and binding rules. Comfort, flexibility, and practicality became key fashion elements. By the mid-twenties jazz was increasingly popular and "flappers" were dancing—and smoking and drinking—in dresses that stopped at the knee.

It was the era of the New Woman, of experimental music, movies, and art. Dadaism had already broken barriers, and Picasso and others cracked more. James Joyce published *Ulysses* in 1922. Silent film stars showed off the current fashions. Novelist Scott Fitzgerald and his wife

Zelda were popular figures who constantly tested society's standards. All this change was, of course, decried by those who were shocked by what they saw as the breakdown of society; they mostly blamed women, calling them morally lax. Women, they insisted, belonged in the home, behind a stove or changing diapers. But the Great War had knocked something loose; change was in the air and it would not be refused. The pretended innocence of the pre-war years was forever lost.

By the year 1920:

- Albert Einstein had defined special relativity
- Ford Motor Company had invented the Model T, and soon after, the first moving assembly line
- last Emperor of China assumed the throne
- Panama Canal had opened
- first Pulitzer Prizes were announced
- League of Nations was founded (and would fail)
- the proton was discovered
- Girl Scout Cookies were being sold
- Treaty of Versailles redrew European borders, and demanded harsh reparations from Germany, which may have set the stage for World War II.

I could go on. The 20th century may have been the busiest 100 years in human history. It isn't just the two world wars and the manifold crises that led to them. The century marks a growth of inventiveness and breakthroughs in multiple fields of science, from quantum mechanics, to the polio vaccine, television, computers, mobile phones, even walking on the moon. Of course a lot of this industry also threatened the planet.

### The Great Depression

Unfortunately, the excitement and progress of the Roaring Twenties was brought to an abrupt halt for over ten years, beginning in 1929. A severe breakdown in global finance, including a crash in the United States stock market (Black Thursday) led to crises in many countries. It was a devastating development that brought high unemployment (23 percent in the U.S.; as high as 33 percent in other places) and falling personal income. International trade fell 50 percent as construction was halted, and exports and crop prices fell. The 1930 Smoot-Hawley Tariff Act and retaliatory tariffs only increased the disintegration of global trade. Between April 1930 to July 1932 the stock market lost 89 percent of its value. Multiple banks closed.

The collapse of a major Austrian Bank and the rise of the National Socialist party (NAZI) in Germany caused financial policies there to fail, putting more pressure on the German people, as well as international banks. This crisis aided Hitler's rise to power.

In the U.S. Franklin Roosevelt was elected president in 1933, the first of three terms (the only president to be so elected). One of the new president's best decisions was to hire a woman, Frances Perkins, as his Secretary of Labor. She greatly influenced his thinking and came to the job with a list of priorities that included:

- an eight-hour work day
- minimum wage
- worker's compensation
- unemployment compensation
- federal law banning child labor
- direct federal aid for unemployment relief
- Social Security
- revitalized public employment service
- health insurance [4]

Could she do all that? She could, almost. Francis Perkins was the first woman to be appointed to a presidential cabinet and she served in that office from 1933 to 1945, the entire time Roosevelt was in office. I vaguely remember hearing her name as a child, possibly my mother, a dedicated Democrat, praised her. But I didn't understand the depth of her contributions until I stumbled across Kristin Downey's book, *The Woman Behind the New Deal.* She was, truly, an amazing woman.

During her years in office Perkins met with continuing criticism and "militant opposition" to implementing her ideas. But she never wavered in her determination, and the New Deal the president is now famous for is the result of Perkins's ideas—ideas that she often had to argue for and convince Roosevelt to undertake. That he was willing to listen, is to his credit.

Francis Perkins graduated from Mount Holyoke College in 1902 with a bachelor's degree in chemistry and physics. She was a class president and while there became interested in the woman's suffrage movement. She also attended the University of Pennsylvania's Wharton School, where she learned economics. She then attended Columbia University where she earned a master's degree in economics and sociology. In 1910 she was the head of the NY office of the National Consumers League, lobbying for better working conditions.

When 146 garment workers, mostly women and girls, died in the 1911 Triangle Shirtwaist Factory fire, Perkins was a witness.[5] It was a pivotal event for workers, unions and, in fact, most of New York, and it moved her to take a job as executive secretary for the Committee on Safety of the City of New York. In 1912 she was instrumental in getting the New York legislature to pass a "54-hour" bill that capped the number of hours women and children could work.

In 1913 she married Paul Caldwell Wilson, an economist and a secretary to the New York City mayor. Perkins kept her maiden name (she had to go to court to do so) in order that her work in New York and Albany wouldn't reflect on her husband. In 1929 Franklin Roosevelt, then New York governor, hired her to be the inaugural NY state industrial commissioner where she supervised 1800 employees. While there she reduced the work week for women to 48 hours and championed minimum wage and unemployment insurance laws.

Though she held numerous positions in state government, confirmation of a female employee was always a problem. But after her time on the Industrial Commission a fellow commissioner said her contributions were "invaluable" and added "from the work which Miss Perkins has accomplished I am convinced that more women ought to be placed in high positions throughout the state departments."[6]

Sadly, Perkins's personal life was not as smooth as her career trajectory. A year or two after their only child, Susanna, was born, her husband began having mental issues and was in and out of institutions throughout their marriage. Later her daughter suffered from bipolar disorder.

But despite what one might reasonably call obstacles, Francis Perkins spent her life working to break barriers and improve the lives of women and men. She initiated much of what we now call the social safety net. She died in 1965.

While researching this era I came across a talk that Perkins gave at Cornell University's School of Industrial and Labor Relations in 1964. It was about the 1911 Triangle Fire mentioned above. The victims were on the 9th and 10th floors of the building. There was only one exit, which was locked; two elevator shafts were immediately engulfed in flames. Perkins, speaking [apparently] extemporaneously, described what she saw:

> "We could see this building from Washington Square and the people had just begun to jump when we got there. They had been holding until that time, standing in the windowsills, being crowded by others behind them, the fire pressing closer and closer, the smoke closer and closer.
>
> "Firemen attempted to get nets out to catch the jumpers, but they couldn't wait, they began to jump." She pauses, then continues, "The window was too crowded and they would jump and they hit the sidewalk. The net broke . . . the weight of the bodies was so great, at the speed at which they were traveling that they broke through the net. Everyone of them was killed, everybody who jumped was killed. It was a horrifying spectacle."

Perkins went on to talk about an open meeting held a week later at the Metropolitan Opera House. A donor had contributed $25,000 from his sick bed in South Carolina urging the city to do something. One of the early speakers was Rose Schneiderman, a young, red-headed woman who was a member of the Ladies' Dress and Waist Union. Perkins praised her speech. "Wonderful what a speech she made, and I remember how moved we all were by this girl who was a member of that union, you see . . . ."[7]

Here's an excerpt of Schneiderman's speech:

> "This is not the first time girls have been burned alive in the city. Every week I must learn of the untimely death of one of my sister workers.

> Every year thousands of us are maimed. The life of men and women is so cheap and property is so sacred. There are so many of us for one job it matters little if 146 of us are burned to death.
>
> We have tried you citizens; we are trying you now, and you have a couple of dollars for the sorrowing mothers and brothers and sisters by way of a charity gift. But every time the workers come out in the only way they know to protest against conditions which are unbearable the strong hand of the law is allowed to press down heavily upon us.
>
> Public officials have only words of warning to us – warning that we must be intensely orderly and must be intensely peaceable, and they have the workhouse just back of all their warnings. The strong hand of the law beats us back, when we rise, into the conditions that make life unbearable."[8]

Rose Schneiderman (1882–1972) was a Polish-born American labor organizer and feminist. Her family migrated to NY in 1890. In 1903 at the age of 21, she started organizing the women in her cap factory, and the union then chartered its first women's local. She also played a role in the 1909 strike of shirtwaist workers led by the International Ladies' Garment Workers Union. Schneiderman later helped pass the NY state law in 1917 that gave women the right to vote. By 1919 she was a key member of the first International Congress of Working Women. She was also a founding member of the American Civil Liberties Union and served on Roosevelt's Labor Advisory board.

The "New Deal" that President Roosevelt instituted included public works projects, financial reforms, and new banking and other regulations. The Civilian Conservation Corps (CCC), the Civil Works Administration (WPA), the National·Industrial Recovery Act of 1933 (NIRA) and the Social Security Administration (SSA) all furnished support for farmers, the unemployed, youth, and elderly citizens.

There appears to be no real consensus on whether Roosevelt's actions brought an end to the Depression, but they eased poverty and hunger, provided much-needed jobs, and surely improved the general morale. He could do this, in part, because he hired and relied on dedicated, determined women who knew what life on the ground was like for men and women, rich or poor. And he was married to Eleanor, a decidedly dedicated and determined woman.

A new Congress in 1938 brought more Republicans to Washington. Conservative Republicans and Democrats then joined an informal conservative coalition that by 1942–43 had shut down the WPA and CCC relief programs. Their work can still be seen in some state and national parks across the country. Roosevelt was reelected in 1940, when it was clear the war in Europe was heating up.

# 17

## THE SECOND WORLD WAR, 1939–1945

Like every war, this was a horror—but worse, thanks to Adolf Hitler and his belief in Aryan supremacy. Before it ended in 1945 war had overtaken nearly every country on the globe. It was the Allies (the U.S., Britain and its Empire, France, and after 1941 the USSR) versus the Axis powers (Germany, Italy, Japan, and parts of North Africa).

It was pure aggression: autocracy versus freedom and independence, fabricated from the fever dreams of two men, Hitler and Mussolini, and later Stalin, who united to feed their egos and satisfy whatever unmet needs chewed at their innards. Unfortunately, the fear they were able to generate meant they had plenty of help.

Its causes were multiple and intricate. Indeed they have filled many a book and are far beyond the scope of this one. But though WWII feels distant, the world we live in today still reflects decisions made during and after that period, some affecting women, so it deserves our attention, if only briefly.[1]

Border issues and disagreements had worried the European continent for years. It's generally thought, but not fully agreed, that the severe treatment of Germany after WWI led that country into deep economic trouble, including the hyperinflation that angered the populace. And that may have opened the door to the 1933 election of Adolf Hitler, head of the fascist Nazi party, as Chancellor. A year later he named himself Führer and dissolved Germany's democracy.

Italy had been led since 1922 by the fascist Benito Mussolini. He had been appointed prime minister by King Victor Emmanuel III but he consolidated power and created a one-party dictatorship. He had earlier joined Hitler in supporting General Franco's civil war in Spain, and quickly joined the war on Hitler's side in June 1940.

In August 1939 Hitler and Stalin, the communist leader of the Soviet Union, created a pact, dividing their "spheres of influence," which included Finland, Estonia, Latvia, Lithuania, and Romania. On September 1, 1939 Hitler invaded Poland. Three days later the UK and France declared war on Germany. Stalin, anxious to grab his share, invaded Poland from the east 16 days later.

After Germany occupied Czechoslovakia and the Slovak Republic, and Italy had seized Albania, the United Kingdom and France expanded their guarantee of support to more nations. In the far east Japan and the Soviet Union were fighting, and Italy moved into Africa where multiple colonies and independent countries were considered ripe for conquering. When the Soviet Union invaded Finland on November 30, almost the whole of Europe was at war.

It had taken just 21 years—one generation—for so-called leaders and their followers to jump from one world war into another. Millions would die.

In the United States President Roosevelt was resisting a strong U.S. right-wing pro-axis movement while searching for ways to help the allies. He eventually invented a lend-lease program that bypassed most objections and allowed arms shipments to Britain. A surprise attack by Japan on America's fleet at Pearl Harbor on December 7, 1941 brought the U.S. into the war.

It's believed over 70 to 85 million people died in WWII, most of them civilians. The eastern front was the deadliest; the Soviet Union alone lost about 27 million people, both military and civilian.[2]

During his relatively short but evil reign Hitler initiated the single-most horrifying episode in all of human history. The Holocaust was the result of Hitler's racist theories about almost everyone, but especially Jews. On his orders multiple camps were built where civilians—men, women, and children—were worked to death or killed outright. Eleven to 17 million civilians died: around 6 million Jews, Roma, and homosexuals; 1.9 million ethnic Poles, and millions of other Slavs and ethnic or minority groups. By the end of the war "there was quite a bit of rivalry among the S.S. leaders as to which was the most efficient gas to speed the Jews to their death." Auschwitz, for instance, set new records, gassing 6,000 victims a day—innocent people whose only crime was being themselves.[3]

**Women and the war**

It was a war that dominated my early childhood. It was on the radio; it filtered down through adult conversations. Towns and cities were changed as more than 16 million American men were drafted and sent overseas to fight and die, their jobs left vacant. Housewives suddenly found themselves in demand as workers.

Women also entered the armed forces. General George Marshall supported that idea—after the First Lady raised it—and Congress instituted and then upgraded the women's branches in the various armed forces. They began as auxiliary units but before long women were in uniform too, as WACS (Women's Army Corps), WAVES (Women Accepted for Volunteer Emergency Service) and WASPS (Women's Airforce Service Pilots). In total about 350,000 women joined the Armed Forces.

By the end of the war there were approximately 100,000 WACs and 6,000 female officers who had full military status, working in non-combatant jobs and in every theater of the war.

In the Navy, the WAVES held the same status as reservists and provided support stateside. The Coast Guard and Marine Corps also had female reservists.

The WASPS, who had pilot licenses prior to service, became the first women to fly military planes, ferrying them from factories to bases, and transporting cargo. More than 1000 served, and 38 died as they flew more than 60 million miles, freeing up thousands of male pilots for active duty. They were considered civil service employees, without military honors or benefits. WASPS finally received full military status in 1977.

"Rosie the Riveter" was a campaign by the U.S. government to encourage women to join the workforce, preferably in jobs benefiting the military. Rosie was fictitious, but she was based on a real-life worker, and the campaign was deemed successful. Such women were crucial to the war effort, but child care and wages (half what men earned) remained a problem. So too was the issue of Black women, who were not always welcomed in the workplace; even if they had the same jobs, their pay was less than for Whites.[4]

The Lanham Act of 1941 gave grants to communities where defense production was heavy, including help with water, sewer, housing, and schools. A 1943 law—passed at the urging of Mrs. Roosevelt—led to the first government-sponsored childcare.[5]

By 1943 women in the U.S. aircraft industry were 65 percent of the total workforce. Though they would later be forced to quit and return home, their work proved to everyone that women could do jobs that had previously been denied them. That idea was easily shoved aside by the post-war landslide of corporate advertising—and misogynistic insistence—supporting the belief that women belong in the home.

I was born a month and a day before the attack on Pearl Harbor, so of course the war had little effect on me until the age of three or four. Then I began to notice things. I remember going with mother to the butcher shop and purchasing our rationed amount of meat with the help of stamps from our ration book. (Other rationed items included sugar, butter, gasoline, tires, and rubber.) I remember carefully saving tinfoil, even the little bits wrapped around candy and gum. Some of those habits extended into late 1940s as the country worked to recover and the Cold War established itself. I suspect these memories and events colored my generation's views about freedom, patriotism, and government in general. Fascism was not a popular word.

I also have a very clear memory of a wartime train trip:

"She stole my watch!" That was the cry of a woman pointing in my direction. She was standing at her seat across the aisle, a few rows ahead of where I was sitting next to my new friend. It was 1945 and I and my parents were on a train heading west after visiting family.

I was probably four and a half; I hadn't yet started school. My friend was probably in her mid-60s. I had stopped in the aisle to watch her knit, fascinated by how quickly the stitches passed from one needle to the next while she paid little or no attention. She invited me to sit with her; with my parents approval I had done so for an hour or so, for three days of the trip.

She told me she was on her way to visit her son in San Francisco, and the sweater she was knitting was for him. I showed her the two little Indian dolls my father had purchased for me during a brief stop in northern New Mexico. She put up with my constant questions, and we chatted while admiring the scenery that rolled endlessly past the window.

It wasn't long before a passenger confronted my parents, questioning their wisdom in letting me sit with "that woman" because "that woman" was a German. If my parents were uncomfortable with the situation they never showed it. Mother explained these actions to me as simply as she could, and said in essence, "just ignore them."

She said "them" because there were many in the car who had shown visible animosity to my friend, deliberately brushing her when they walked by, talking more loudly than necessary about the awful Germans, or muttering "Nazi" as they passed. Those actions had not escaped me, but I was confused, or maybe dumbfounded, over their dislike. I knew a friendly, kind, gentle woman. How could they not like her?

I was aware of the war only as a peripheral matter. My father's hearing loss kept him from serving despite two attempts to enlist, so except in minor ways, the war hadn't touched me. But this was different. This was coming face to face with something ugly.

"She stole my watch!" The woman yelled again. "She should be put off the train, she's a thief!" The conductor was called. He tried to calm the complainer, and asked how she knew this. The whole car was listening.

"When I was in the bathroom I took off my watch to wash my hands. I must have left it there. And that woman came in as I was leaving. After she left I went back to get it and it was gone! She took it!"

The discussion went on; various suggestions were made. I sat with my parents as my friend was questioned by the conductor. A cursory search of her belongings yielded nothing. But that did not satisfy the growing number of accusers who were now taking advantage of the situation. They wanted her off the train or at least out of "our" car. The conductor said there was nothing more he could do, but the complaints only got louder. He left, but a few hours later he came back and moved my friend and her belongings into another car. I waved a sad goodbye.

The next afternoon the accuser discovered her watch hadn't been stolen after all.

The bigotry expressed by the train's passengers was not unique for that time, in fact it permeated much of the populace. It was reinforced every day by news of battles fought, of yet more American soldiers, sailors, and airmen dead or wounded. The brutal slayings of innocents by Germans were documented and mourned; and later came news of the extermination camps and the evil they hid.

But the bigotry didn't end with Germans. Japanese-Americans had been forced into camps on American soil, "just in case" they might be aiding our enemy. Stalin and the Communists were hated too, their brutality in war well known—even against their own citizens.

For me this experience was, of course, a lesson. A good one. That doesn't mean I'm free of bigotry or intolerance; I'm sure it's there in the multiple folds of my brain, it hides in all of us. It's a very human feeling. Perhaps it formed in a distant age when anything "not me" could be dangerous. Probably we learned suspicion to protect ourselves. And maybe that ancient habit embedded itself in our DNA. Whatever its cause it remains to haunt us. And yes, I believe bigotry and fear of the "other" align with the patriarchal tendencies that have harassed and threatened women forever. I can hear you muttering. "Good grief. Does everything have to relate to patriarchy?" And I say no, not everything. But a lot.

# 18

## THE NINETEEN FIFTIES

On April 29, 1945 Adolf Hitler married his long-time partner Eva Braun. The next day, April 30, the couple committed suicide in his Berlin bunker, confirming the collapse of Nazi rule and the end of the European war.

World War II officially ended in May, 1945. President Franklin D. Roosevelt, the man who had guided the United States through that terrible time, had died April 12. His Vice President, Harry Truman, had been in office only a few months, and until his swearing-in he knew nothing about the first atomic bomb, now ready for use.

On June 26, in San Francisco, the United Nations Charter was agreed upon by 50 of 51 countries. It was an act of desperation, of faith, and of hope that humans could work together to prevent future wars. The devastation and savagery of two world wars in 45 years had leached into the lives of almost everyone on the planet. Maybe a United Nations would be the answer.

But war still raged in Japan and the Far East. The new president weighed the costs of using the first atomic weapon. How many American lives would be lost during a military invasion large enough to bring Japan to its knees? What was the estimated number of innocent lives lost in an atom bomb attack? How would the world, and especially the Soviet Union, react to this dreadful weapon?

The Allies called for an unconditional surrender of the Japanese armed forces in July, 1945 with the alternative being "prompt and utter destruction."[1] Japan ignored the ultimatum. So four months after taking office Harry Truman ordered the first and only use (so far) of atomic weapons over two Japanese cities: Hiroshima and Nagasaki, on August 6 and August 9, 1945. And the world was changed.

Estimates are that between 150,000 and 246,000 died in the two bombings. There was no warning given and as they went about their day the victims had no idea what would soon happen. Both cities had significant military facilities, but most of the dead were civilians. Debates about the ethical and legal justifications of that action continue, as they should.

On August 15 Hirohito, the emperor of Japan, surrendered, citing the two bombings and his acceptance of the Potsdam Declaration—an agreement between the United States, the United Kingdom, China, and the Soviet Union. The use of atomic weapons and their enormous destructive power would influence world events far into the future. (The Soviet Union detonated its first atomic bomb in September 1949.)

In the United States both Hitler's defeat and Hirohito's surrender were wildly celebrated. And as in every other country involved in the war, political and social changes were soon underway. In 1947 the president established the Truman Doctrine, an effort to contain Communism and another harbinger of the Cold War. Also in 1947 the Central Intelligence Agency (CIA) was established, the sound barrier was broken, a transistor was demonstrated for the first time, and Jackie Robinson became the first African American player in Major League Baseball.

Everywhere people were easing back into life without war, without rationing, without worry about loved ones fighting abroad. Women whose jobs had supported the war effort were told they were no longer needed; they should return to their homes. Rosie the Riveter was recast as Rosie the Homemaker.

## The post-war years

What followed was a prosperous and optimistic period. Growing up in California I and my classmates had good reasons to feel hopeful; the world was at peace and life could only get better. It's safe to say that all of us—steeped in patriarchal tea—accepted that women belonged in the home, and that women's lives happily circled around marriage and raising children. A few managed to ignore those expectations, however.

My mother worked, as did the moms of a few friends. I was in the second or third grade when she accepted the position as secretary to the elementary school principal. She held that job for many years, resigning twice and coaxed back twice. I took it for granted that women could work outside the home. My father's job with the Forest Service often meant he was home only on weekends, so Mom not only ran the house but paid the bills and made all but major financial decisions. Given that women couldn't obtain credit without their husband's permission (until 1974!) and credit cards were still in our future, every bill and purchase was paid with cash or a check. Looking back from our now effortless automatic bill pay and "tap and go" card purchases, that feels awfully inconvenient.

The U.S. was experiencing an economic recovery. Businesses were rebuilding, employment and wages were up and inflation was low. Between 1945 and 1960—coincidentally my school years—the gross national product more than doubled, growing from $200 billion to more than $500 billion. The G.I. Bill subsidized education and low-cost mortgages for returning servicemen, new homes sprang up everywhere, and the baby-boomer generation began to make their appearance. Disparities remained, however, for Black servicemen and women, who continued to be limited by the Jim Crow laws of the South, and redlining in the North.[2]

In 1948 Harry Truman ran for President, winning a surprise election over the Republican Thomas Dewey. During his campaign Truman crisscrossed the country by train on a 21,928-mile "whistle stop" tour, stopping in big and small towns and speaking to crowds from the rear platform of the presidential car.[3] I remember walking the few blocks through town with my parents, our destination a park next to the railroad tracks. I thought it terribly exciting to get to see a President, and since I was still small I had a perfect view, sitting on Dad's shoulders throughout Truman's brief talk. The train was decorated with red, white, and blue bunting and the crowd was enthusiastic. I thought he seemed like a nice man.

Despite the general optimism of the period, events behind the scenes remained unsettling. The Cold War between the West and Communism would percolate for 44 years, producing stresses, sometimes violent, that often involved recently colonized nations fighting for independence or caught in a civil war. Both America, its allies, and the Soviet Union sought to bring such nations into their fold of influence. The invisible but always present worry was the fact of the atomic (and after 1952, hydrogen) bombs that both sides stockpiled. I don't remember practicing hiding under my school desk but we may have; there were such drills elsewhere. The fact that a school desk wouldn't save us was never mentioned.

The invasion by North Korea into the South in 1950 soon drew the U.S. military back into a war that President Truman called a police action. An armistice in 1953 created the current border between the two; over 70 years later it is stable, but remains a potential flashpoint.

At home in the 1950s television was overtaking radio and playing its role in supporting the "women belong at home" platitude. Besides *Father Knows Best,* we watched *Leave It to Beaver, I Love Lucy, and The Adventures of Ozzie and Harriet,* all shows representing "traditional" families. And oh yes, *Queen for a Day,* a show that "turned unhappy housewives into TV royalty."[4] Westerns were also popular beginning in the late 1950s: *Wagon Train, Maverick, Gunsmoke,* and others. Not surprisingly women played only minor roles: the pretty (and modestly sexy) saloon girl, the pretty homesteader, or the pretty wife.

For me this was a time of growing and learning. Life felt safe, comfortable, and mostly fun, but I was discovering that bad things happen too. My neighbor, friend, and playmate, a few years older, contracted polio. She recovered, but wore a leg brace for over a year, and our time together shrunk to almost nothing. The school had given her permission to wear slacks to cover her brace; some of us were, admittedly, envious.

Long pants and jeans were considered unladylike; girls must always wear dresses or skirts. Which made climbing and swinging on playground equipment a bit of a struggle and an open invitation for teasing. In sixth or seventh grade we girls were finally given permission to wear pants or jeans—on Fridays only—which we thought the greatest treat. Seventh grade was also the year I and a group of friends took classes in gun safety and shooting, sponsored by the NRA. By summer I'd earned my sharpshooter badge and Dad bought me a 22 rifle. I felt very grown up.

It wasn't uncommon in small farming towns like ours for people to have guns. We were on a major flyway and I remember falling asleep on Autumn nights to the unending cries of geese passing overhead. Duck and pheasant hunting were especially popular and financially important to the community. Pheasant season brought hunters from all over, and many of the churches held "hunter breakfasts" on the weekends. As a kid I helped wash dishes and serve food in the church basement while hoping Tennessee Ernie Ford might show up. He visited nearly every Fall in the late '40s and early '50s.

There are many good reasons to look back at the 1950s and laugh; including the lack of everything we now consider essential. But for a child living in a small town it felt stable and peaceful, and very unlike the stresses felt today.

### The Second Sex

Meanwhile across the Atlantic a brilliant French woman named Simone de Beauvoir published a book in 1949 that became a benchmark in the history of women and a needed shove toward female equality. A translation of *The Second Sex* was published in the United States in 1953, and as Judith Thurman notes in her introduction to a more complete 2009 translation, it "marks the place in history where an enlightenment begins."[5]

The book is both a wide and deep look at female lives from birth to adulthood, and an analysis of how one gender influences the other. Put simply, for most of recorded time society has portrayed men as representing the Norm. Women have been and still are, Other. Misogyny and patriarchy are the result.

Born in 1908, Beauvoir was an existentialist, a feminist, a philosopher, a social theorist, and one of the most influential thinkers of her generation. The youngest person ever to obtain the *agrégation* in philosophy at the Sorbonne, the jury placed her second to Jean-Paul Sartre (excuse me while I question the jury) with whom she soon formed a lifelong partnership. Beauvoir was bisexual and she and Sartre never married, though they shared what he called an "essential" love.[6] She died in 1986.

Simone de Beauvoir undoubtedly dove deeper and more systematically into her investigation of women, and their ineluctable link to men, than anyone before or since. All the intricacies of being a prepubescent girl growing into a woman: her introduction to sex, marriage, becoming a mother—every aspect of female life is open for examination. Her book is divided into two volumes. Vol. One, Facts and Myths, includes chapters on Destiny, History, and Myths. Vol. Two, Lived Experience, contains Formative Years, Situation, Justifications, and Toward Liberation.

Perhaps not surprisingly, it was her chapter on history that drew most of my interest, specifically early man's break with the mystical. As man becomes master of the fertile earth, woman "is destined to be subordinated, possessed, and exploited, as is also Nature, whose magic fertility she incarnates. . . . Thus the day agriculture ceases to be an essentially magic operation and becomes creative labor, man finds himself to be a generative force; he lays claim to his children and his crops at the same time."[7]

This change, from beings who were awed by the natural world, esteeming Earth as their mother, to a materialistic view of the planet as a source of wealth and power—this idea is a critical change and one that puzzled me. Our casual destruction of forests, of lands hiding oil, gas, coal, gold or other metals, felt cruel to my young self, and still does. Today, of course, I recognize the role that destruction had in creating the conveniences and way of life we now enjoy. I also understand its role in the climate crisis. But until I read Beauvoir's words I had not associated that loss of respect for nature with patriarchy.

I found its echo in physicist Marcelo Gleiser's book, *The Dawn of a Mindful Universe.* "Gradually," he writes, "the age-old sacred alliance between humans and Nature turned into an open conflict. Nature, once the life-giving mother goddess, became Nature, the enemy. Ancestral religions that worshipped Nature were deemed pagan and sinful." In a later chapter he states, "The severance of our spiritual bond to the planet made our unchecked growth possible. Nature changed from being a sacred realm to disposable garbage . . . this growth is choking our future."[8]

I'm not ready to blame men for depriving us of that spiritual link with the natural world; after all they lost it too. But I do wonder what our world would be like today if women had remained equals, instead of evil Eve.

There's no doubt *The Second Sex* had an impact on all who read it, and even those who only heard about it. Though women had written about women's issues for years, no one before Simone de Beauvoir had taken that task so seriously. No one had thought so deeply or written so intelligently on a subject that most in that period found silly and frilly. Women had not had so much attention paid them since Freud declared they suffered from penis envy.

My copy of *The Second Sex* is 766 pages, and I confess I haven't read it all. It's dense and wide-ranging, and much is beyond the scope of this effort. She ends, however, with a thought I heartily agree with: "What is beyond doubt is that until now women's possibilities have been stifled and lost to humanity, and in her and everyone's interest it is high time she be left to take her own chances."[9]

So how are women doing halfway through the 20th century? We've worked our way through several thousand years of history to the 1950s; are women better off? Is Eve's shadow still hanging around?

It depends on who you ask. Around the globe, despite female success in fields like nursing, teaching, and writing, women remain second-class citizens. They are still bound by laws, both cultural and religious, demanding they cover their heads, or their entire bodies, in order that males not be tempted by desire. In various parts of the world, including the U.S., some young girls are forced to succumb to painful genital mutilation, a "traditional" process usually done by women. They might be forced to marry whomever is chosen for them. They are, in many places, still denied education. And women still work long hours in the home and in the fields, caring for and feeding their families. They are expected to put up with men's frequent disdain, demands that they smile, sexual innuendo, and unwanted touching. They remain vulnerable to abuse, violence, and rape.

In the U.S. of the fifties, where middle-class women have the advantages of whatever modern appliances are available to them, patriarchy and misogyny continue to limit their life choices. Most are educated, usually up to 12 years; some go on to college if they choose (to get their Mrs. degree, it's said). In the 1950s women can hold jobs in approved fields, like office worker, nurse, teacher. If they're talented enough they may find a career in music or the arts. They are expected, and most wish, to marry before age 25 and to soon have children. But affordable birth control is not yet available; women are dying from miscarriages or botched, illegal abortions. Poor women struggle more, suffer more abuse, work for a pittance. White women can vote. Black women and men in the Jim Crow south can't, without ace-ing some version of an unpassable test (how many jelly beans are in this huge fishbowl?). Segregation limits where they sit, eat, or pee.

So no, women's lives have not improved; but yes women's lives have improved. And yes, Eve's shadow is dark and gloomy.

Writer Dale Spender, in *Women of Ideas,* references anthropologist Margaret Mead's 1950 book *Male and Female,* writing that "Mead recognized . . . that even where women engage in the same activities as men, and even where their performance may be comparable (or better), they are not considered of the same nature." Women were simply appendages to men, and if men were the homemakers, that job would be considered "prestigious."[10]

Indeed, women who protested or complained about their lack of life choices were told that true happiness lay in marriage and motherhood.

It was understood that the only socially accepted role of women in the 1950s denied them a life outside marriage and children. No career, no anything. For women who came of age in the late '40s or early '50s, life didn't offer much else unless you were ready to withstand society's displeasure or open vilification. To exist happily in the 1950s you had to believe that being a homemaker was the most wonderful, the most fulfilling life a woman could have. No complaining allowed.

Not everyone had the drive or necessary courage to buck social dictums, and marriage was the obvious alternative. Indeed, some of us weren't even aware we were being held back—that our minds, our capabilities, our hopes for an interesting life were unimportant, even nonexistent. As Spender says, "An ungrateful woman, an unhappy woman, was a 'sick' woman; there was stigma and shame attached to her personal failure to be happy and fulfilled."[11] Unless you were male, life was just one thing. And what could be better, young women were told (and sold) than being a cared-for wife to the ideal husband, and mother to charming and beautiful children?

Thanks to writer Sally Petersen's unpublished memoir I learned how hard that option could be when what you really wanted and needed was the career you had trained for and were good at. Petersen, a journalist and friend, included a quote in *From Society Page to Front Page* by Eileen Wirth. "In a decade by decade look," writes Petersen, "she notes that 'newspapers of the 1950s offered the fewest insights into the daily lives of women of any decade examined.'"

Wirth suggested women's marginalization would "change drastically with the coming of age of the baby boomers . . ." She was right about that.[12]

"But before the boomers," writes Petersen, "came increasing numbers of women like me in many fields, college-educated, career-minded, pushing back against 1950s stereotypes that said all women wanted to wear aprons, polish appliances and care for their men. We were in the vanguard of women who worked from desire, not need, and we helped push open doors for those baby boomers."[13]

There are women in every age who, like Petersen, "worked from desire" and succeeded despite society's restrictions and inflictions. One of the well-known exceptions was Ruth Bader Ginsburg, who helped free women from the laws that held them back. If you've seen the movie *On the Basis of Sex*, you may recall the scene when Ruth Bader and eight other young women, just starting at Harvard Law School in 1955, are invited to dinner by the dean, Erwin Griswold. After welcoming them to his home, he asks each one, "Why are you at Harvard Law School, taking the place of a man?"[14]

They were nine women in a class of about 500 men, but apparently nine was too many. It's no surprise that Ginsberg was one of them. She had graduated from Cornell in 1954 as a member of Phi Beta Kappa, and the highest-ranking female in her class. A month after graduation she married Martin Ginsburg. At the age of 21 she was working for the Social Security Administration in Oklahoma while her husband was in the Army Reserve. When she became pregnant she was demoted.

She then spent two years at Harvard Law, and was on the Law Review. When her husband took a job in New York City she asked the dean for permission to complete her third year at Columbia Law School under the auspices of Harvard. He refused. So she transferred to Columbia and made it onto their Law Review, tying for first place in her graduating class in 1959. Despite these impressive credentials she had difficulty finding a job.[15]

In 1972 she co-founded the Women's Rights Project at the American Civil Liberties Union and in '73 became the Project's general counsel, arguing six gender discrimination cases before the Supreme Court and winning five. In 1980 she was appointed to the D.C. Circuit Court by President Carter, and in 1993 was named a Supreme Court Associate Justice by President Clinton. Her husband Martin died in 2010 after 56 years of marriage.

Ginsburg played a role in many important decisions while on the Court, but her interest in gender justice never left her. She was inducted into the National Women's Hall of Fame in 2002, and received a long list of other awards, including honorary degrees from 30 colleges and universities. She became a pop icon over time, and the only apparent blot on her long career was her decision not to retire during President Obama's terms, which allowed President Trump to name her replacement (who later voted to end Roe v. Wade). Ruth Bader Ginsberg died September 18, 2020, at age 87, adding to her list of "firsts" even after death. She was the first woman to lie in state at the Capitol.

Justice Ginsburg opened doors for all women, not just those who chose to follow her into law. She spoke out. She worked hard to change the laws that were holding women back and in many cases she succeeded, making all our lives better.

When Ginsberg was appointed to the Supreme Court she joined Sandra Day O'Connor, who had been the Court's first female justice who served from 1981 to 2006. O'Connor had graduated magna cum laude from Stanford University in 1950, and continued at Stanford Law School, receiving her degree in 1952. She served on the Arizona Court of Appeals and was appointed to the Supreme Court by President Reagan. A moderate conservative, O'Connor was one of three co-authors of the lead opinion that preserved legal access to abortion in Planned Parenthood vs. Casey. In 2009 President Barack Obama awarded her the Presidential Medal of Freedom.

As I write today there are four female justices on the Supreme Court: Sonia Sotomayor (2009) the first Hispanic, Elena Kagan (2010), Amy Coney Barrett (2020), Ketanji Brown Jackson (2022) the first Black woman.

Unlike those distinguished women, I had no plans when I graduated from high school in 1959, but at my parents' insistence I agreed to attend nearby Chico State College (now California State University, Chico) for a least one year. They hoped I'd love it and continue. I majored in music, primarily because I had a voice that kept me singing in choirs and performing solos from about the age of five. Voice teachers told me I could sing at the Met if I was willing to work. I wasn't. I had no interest in being a performer, but neither did I have any other career goals. And while performing was fun and easy for me it wasn't, I thought, worth pursuing. I wanted more, but more "what" was a mystery.

I found college just okay. No classes inspired me and I thought campus life limited. I wanted to be out in the "real" world. After my cousin went off to airline school in Kansas City, Missouri, I decided to follow her, inspired by the free passes airlines offered employees.

Another high school classmate was going too, and we took our first flight together, from Sacramento to Kansas City, feeling extremely grown up and looking forward to the adventure.

Most of the women in the 30-day class wanted to be airline stewardesses (the term used at that time) and the focus was clearly on that goal. My goal was to get an office job, but like all the other women I was taught various grooming tips: how to look good when a photo is taken (stand sideways to the camera then twist your head and shoulders toward it), and how to swish your nylon-stockinged legs together when walking. This is how women got jobs in 1960.

But I did learn how to operate a teletype machine and read the tape that flowed from it. A few months later that skill got me a job with United Air Lines in San Francisco. I found an apartment within walking distance of the Union Square office, kissed my parents goodbye and left my small town for a city I'd been to only once on a high school field trip, and then the job interview. I was 19 and on top of the world.

# 19

## THE SIXTIES

San Francisco was not yet famous for its hippies when I moved there in 1961, but it soon would be. The decade known as the Radical Sixties, the Swinging Sixties, or the Counterculture Decade cannot easily be defined. It began with the 1960 presidential election, Kennedy vs. Nixon. It ended with Richard Nixon's inauguration in January 1969, promising "peace with honor" and an end to the Vietnam War. Those ten years were buffeted by the kind of changes that left some feeling expansive and inspired, and others angry and fearful. Most of us swung from one end of the spectrum to the other as events overtook our lives.

The '60s did bring the hippies, along with psychedelic drugs, anti-war protests, the first American to orbit Earth (John Glenn), civil rights marches and legislation, music (the Beatles, the Doors, Joan Baez, Jimi Hendrix, Janis Joplin, Bob Dylan, Pete Seeger and many others), war, multiple assassinations, and not least, second wave feminists. And so much more.

The changes in my personal life felt just as intense. I had been too young to vote for John Kennedy, but I was delighted when he was elected; his energy and youth reflected my post-war confidence and hope.

On November 22, 1963, I was home preparing for an afternoon shift at United when I turned on the TV. A few minutes later a voice-over interrupted the soap opera I was watching to report that three shots had been fired at the president's motorcade. I returned my uneaten lunch to the kitchen and sat down to watch and wait. Thirty-eight minutes later Walter Cronkite announced the president's death.

The days that followed were filled with an omnipresent sadness. Even the chatter of our busy office was muted for weeks. It didn't help that we saw it all on live television, including the murder of accused assassin by Jack Ruby, the swearing-in of President Johnson aboard the plane, and the blood-stained suit of Jackie Kennedy standing witness.

The assassination of President Kennedy seemed to draw a line across time, replacing hope with gloomy pessimism. It's no wonder so many turned away from the staid and demure years of the 1950s to indulge in psychedelic escapism and loud, angry protests.

After three years in San Francisco, after using every yearly travel pass United offered—including a first trip to Europe—and at the urging of an old friend, I moved to San Jose. As told in Chapter 1, my plan was to get a job and finish college. Instead I fell in love on a blind date, married a year later, and in November of 1965 had a daughter.

But before all that I had to find a job. I turned to the help-wanted ads where jobs were categorized under Male or Female headings, a distinction that limited us right from the start, but one we took for granted. I also signed with an employment agency that regularly sent me to interviews. Women like me, looking for office work in the early '60s, dressed professionally, wore nylons and heels, and hoped we would be treated with respect. My qualifications were never questioned, but how I looked was. I was turned down for being too sophisticated for the clientele, which made me laugh, and a distraction in an office of mostly young men who openly ogled me on the way out.

But the one I remember most took place in the agency office. I was taken into a room to be interviewed for a secretarial job by a youngish man. It was a typical interview until he asked me to stand and turn around. I complied. I also knew I didn't want the job. He then asked if I would be interested in a different job—as a "traveling secretary" for his boss in Las Vegas. I was naive but not that naive. I said no, and got up to leave. He walked me to the door and kissed me. I was too shocked to say anything, and promptly left.

The next morning he called and offered me the job. I had earlier clued in my roommates who had been equally shocked, and they stood by grinning and giving me thumbs up as I repeatedly said no, though the salary he offered was far above normal. I later learned he had kissed at least one other candidate. The agency assured me they would take steps so such things could no longer happen. It was a relief, a few days later, to be hired as a secretary in a bank's loan department. It was a good job where I was respected and treated well.

I tell you that story because I doubt it was untypical. Women were (and are) too often judged on their appearance first and their skills and interests second. Esther Peterson, director of the U.S. Women's Bureau, convinced President Kennedy, who had endorsed equal pay for equal work, to establish a Presidential Commission on the Status of Women, which he did in 1961. It included former first lady Eleanor Roosevelt and Dorothy Height, president for 40 years of the National Council of Negro Women. Height was one of the first to recognize the value of uniting the struggle for women's equality with that of African Americans.[1]

Many progressives favored what was then called "protective legislation," which essentially promoted gender-based workplace restrictions designed to halt exploitation and workplace injury. In reality such legislation provided employers with justification to avoid hiring women altogether, or to not pay the same wages men received. In other words, very little such legislation was ever drafted, let alone passed.

President Kennedy later signed the Equal Pay Act of 1963 that stipulated women could no longer be paid less than men for comparable work at the same job. There were no laws against sexual harassment until it was made illegal by Title VII of the Civil Rights Act of 1964, signed into law by President Lyndon Johnson.

## The Second Wave

In 1963 Betty Friedan published *The Feminine Mystique,* changing minds, eventually including mine, and stirring up the second feminist wave. Based on her own experience of moving from a career journalist into the sphere of homemaker, Friedan described "the problem that has no name."

As discussed in the previous chapter, women in the 50s became—after the newness of marriage wore off—unhappy being just homemakers. Men in general didn't care. In fact, they openly ridiculed women who expressed dissatisfaction and wanted more from life. When Friedan, after leaving her journalist job, experienced that unhappiness, she wondered if she was alone. Women were mostly silent about disliking their housewife role; it felt unacceptable to deny what society clearly demanded. While at a class reunion Friedan interviewed former classmates, then others over a five-year period. Then she sat down and wrote persuasively about what she'd learned, telling and showing us why we were unhappy. And she proved her point. Sales of the book (over 3 million in three years) revealed that indeed, there was a problem.

Another writer in 1963, Gloria Steinem, went undercover as a Playboy Bunny and wrote an exposé for *Show* magazine. Published as "A Bunny's Tale," it revealed the low pay and sexism—which bordered on illegal—that she and other women were forced to endure. The article and the splash it made eventually led the owner to improve working conditions.

"A Bunny's Tale" was an eye-opener for many. Steinem was a reporter for *New York* magazine and in 1969 published another article that earned attention: "After Black Power, Women's Liberation." In 1971 she co-founded the National Women's Political Caucus with Betty Friedan and Congresswomen Bella Abzug and Shirley Chisholm. Their goal was to ensure gender equality in governments and to provide training for women seeking office. That same year she co-founded the Women's Action Alliance working to advance feminist causes.

Steinem also co-founded the magazine *MS* with Dorothy Pitman Hughes, who was active in the civil rights movement and with child welfare. The magazine has covered a broad range of women's issues over the years, provided by writers from an equal range of backgrounds. Steinem has continued throughout her career to be involved in multiple women's issues.

All these women and so many more built the liberation movement of the 1970s. It was a heady time for women; their words, writing, and fights for rights were regularly in the news, and whether we were home raising a family or working full time, we were aware that things were changing. For the better.

Other influential authors at the time included Kate Millett, *Sexual Politics* (1969), Juliet Mitchell, *The Subjection of Women* (1970) and Shulamith Firestone's *The Dialectic of Sex: The Case for Feminist Revolution* (1970).

Angela Davis was making a name for herself too, publishing in 1972 an article on the harmful stereotypes of Black women in society.

Frances Beal's book *Double Jeopardy: To Be Black and Female*, added to the frustration of exploited Black women, and, as in the post-Civil War period, caused fissures between Black and White women fighting for the same issues: to be taken seriously as free and independent individuals.

All this attention (undue attention according to some) meant that being a "women's libber," like "bluestocking," quickly became a negative appellation.

### Our changing focus

Learning that women were treated unfairly, earned less than male peers, and too frequently faced harassment, rape, and illegal, dangerous abortions may have been hard for Americans to accept, but that was put aside after the shocking assassination of Martin Luther King, Jr. in April 1968. Riots broke out in hundreds of cities across the nation, destroying all semblance of the peace King had stood for.

Two months later we watched Robert F. Kennedy speak after winning the California primary, only to learn hours later that he too had been shot. He died the following day.

With the 1963 assassinations of President John F. Kennedy, the NAACP's Medgar Evers, and in 1965 Malcolm X, a hero to many Blacks, the country had lost five prominent leaders in six years.

Less prominent but equally devastating were the 1963 bombing deaths of four little girls attending Sunday School in Alabama. In 1964 three young men, voting-registration activists, were kidnapped and murdered in Mississippi. In 1965 the Watts Rebellion in Los Angeles resulted in 34 deaths.[2]

One of President Johnson's first acts was to pass and sign the 1964 Civil Rights Bill, which ended legal segregation and "would alter the legal, political, and social landscape of America as radically as any law of the twentieth century."[3] While many of Americans cheered that action, the legislation itself sparked continued violence and mayhem, especially in the south.

Newly inspired Blacks brought a new focus to their civil rights, so did a planned march from Selma, Alabama to Montgomery on Sunday, March 7, 1965. Six hundred peaceful marchers crossed the Edmund Pettus Bridge to find helmeted, gas-masked state troopers blocking their way. The marchers were ordered to disperse. When they refused they were brutally and deliberately attacked with nightsticks, whips, tear gas, and finally men on horseback "trampling over bodies and lashing the retreating crowds with nightsticks. Over the screams and cries of the marchers could be heard the crazed whoops and cheers of white spectators waving Confederate flags."[4]

"Bloody Sunday" was seen and re-seen across the country, and as historian Doris Kearns Goodwin writes, "Few public events in my lifetime have caused the ground to shift, as if the ocean had pulled the sand out from underfoot, leaving you unbalanced."[5]

A week later, on March 15, President Johnson addressed a joint session of the Congress and in a moving speech presented his Voting Rights bill. It passed August 6, 1965. These two "Great Society" bills changed

American life for all of us, but especially for those who had been limited for years by the South's regional Jim Crow laws. As a result of Johnson's efforts the United States made impressive advances in fairness and equal opportunity, until the growing costs of the Vietnam War—in lives and money—ended almost all social progress.

During this decade thousands of young women joined and marched for liberation, civil rights, and an end to the war. Others, cynically frustrated by a lack of progress "anywhere" turned to the hippie lifestyle, became rabid activists or, in the language of the day, "tuned in and dropped out."

Meanwhile, the government was still drafting young men my age and shipping them off to Vietnam (Ray was in the National Guard at the time). I became Another Mother for Peace, with a bumper sticker on my car and a necklace I wore on those days I wasn't wearing a peace sign. Instead of going back to college I took a half-time job working for a sociology professor.

On July 30, 1965 President Johnson signed a bill that led to the creation of Medicare and Medicaid, a huge step forward for seniors, the handicapped, and the poor. The same year he federally insured student loans and signed the Immigration and Nationality Act of 1965.

But it was the anti-war and civil rights protests that were continually in the news. By 1967 there were 435,000 troops in Vietnam. I had praised Johnson's efforts on civil and voting rights but had little patience with his actions in Vietnam, which consisted of more troops and more bombs. Then on March 31, 1968 President Johnson shocked us all by announcing he would neither seek nor accept the nomination of his party.

Throughout the decade the news of the war had grown from an occasional on-air mention to filling most of the evening news. In 1967 more than 150 anti-war riots erupted across the U.S., with numerous deaths, injuries, and arrests. By the middle of 1968 almost 70,000 Americans had been killed or wounded in the war.[6] I clearly remember the chaos of the Democrats' 1968 convention in Chicago; I watched police beating anti-war protesters on live TV and felt as betrayed and angry as the protesters.

Ray and I had married in March, 1965, and despite the dramatic changes occurring all around us, we happily adjusted to our new life, moving from our first tiny apartment to a larger one and then to our first house in 1968. Our daughter was healthy and growing, we had a cat and a dog to keep us company, and in many ways we were a typical young, busy family. My life left little time for thinking about discrimination against the female sex; besides, I had the pill. I thought I was free of Eve's shadow.

But others weren't. That shadow lurked, dark as night, over outlawed abortion and it shadowed every girl or woman who suffered a sexual aggression like rape or incest, who had a drink and "went too far," who chose love over virginity—or a hundred other reasons people have sex. That shadow darkened the days and nights of every female who was fearful of having an unwanted child—for whatever reason.

But if she was lucky, if she or a friend or family member found a reliable nurse or doctor, and if they had the money to pay, this might happen:

"It was in 1966," said my friend. "My mother and I flew to San Diego. We'd been instructed to look for a gentleman in a blue and white pinstriped suit with a red rose, or carnation, or something, in his lapel, and he had a fedora."

Imagine being that 17 or 18-year-old, alone with your mother, flying into a city you don't know for a medical procedure that scares the hell out of you. You might have laughed at his fedora if you hadn't been so afraid. You are from a prosperous family, knowing only the best care, and yet here you are, sneaking into town and searching out a stranger for an intimate procedure.

"He was instructed, of course, to look for us, and we met, and we got in his car and he drove us to kind of a seedy neighborhood in San Diego."

You watch from the car window as unknown street names flash along the road that is leading you closer to your fear. And then the car stops and anxiety grows, and you reluctantly climb out and are led to a door. A woman opens it.

"She let us in, and then we went out the back of her house and into this room, this space, like a detached garage, or just like a little shed, in back of this woman's house."

Imagine yourself walking into that space, that shed, not knowing for sure what was next. Wanting desperately to disappear, to make it all go away; to just have it over and behind you.

"It was set up like an operating room. The doctor was from Mexico; he came over the border and performed my abortion." Was it as simple as that? "He performed my abortion."

After the procedure she and her mother reversed their path and flew home.

"It was a humiliating and demeaning and terrifying experience," she said 58 years later, "that no woman should have to face."

(That 1966 abortion cost $2000. In late 2024 dollars that is $19,485.)

In the fall of 1969 our daughter turned four and we were talking about moving again. A couple who were close friends had chosen to get their Ph.Ds at the University of Oregon in Eugene. They raved about the town and the surrounding beauty, and reported positive news about the local schools. We were unhappy with the astonishing growth taking place around us. The Santa Clara valley had been home to hundreds of orchards and thousands of trees, their blossoms lighting up the spring and filling the valley with their scent. But now they disappeared seemingly over night and new houses made of "ticky-tacky" sprang up in their place.

We temporarily subscribed to Eugene's local paper and were impressed with what we read. So, leaving Jennifer with her grandparents for a week, we paid our friends a visit. Just for fun we decided to look at houses. And we bought one. It wasn't the first of our many moves, but it confirmed our comfort in acting on the spur of the moment, which would continue to reveal itself.

# 20

## NEW HOME, NEW LIVES, NEW EVERYTHING

Our move to Oregon in March, 1970 was promising. Ray had arranged a job transfer during our visit, and Jennifer immediately found playmates. Our new neighbors wasted no time inviting us over, so after unloading our belongings we trekked next door, tired but happy to meet them, their three children and another couple who lived nearby. We soon felt part of the neighborhood and our new acquaintances would become lifelong friends. Oregon very quickly felt like home, and we never regretted our decision to move.

As Ray settled into his new job I took on the role of housewife. We'd agreed that I would stay home until our daughter started school. I was fine with that; there was plenty to do and learn about the small city we now called home, and of course with any move there are multiple tasks to complete before a new space feels comfortable. I discovered a local bookstore and finally bought Betty Friedan's book.

As the traumas of the sixties began to fade into background noise, the counterculture continued to grow. The 1970s took on a decidedly different shape: like a balloon that keeps expanding it made room for the growing war in Vietnam and a rapidly expanding movement for women's rights. The protests for and against both actions continued. On

May 4, 1970 Ohio National Guards opened fire on a group protesting the war. They killed four Kent State University students and injured nine. That horrifying action led to student protests across the nation and many campuses temporarily shut down.[1]

Meanwhile, the Equal Rights Amendment (ERA) surfaced again and was approved by the House on October 12, 1971, by the Senate on March 22, 1972, and submitted to the state legislatures for ratification. This Constitutional amendment would end legal distinctions between men and women in matters of divorce, property, employment, and more. Women and their supporters celebrated, believing that real progress was being made. We forgot, or didn't know, that the same amendment had been introduced in Congress in December 1923 and reintroduced numerous times. Between 1948 and 1970 the House Judiciary Committee refused to even consider it.

Because the amendment is often misunderstood, or attacked due to misinformation, I'm including it here. It's not long:

"Resolved by the Senate and House of Representatives of the United States of America in Congress assembled (two-thirds of each House concurring therein), That the following article is proposed as an amendment to the Constitution of the United States, which shall be valid to all intents and purposes as part of the Constitution when ratified by the legislatures of three-fourths of the several States within seven years from the date of its submission by the Congress:

ARTICLE

*Section 1. Equality of rights under the law shall not be denied or abridged by the United States or by any State on account of sex.*

*Section 2. The Congress shall have the power to enforce, by appropriate legislation, the provisions of this article.*

*Section 3. This amendment shall take effect two years after the date of ratification.*[2]

The deadline for ratification was March 2, 1979. By the end of 1977 it had received 35 of the required 38 state ratifications and was expected to pass with support from both major parties. But in 1972 Phyllis Schlafly, founder of the ultra-conservative Eagle

Forum, whose "career contradicted the very rules she fought to defend,"[3] had mobilized conservative women against the ERA, and a number of states rescinded their ratifications (there is no legal route for doing this).[4] President Carter extended the deadline to June 30, 1982, to no avail.

Inspired by words from people like Representative Bella Abzug, Gloria Steinem, Shirley Chisholm, Betty Friedan and others, I and women like me across the country slowly began to take ourselves more seriously. We didn't all know what we wanted but there was no doubt ideas were changing and being shared. What helped was the popularity of those small, informal women's groups—built strictly for conversation—that sprang up across the country as if impelled by an unknown force.

Informally, in big houses and small, in apartments of every size, in dorm rooms or spare rooms, women met to talk about women's issues—however defined on any given day—and discovered that others felt the same. We were sad, happy, content, angry, upset, pissed off, or too busy. Or we didn't have enough to do, or it wasn't what we wanted to do. Maybe we were bored. Maybe we yearned for adult conversation. Or maybe we wanted to go back to school, to finish our degrees; or yes we were perfectly content and were afraid of the changes we saw coming. It was all open to discussion and argument. We didn't solve every problem but we learned, and our confidence grew.

It was around this time that I had an epiphany.

I was on my hands and knees scrubbing the kitchen floor. I don't remember why I thought this necessary, but there I was. As I wrote in an earlier book, "I wasn't unhappy that day, but I was disenchanted with the life I saw stretching before me. The feminist revolution was gaining ground, and like other women of my generation, I was encouraged by news of growing opportunities, but felt restrained by my 1950s conditioning. It was confusing. I loved my husband and young daughter and had no interest in pursuing a life without them. But still, was this all there was?" It was the housewife's cliché lament. But this time it was mine, and Betty Friedan had nailed it.

"It came to me then, sitting back on my heels and admiring my work, that Life—it was capitalized in my thoughts—was not going to hand me roses or wealth or adventure. Life was not a generous uncle. If I wanted Life to be exciting I was going to have to make it so myself."[5]

That unexpected thought cracked open a door. I spent many months thinking about what it meant, and looking for gaps in my world that I might explore. As you'll see, that experience changed the trajectory of my life, and that of my family.

But it was still the 1970s and everyone had a cause. While women, African Americans, Native Americans, gays and other marginalized people were hopping on the protest bus and demanding their rights, the war in Vietnam continued. Another movement was growing too, claiming conservatism and traditional family values. These ideas were advocated, rather angrily it seemed to me, by Phyllis Schlafly and her Eagle Forum. Jerry Falwell and his Moral Majority followed in 1979, and a host of other religious right and social conservatives raised their voices against those they saw as far leftists, socialists and communists. It was and continues to be a broad movement that covers a spectrum from center to far right. These groups and others like them were anti-abortion and anti-feminist. Traditional family values demanded that women belonged at home and in the kitchen. None of them asked women what they wanted. Eve's shadow rotated through shades of gray to black as one cause or the other dominated the zeitgeist.

But for the time being, women and their "Lib" movement were still the primary story, and when lesbian women protested their treatment, or rather nontreatment, to the National Organization for Women, they quickly adopted a resolution that recognized lesbian rights. Then, while feminists books were still being written and read, the country suddenly found itself engrossed in the 37th president's problems: something called Watergate?

Before Richard Nixon let his ego take control of his common sense he had done some good things for the country. Anti-war people like me were outraged when he ordered carpet bombing in Cambodia, hoping to bring the Vietnamese to the negotiating table. It didn't work, but he did, finally, end the long, unnecessary war in 1973. He visited China, leading the way to diplomatic relations. He finalized an anti-ballistic missile treaty with the Soviet Union. Under pressure from a growing environmental movement he created the Environmental Protection Agency (EPA) and the National Environmental Policy Act. He signed the Endangered Species Act and the Clean Air Act. Relations with Native Americans improved (they still have a long way to go); on July 1, 1971 the voting age dropped from 21 to 18. All that happened in his first term.[6]

In 1972 Nixon won re-election against George McGovern, and soon after came rumors and reports of a scandal during the run-up to the election. It began with a break-in at the Democratic National Committee office in the Watergate complex and escalated after arrests of the burglars and their revelations. Martha Mitchell, the wife of Attorney General John Mitchell, was kidnapped in June 1972 because she knew one of the burglars and threatened to tell the media. She was held captive and was tracked down by a reporter for the *New York Daily News*, Marcia Kramer.[7] Mitchell said she was threatened at gunpoint. (In 1975, James McCord, convicted of conspiracy in the Watergate affair, confirmed the kidnapping.)

More information followed after Carl Bernstein and Bob Woodward, hungry reporters at the *Washington Post,* pursued leads, followed the money, uncovered illegally funded contributions, and exposed a massive cover-up that included hidden audio tapes.[8]

When Nixon denied the accusations the Senate established a committee to uncover the truth. Called the Watergate Committee,[9] its live-broadcast hearings captivated the American public. A special prosecutor was appointed who subpoenaed the tapes Nixon had refused to hand over. The president ordered him fired. The Attorney General refused to fire the prosecutor and quit. So did his deputy. The Solicitor General finally carried out the order. These actions were soon dubbed the "Saturday Night Massacre." The House Judiciary Committee recommended impeachment of the president for obstructing justice, abuse of power, and contempt of Congress.

During these months of scandal and endless surprises, I would rush home from work to turn on the TV. It was like watching an engrossing legal series, but with real people and real consequences. Everyone breathed a sigh of relief when Nixon resigned the presidency on August 9, 1974. His Vice President, Gerald Ford, became president and pardoned Nixon on September 8, an act now thought by some to have contributed to the weakening of America's hold on the rule of law.

While all that was happening the Supreme Court, in 1973, ruled on Roe v. Wade, legalizing abortion rights for the first time. Wow! It was an amazingly freeing decision. Though abortion had been condoned—until quickening—in most of the United States until the early 1800s, this was the first time U.S. women had safe, secure, and legal options over pregnancy, and the freedom to make decisions about their own bodies. Even I, married with legal access to birth control, celebrated the decision. That freedom would, and did, change our lives and our culture.

The biggest televised event in 1973 was the "Battle of the Sexes," a tennis match between Bobby Riggs, a self-defined male chauvinist, once thought to be the best tennis player in the world, and Billie Jean King, who had won six Wimbledons and four U.S. Opens.

Riggs, 55, challenged King, 29, to a $100,000 winner-take-all match, bragging "I'll tell you why I'll win. She's a woman and they [sic] didn't have the emotional stability."

King called him a "creep."

He loved attention and kept talking: "women belong in the bedroom and kitchen, in that order," and "women play about 25 percent as good as men, so they should get about 25 percent of the money men get."

The match was held in the Houston Astrodome on September 20, in front of an estimated 50,000 in Houston and 90 million worldwide watching on TV. Under incredible pressure Billie Jean beat Bobby in straight sets and the cheers and applause of happy women echoed around the world.

King later said, "I thought it would set us back 50 years if I didn't win that match." Riggs graciously said she "played too well." The two later became good friends.[10]

In 1976 Apple Computer Company was founded, but the more visible electronic advance was the Sony Walkman. Long hair, bell-bottomed pants and granny dresses were still the rage. So were leisure suits. Music lovers tuned to Dolly Parton, Elton John, David Bowie, the Rolling Stones, Fleetwood Mac, and Bruce Springsteen. And the Boston Women's Health Book Collective hit the best seller list with *Our Bodies Ourselves* in 1973.

James E. Carter was elected president in 1976, America's Bicentennial. The patriotic celebration relieved some of the stresses brought on by the Nixon debacle, but Carter was left to face an energy crisis and inflation. One of his first acts was to grant amnesty to Vietnam-era draft evaders. He put solar panels on the White House. Reagan took them down.

Carter is perhaps best known for bringing together the Egyptian president Anwar Sadat and Israeli prime minister, Menachem Begin—two men who couldn't stand one another—at Camp David. The 12-day meeting resulted in the Camp David Accords, finally ending war between the two countries.

During his final year he faced what became the Iran hostage crisis, when 53 U.S. citizens were taken by armed Iranian students and held in the U.S. embassy in Tehran from November 4, 1979 to January 20, 1981. Carter tried a rescue operation; it failed. The prisoners were released as Ronald Reagan took the presidential vow to protect the Constitution. Persistent rumors alleged that people on Reagan's campaign had convinced Iran to hold the hostages to reduce Carter's chances for reelection.[11]

As I was writing this I learned that President Jimmy Carter died today, Sunday, December 30, 2024, at his home in Plains, Georgia at the age of 100. He was a man ahead of his time in many ways, particularly in seeing the oncoming environmental crisis. He was also a great supporter of women, appointing 40 women to the judiciary, including Ruth Bader Ginsburg. Eight were women of color—an almost unheard-of achievement at that time.

And despite being a dedicated evangelical Christian who taught Sunday School throughout his long life, he wrote that the alleviation of women's abuse "is made less likely by the mandated subservience of women by Christian fundamentalists. What is especially disappointing to me is the docile acceptance by so many strong Christian women of their subjugation and restricted role."[12] In 2009 Carter left the Southern Baptist Convention saying: "Women and girls have been discriminated against for too long in a twisted interpretation of the Word of God."[13]

Both these statements seem surprising given his life-long dedication to his church, but he was an intelligent man who often saw things more clearly than the rest of us. If Eve is anywhere, she is surely welcoming him home today.

As a former California resident I was familiar with Ronald Reagan. As our governor (1967–75) he had raised taxes and cut spending to schools. The homicide rate doubled as he signed tough criminal sentencing and supported capital punishment. He did do one good thing for women though: in 1967 he signed the (pre-Roe) Therapeutic Abortion Act, allowing legal abortions in cases of rape or incest when "a doctor determined the birth would impair the physical or mental health of the mother." He later said he regretted signing it.[14]

President Ronald Reagan is still loved by many. Republicans still quote his famous ". . . nine most dangerous words: I'm from the government and I'm here to help." Unfortunately those words and that attitude continue to encourage a general loss of trust in government. Reagan supported supply-side economics (known pejoratively as trickle-down economics) and in 1981 he cut the highest personal income tax rate from 70 percent to 50 percent. In 1986 he again cut the personal income tax from 50 to 38.5 percent, decreasing to 28 percent in the following years. But, his supporters would eagerly assure us, he increased the highest capital gains tax rate from 20 to 28 percent.[15]

The boost that women received from the second wave of feminist activity in the late sixties and early seventies was essentially buried by the Nixon and Reagan presidencies. Reagan was an avowed conservative whose influence is still felt today. Other than the abortion law he signed in California and then disavowed, he did little or nothing to help women.

Eve's shadow slid silently back over the land as its inhabitants slowly but inexorably ignored or sidelined women's freedom. Yes, there were always outspoken women who wrote, and told stories, and inspired us. But they weren't in control. We did, however, have the right to make decisions about our own bodies.

# 21

## GOOD YEARS AND BAD

Still thinking about the epiphany I'd had a few years earlier, I decided in 1974 to return to school. My long-time interest in Russia after reading Tolstoy's *War and Peace* and other Russian authors hadn't worn off, and I wondered what I was missing in the translations. Maybe I should go back to school and learn to read them in Russian? In September, 1975, at 34, I enrolled at the University of Oregon.

I found the Russian language difficult, but what stirred my heart was discovering *samizdat* and learning about the writers who created the brave underground books, booklets, and articles being illegally passed from hand to hand in the Soviet Union. One of them, Vladimir Bukovsky, spent 12 years in prisons, labor camps, and psychiatric prisons (because if you don't love the Soviet Union you must be crazy). He was expelled in 1976 but remained a vocal critic of the system. In 1977 he published *To Build a Castle: My Life as a Dissident.* As a writer I've always appreciated his rather prescient lines, though without, one hopes, the final distortion:

"I would erect a monument to the typewriter too. It brought forth a new form of publishing, *samizdat*, or 'self publishing': write myself, edit myself, censor myself, publish myself, distribute myself, go to jail for it myself."[1]

I had cut my work hours to half time, working as a secretary in the mornings, then rushing daily to my 12:30 two-hour class. I had other classes too, History was a favorite. It wasn't easy being back in school after so many years, surrounded by bright kids—I felt completely out of my depth. Could I keep up? I had no idea; but I had to try.

At some point during that year Ray and I were at a bookstore and I came across *Europe With Two Kids and a Van.* I picked it up and flipped through it. "Wow," I thought, what a great idea!" I promptly showed it to Ray, saying "we should do this."

He looked at me like I was crazy. "No, really," I said. "We could do this." I bought the book and immediately read it. Then, because I doubted he would read it, I read sections to him. He listened, but he didn't believe. I kept talking it up—"those people did it, so could we. It's not that hard. We plan and we save." Yada yada.

Ray had never been especially interested in travel, and while he'd frequently visited Mexico from his home in Arizona, he'd never been to Europe. Eventually he agreed to think about it. But Ray was an activist, always involved in one issue or another, trying to save or make better. Travel wasn't on his list. And he reminded me, more than once, that we had a child in school, a dog and two cats, a mortgage, a car payment, and other obligations. I kept talking. When he learned he was eligible for a leave of absence through his union, I saw no excuse for not going. He finally agreed.

Without boring you with the details such a trip demands, let me just say that we set a date about ten months out, sold our car to save money (Ray already cycled to work, Jennifer walked to school, I adapted to biking), and arranged to rent our house, unfurnished. Then we ordered a VW camper to be picked up in Brussels. The dollar was strong then, greatly to our advantage. Now in my second year at school I suggested that since I spoke some Russian, maybe we could add that country to our itinerary. It was that idea that got Ray excited about the trip.

In 1977 we spent six months traveling through Europe. Our route was a circle, taking us from Germany, where we visited with old friends, through England and Scotland, then north and east through Scandinavia and into the USSR in June. There we traveled on our own for 39 days, exiting through Romania and continuing to points west. While in the Soviet Union we had to check in every night, were frequently followed by police and stopped twice. As our then 11-year-old said later, "I learned the difference between free and not free."[2]

It was an exciting, fulfilling trip that fostered a confidence in all of us I doubt we would have gained any other way. And we learned an important lesson. While in Moscow we spent an evening at the famous Circus and were seated next to a tour group of Americans. During intermission we chatted. They were astonished and curious when they learned we were in the country on our own, and after answering numerous questions we went on to talk about the various the sites we each had visited.

They were seeing places and events we couldn't, either because our schedule was too tight, or we didn't know about them, or they were too expensive. But we saw and did things they couldn't, or wouldn't venture on. Besides exploring the famous sites and museums, we stood in line with the Russians to buy bread, visited local parks, ate food from vendors, wandered the streets and stores, talked with strangers, and frequently said, "No, we don't want to sell our jeans."

Yes, we envied the tour's four- or five-star hotels and seats to the ballet, but we realized that we were seeing a very different country, and learning about the Soviet Union and its people in a wholly different way. Ray described it as "the cheaper the trip, the richer the experience." Those words soon became a life-long mantra.

The six-month journey that was supposed to satisfy my urge to travel worked only to the extent that both Ray and Jennifer were severely infected. It would not be our last.

I've said that I never had career goals, but felt confident that whatever I was looking for would somehow show itself. I'd always loved writing, but whenever it surfaced as a possible career I thought of people like Tolstoy and Steinbeck and knew I could never do that. As I grew older I watched female writers surfacing; even becoming best sellers, but again it remained a bridge too far. My only goal remained a consistent one: to see as much of the world as I could.

I'd planned to continue college classes on our return but we were already thinking of our next trip. I found a new half-time job instead and took a freelance writing course at the local junior college. Completing an article was required, so of course I wrote about our trip through the USSR in a VW bus. The teacher thought it good enough to submit so I sent it to *Small World,* a Volkswagen magazine. To my surprise they bought it for $300, real money in 1978. I decided maybe I could be a writer after all, and set about trying to prove it to myself.

The 1980s began with a bang—the May 18 eruption of Mt. St. Helens in southern Washington. The eruption took the lives of about 57 people, destroyed hundreds of square miles of forest and range land and killed thousands of animals. It was the kind of event that seems impossible until it happens, though seismic monitors had sounded plenty of warnings. Eugene had only limited ash fallout, and we were happy to hear—after phone calls home—that our daughter and her grandmother were doing fine. This was a relief since Ray and I were on Highway 1 riding our bikes to San Francisco. Looking back, the eruption feels like a portent.

In 1984, in Bhopal, India, a Union Carbide plant suffered a gas-leak explosion that killed about 2000 people. Far more died throughout the area when poisonous gas escaped.

In 1986, the first female astronaut, Sally Ride, was killed with six others, including a teacher, when the Challenger spacecraft blew up shortly after launch. Our sadness was compounded knowing that many school children were watching at the time. It was a horrific event that affected everyone who saw it.

Also in 1986 a reactor at the Chernobyl Nuclear Power Plant in Northern Ukraine exploded, sending radiation across Europe and beyond. A 10-kilometre (6.2 miles) exclusion zone was established 36 hours later and 49,000 were evacuated. The zone was later expanded to 30 kilometers, with about 68,000 more people evacuated. It remains the worst nuclear accident and the costliest in human history.

The AIDS epidemic was a different kind of disaster. The disease swept through the country and beyond, especially affecting the gay community and initiating far too many personal tragedies before it was brought under control. Sadly, it took years to find relief, and though great progress has been made, AIDS continues to inflict pain and death on areas where medication is not always available.

The politics of the Right gained power, and the eighties were soon thought of as the Me generation, with how-to books filling the best-seller lists, a passion that continued into the nineties. Yuppies became a word. Yuppies were highly materialistic young urban professionals who liked to spend money. Given the turn to the right that the country was taking under President Reagan, that was probably not surprising.

In Britain, Margaret Thatcher became the first female prime minister, and Corazon Aquino, after her husband's death, was elected the first female president of the Philippines in 1986. Sandra Day O'Connor became the first woman named to the Supreme Court.

New books by Black women made the best-seller lists and changed the way many of us thought about feminism. One of those authors was Gloria Jean Watkins, known by her pen name bell hooks. In 1981 she published *Ain't I a Woman? Black Women and Feminism.* hooks believed that feminism, and especially Black feminism, must be a tool for achieving liberation of all people, men and women. She was a distinguished professor in residence at Berea College, known for her scholarly work on the interactions of race, gender, and capitalism. She received her B.A. at Stanford, and her doctorate in English at the University of California, Santa Cruz. She published about 30 books, as well as essays, poetry, and scholarly articles.

Alice Walker published *In Search of Our Mothers' Gardens: Womanist Prose* in 1983 and introduced us to new words: womanism and womanist. The latter is defined as "committed to the survival and wholeness of entire people, male and female." She is best known, however, for her novel *The Color Purple,* which later became a popular movie.

The success of these women, and others like them, made many of us happy. Every woman's success, but especially that of Black women, seemed to confirm that women were finally coming into their own and making progress. And it continued. In 1990, for the first time, four Black women appeared on the same *Publishers Weekly* best seller list: Toni Morrison, Alice Walker, Maya Angelo, and Terry McMillan.[3]

What I didn't credit enough at the time was the anti-woman pressure slowly building on the right.

In 1981 we were back in Europe for the summer. Jennifer, 15, had a two-week homestay in Avignon, France; Ray and I went to Italy. Then we all turned southeast in a leased car, with a tent, to explore Portugal and southern Spain. There was a severe drought in southern Portugal and we each got sick from the unclean water, but that stole only a week or two, and the trip confirmed our shared love of travel.

In 1985 Mikhail Gorbachev became the General Secretary of the Communist party of the Soviet Union—essentially the country's leader. In 1988 he was named Chairman of the Supreme Soviet and in 1990 he became President. Despite introducing glasnost (openness) and perestroika (restructuring), neither his titles nor his ideas were able to save the Communist government. In 1989 the Berlin Wall came down amidst crowds of cheering and determined East and West Germans. The world also cheered; it was a long-wished-for leap to freedom for the German people. It was also a death knell for the Soviet Union, which collapsed two years later. I thought about Andrei Amalrik's smuggled book, *Will the Soviet Union Survive Until 1984?* It had, but barely.

Four years after that surprise we watched on television as student-led demonstrations calling for democracy and a free press in China led to the Tiananmen Square disaster. The bravery of the students and protesters failed to impress the leaders, and the outcome was bloody and cruel. Freedom in China was once again denied.

The arrival of technology in our lives meant a big change for everyone. In the '70s I had occasionally worked on a computer that filled a medium sized room. In 1981 IBM released its first personal computer; in 1982 the Commodore 64 personal computer debuted and in 1983 *Time* magazine named the computer "Machine of the Year." Apple's Macintosh debuted the following year. The devices that were predicted to save time and simplify our lives had finally arrived.

I'm still waiting for all that saved time.

The second half of the eighties were a busy time personally, filled with happiness, shock, pain, and relief. In 1983 our daughter graduated from high school and went east for college. About two years later Ray took a buyout from his long-time employer. Wondering what to do next, we learned that a casual friend with several local businesses had one to sell, as a partnership. Owning a business had a been an idea of Ray's for a number of years, so thinking this would be a way to learn retailing without too much risk, we handed over the cash and became co-owners of two small natural-fiber clothing stores—a new idea at the time. Then we discovered that our "friend" hadn't been entirely truthful and was being sued by a number of vendors. Yikes!

We hired a lawyer who got us out from under one lease and gave us full ownership of the other, a small space in a building consisting of about 15–20 shops. We avoided the bankruptcy that looked inevitable at one point. But desperation had forced quick learning and though it wasn't easy, when we sold the store three years later we had the highest profit per square foot in the market.

A few months after the sale closed our daughter graduated from college. It was 1987. She'd arranged for a six-month work visa in London. I'd just had a cancer scare and surgery; Ray was recovering from three years of intense emotional and physical activity. Another trip was called for, and France beckoned. I took a leave from my full-time job; we stayed six months and made our first visit to Turkey.

Two years after our return we decided it was time to move. We'd lived in Eugene 20 years. Ten years earlier Ray had started a nonprofit bike ride (the Willamette Flyway Century) that had more than achieved his goals; he'd recently turned it over to another nonprofit. The city of Eugene had a habit of replaying the same issues while little changed; we were tired of it. But where to go? We talked about it for months and finally settled on options. I covered three glass jars with paper, labeled them, and set them on the kitchen counter with a bowl of dried beans. We voted diligently twice a day, morning and night, for 30 days. Then we poured two glasses of wine and tore off the paper.

# 22

## THE NINETIES

We moved to Portland, Oregon, in January 1990, and settled down to enjoy our new "big city" lifestyle. We both found jobs within a few months and once again I was in a college environment, and for the first time I had a female boss.

A year later Anita Hill and Clarence Thomas were in the news. Hill received her Juris Doctor from Yale Law School in 1980 and worked at a D.C. law firm until 1981 when she became an attorney-advisor to Clarence Thomas, who was in the U.S. Department of Education's Office of Civil Rights. When he became chairman of the Equal Employment Opportunity Commission in 1982 she served as his assistant, leaving the job in 1983. She went on to teach at Oral Roberts University and the University of Oklahoma.[1]

Thomas had been a federal circuit judge for about a year when in 1991 he was nominated by George H. W. Bush to succeed retiring Associate Supreme Court Justice Thurgood Marshall. His position on abortion and other conservative beliefs meant there would certainly be opposition, and the American Bar Association had rated him only "qualified"—a very low rating for a Supreme Court nominee. The NAACP, Urban League, and National Organization for Women worried that he would swing the Court to the right. (Thomas asserted no opinion on Roe v. Wade.) [2]

The Judiciary Committee voted 13–1 to send his nomination to the Senate without recommendation. Despite these concerns there was no reason to expect he would not be confirmed. The hearings had run 10 days and were considered complete; the Senate was preparing to vote. Then a report of an FBI interview with Hill was leaked to the press and Senator Biden was pressured to reopen the hearings. The Senate vote was postponed and Hill was called to testify.

I just listened again to her testimony, and it was as gripping and upsetting as it was in 1991. The following excerpts are from that testimony.

At first Hill reported that her working relationship with Thomas was "positive." After about three months on the job Thomas asked Hill out and she refused, saying she feared "it would jeopardize" what she considered "a very good working relationship." She thought having a social relationship with her supervisor "would be ill-advised." However, he continued to ask her out.

"My working relationship became even more strained when Judge Thomas began to use work situations to discuss sex. . . . After a brief discussion of work, he would turn the conversation to a discussion of sexual matters.

"His conversations were very vivid. He spoke about acts that he had seen in pornographic films involving such matters as women having sex with animals and films showing group sex or rape scenes. He talked about pornographic materials depicting individuals with large penises or large breasts involved in various sex acts. On several occasions, Thomas told graphically of his own sexual prowess."

Despite asking him to not speak on such subjects, and trying to change the subject when he did, Thomas continued to ask Hill out. Then for a time the situation eased and she moved to the Equal Employment Opportunity Commission (EEOC) job with him because, she said, "I was dedicated to civil rights work, and my first choice was to be in that field." Thomas began again to ask her out, commenting on her clothes and appearance. What follows is the statement that ripped through the headlines: "He got up from the table at which we were working, went over to his desk to get the Coke, looked at the can and asked, "Who has put pubic hair on my Coke?"

Following that incident Hill began looking for another job, and "was hospitalized for five days on an emergency basis for acute stomach pain, which I attributed to stress on the job."

Hill had not volunteered any of this information and only came forward when she was asked to do so by a representative of the committee. "I felt that I had to tell the truth. I could not keep silent."[3]

After her testimony Hill was questioned by committee members. They were openly skeptical and frequently rude. They also questioned Thomas, who denied every allegation and called the hearing a "high tech lynching," an expression guaranteed to raise hackles and perhaps gain him, a Black man, some sympathy. [4]

The press was filled with support for and against both sides. Two women had supported Hill through statements made to Senate staffers. One claimed similar experiences, but both were dismissed by the committee without testifying. A third woman told staffers that "if you were young, Black, female, reasonably attractive and worked directly for Clarence Thomas, you knew full well you were being inspected and auditioned as a female."[5]

The failure to call those witnesses for public testimony led later to complaints about the committee's fairness and judgement. Over the next three days five women spoke in defense of Thomas. One said Thomas would not tolerate "the slightest hint of impropriety, and everyone knew it." Another said "At no time did Professor Hill intimate, not even in the most subtle of ways, that Judge Thomas was asking her out or subjecting her to the crude, abusive conversations that have been described."[6]

Clarence Thomas won confirmation and took the oath of office as the 106th member of the Supreme Court on October 23, 1991. The charged hearings brought to the surface again—and in vivid language—the ways in which women were vulnerable in the workplace despite a series of regulations and, in my opinion, weak laws.[7]

Numerous articles and commentaries kept the issue going for weeks and at least two books were soon published. *Strange Justice,* by Jane Mayer and Jill Abramson, was a National Book Award finalist in 1994 and was made into a movie. David Brock wrote an article and a 1993 book of the same name, *The Real Anita Hill,* arguing against her truthfulness. In a 2003 book, *Blinded by the Right,* Brock admitted he had lied in print to protect Clarence Thomas.[8]

Outrage from women and men across the country brought about a significant rise in awareness of sexual harassment and aggression, and of the vulnerability of women in the workplace. The general assessment by the public seemed to be that Hill had indeed told the truth. Given that Thomas lied to the committee about having no opinion on Roe v. Wade, and seeing his subsequent behavior as a Supreme Court Justice, I have no problem believing Anita Hill.

As mentioned earlier there were only two women in the Senate at the time the hearing took place. At the next election (1992) four more women were sent to the Senate, an event so astounding, apparently, that 1992 became known as the Year of the Woman. California had two female Senators for the first time in history, and Carol Moseley Braun of Illinois was the first Black woman elected to the Senate. A special election in 1993 brought in Kay Bailey Hutchison of Texas. In the House 106 women ran for office, with 23 percent winning. Many of these women cited the Hill-Thompson hearings as a motivating factor. In response to the publicity given these events Maryland Senator Barbara Mikulski said, "Calling it the Year of the Woman makes it sound like the Year of the Caribou or the Year of the Asparagus. We're not a fad, a fancy, or a year."[9]

The 1990s were in general a decade of loosening inhibitions and social liberalization. Tattoos and body piercings became common over the decade, and the styles of the '60s and '70s reappeared for a time. But life did not necessarily get easier. The '90s reintroduced us to the seriousness of global warming and need for environmental protection. In 1992 an Earth Summit was held in Rio de Janeiro, and attendees pleaded for action. Several countries signed a Convention on Biological

Diversity. In 1997 the Kyoto Protocol was adopted, binding signatory countries to limit emissions.

The decade was, in fact, a good one for women. The Violence Against Women Act (VAWA) was sponsored by Senator Biden as part of the Violent Crime Control and Law Enforcement Act of 1994. It passed with bipartisan support. Among other protections, it strengthened federal penalties for repeat sex offenders and included a federal "rape shield law," which prevents offenders from using victims' past sexual conduct against them during a rape trial. Eve's shadow turned a lighter gray.[10]

A year later a separate office within the Justice Department was created, the Violence Against Woman Grant Office (VAWGO). The Act has been in continual use, creating a hotline, a special program for Native American Women, grants for combating violence against women on campuses, and much more. In 2024 VAWA celebrated its 30th anniversary.

In the late 1980s a kind of proto-internet was in use by government offices, universities, and similar organizations, but on March 12, 1989 Tim Berners-Lee, a British computer scientist working at CERN (European Organization for Nuclear Research) in Switzerland, proposed a new type of information management system. In mid-November he linked nodes across the network and created the World Wide Web. That development was dramatic, and the rollout of fiber optic cables in the mid 1990s was a revolution.[11]

Slowly and then quickly, the Internet changed attitudes and work habits. Mosaic, the first popular web browser, came out in 1993, followed by Netscape Navigator in '94 and Microsoft's Internet Explorer in '95. The realization that we could find information and talk freely to people across the nation, and soon the world, was slow to take hold. But as personal computers became more accessible, what had seemed impossible just a few years earlier was suddenly commonplace. It's hard to believe that one of the original ideas was to keep the internet free of commerce. We knew it would change things; we had no idea how much.

I was working in the News & Publications office at a local college, originally hired to layout the school's weekly broadsheet, done in Pagemaker on the tiny screen of an early Mac. That eventually upgraded to a large screen, and with the introduction of Photoshop my skills expanded and so did the variety of work. When I took the job in 1990 the public internet didn't exist. Six years later it was taken for granted, and *You've Got Mail,* a popular comedy built around email, came out in 1998.

In 1993 a three-week vacation in Turkey found Ray and I revisiting friends in Bodrum and once again falling in love with the country and its people. Driving from Istanbul south and back again, we stopped along the way to explore numerous ancient ruins. It was a wonderful vacation. Jennifer was also on the move. Before starting grad school she spent nine weeks traveling on her own around Thailand. If we worried, we had only ourselves to blame.

At home again I started work on what became our first book. It was meant to be a brochure, but it just kept growing. We were by now experienced independent travelers and had given talks at various venues, mostly for travel agency customers; the brochure project grew from that. When it was clear I had enough material for a book, I tested the idea of working half time and suggested job-sharing to my boss. She agreed. A month or so later my co-worker was hired. We soon became good friends, comfortably managing the coordination of our work and enjoying our four-hour days.

In 1995 we published *How To Plan Your Trip to Europe,* a 133-page workbook. We named our little publishing company Artha (Sanskrit for earth) and jokingly appointed our cat Winston to be our "office manager." We laughed when a UPS driver knocked on the door and said he had a package for a Mr. Winston Feline?

When 3,300 books are deposited in your basement you have great incentive to market. Ray took on most of that effort, and by the end of the year we had sold all but about 200 books. Which was a good thing because soon after, in the middle of the night, the hum and beep of the fax machine woke us both.

I got out of bed and retrieved the fax. It was from our Bodrum friends, with news that a couple in a village down the coast were planning to sail around the world. They wanted to rent their apartment for a year. Were we interested? It would be $125 a month, in advance. I went back to bed and read the fax to Ray. When we turned out the light 15 minutes later we'd decided.

I don't remember exactly how long we had before departure—six months maybe?—but I remember a large piece of butcher paper tacked to my office wall with lists of to-dos. We seemed to add more than we scratched off, but eventually it became manageable. We told our employers we were leaving, put the house on the market, sold it, packed everything into another storage unit, sold the car, said goodbye to family and friends, and flew to Istanbul on July 4, 1996.

It turned out to be a wonderful year; Ray called it the "best year of our lives." We soon made friends with our neighbors and others in the village. It was a popular sailing venue and it filled with tourists in summer. The winter was quiet; many of the stores and restaurants shut down. Jennifer flew over to spend the holidays.

It was a delightfully long, slow year. Occasionally we rented cars and explored other parts of the country. Every three months we had to renew our visas, which meant taking the daily ferry to the nearby Greek island of Kos—or another island—and often spending a night or two, a break we always enjoyed. Despite an unreliable internet we managed to send trip reports home to friends and relatives. That material led to our second book.[12]

We felt sad leaving Turkey, in July '97, but we didn't rush home. We spent a month camping around France, looking for places we might want to live part time, and talking to realtors. Then we went north to England to spend a month housesitting for friends.

President Clinton had been re-elected in 1996, and his sexual misadventure had not yet occurred when we arrived back in the states. In fact everything felt normal and unchanged, though the two of us were surely changed by our experience. Not in a noticeable way, I think, but changed nonetheless. Extended travel is a growth experience like no other, and we were reaping the benefits. We were also temporarily unprepared for stepping back into life in the busy U.S.

Here's an excerpt of something I wrote in a journal a few weeks after coming home:

*When I left Turkey to return home I felt content. For the first time in a long time I knew who I was. Superfluousness had been carved away during that year, and meaning had been revealed. Life was really very simple.*

*During our year in the village I had—unplanned—reshaped my thoughts, values, reading, conversations, and writing into limbs and branches that enveloped me in a protective shelter of warmth and peace. I loved the simplicity I found in Turkey, and when I left I loved the feeling of knowing who I was and where I stood. My sense of self was firmly in hand.*

*I hung on to this belief through France, where I remember saying that all I really want or need is a pair of winter shoes, a pair of summer shoes, and occasional access to an L.L. Bean catalog.*

*Then we arrived in the U.S.*

*My feeling of certainty lasted about one week. And then I began to want things. Silly things. Things I couldn't use and had no need of. I turned on the TV and wanted a bigger one. I picked up a magazine and wanted a subscription. I walked down the street and wanted a new car. I entered a department store and wanted clothes I'd never wear, and exited a bookstore carrying books I'd never read. The advertisers and marketers are so good at what they do that even when we know they're doing it we succumb.*

*My love of simplicity remains, but I feel as if a sinister form of mind control is chipping away at my core. I seek shelter in imagination and meditation and avoid advertising when I can, but daily my willpower grows weaker and I fear I'm losing the battle.*

*This feeling can't be unique. So what are we doing to ourselves? When it's impossible to be who you know yourself to be, and to live the way you know you want to live, what is possible? Must we run for our lives—and our souls—away from marketing wizards and globalization experts and market share concerns and high-tech hijinks? At the moment I can think of no other answer.*

If nothing else those paragraphs are proof that: (a) it's incredibly easy to deceive oneself; and/or (b) it's a given that one will succumb to the dominant culture, no matter what its values. Both scary thoughts.

President Clinton saw the "longest period of peacetime economic expansion" in American history, helped by the "dot.com" startups. In 1995 Newt Gingrich and the Republicans took the House of Representatives for the first time in 40 years, which was like lighting a cannon under the nascent right-wing political movement.

In contrast, Clinton helped American women during his two terms. For the first time a President made room in his administration for his wife, Hillary Clinton. She led an unsuccessful effort to restructure U. S. healthcare, traveled to 82 counties as a State Department representative, and was certainly the most powerful/influential First Lady I had ever known.

Clinton also elevated Madeleine Albright to U. S. Secretary of State, and Janet Reno to Attorney General. Both were firsts for women. Sheila Widnall became Secretary of the Air Force; another first. Besides appointing Ruth Bader Ginsburg (and Stephen Breyer) to the U.S. Supreme Court, he revoked a gag order preventing abortion counseling in federally funded clinics. He signed an executive order allowing fetal tissue to be used in medical research, signed a law making it a federal crime to obstruct abortion clinics, and vetoed the Partial-Birth Abortion Ban Act of 1995. He also expanded health insurance for children (CHIP).[13]

Clinton was impeached in 1998 after he denied under oath an affair with Monica Lewinsky. He was acquitted by the Senate. At the end of his term he left office with a 66 percent approval rating, the highest of any president since WWII.

Throughout the 1990s Pope John Paul II extended apologies to groups the Catholic Church had harmed over the years. Many of them included women and one was specific. In a July 10, 1995 letter to "every woman" he apologized for: "The injustices committed against women, the violation of women's rights and the historical denigration of women." The same year he apologized for the church hierarchy's role in burnings at the stake and the religious wars that followed the Protestant Reformation. He also apologized for the involvement of Catholics in the Atlantic slave trade, and for the inactivity and silence of "many Catholics" during the Holocaust. Of course women too were victims in all those actions.

A fifth apology went to Galileo Galilei.[14]

I was not aware of these at the time; if they made it into the daily news I missed it. I'm happy to know that the Pope recognized the Church's horrible deeds, but for some reason I don't find it particularly meaningful to apologize once for the thousands of innocents tortured and/or burned as witches or heretics over centuries, or denying women leading roles in the Church hierarchy. As the Church leaders surely knew, it was all wrongly done, but they continued to do it.

As for the violations of women's rights and the historic denigration of women, no apology will stand, despite John Paul's good intentions. Such "denigrations" have, for centuries, devalued women unnecessarily; fostered and encouraged a male attitude that continues to find reasons to demean, insult, and sexually harass women; and reduced or eliminated opportunities of all kinds for every member of the female sex. All of this has been done to maintain power, influence, and money for the holy institution.

I'm aware, of course, that the Church has also provided consolation and meaning to millions who claim the Catholic Church as home. I have no issue there. My issue lies with the deliberate steps away from women toward the end of the 3rd century and the beginnings of the "official" Church, its hiding of the truth about its beginnings, and its continued denial of half the human race.

Returning from our extended year abroad we landed back in Eugene, in a tiny garage apartment belonging to old friends. We planned to be there a month but it ended up closer to three. We spent our time catching up with family and friends and lining up a few house-sitting jobs. I noticed an "office for rent" sign in a nearby building; the rent was affordable so I took it for two months and spent most of my days working on our next book.

We also bought a used car from friends, a white Dodge Colt that we planned to take to Mexico, which we did, leaving in January for about three months, criss-crossing the country and visiting Mayan, Aztec, and other ruins. English friends flew into Mexico City and traveled with us for two weeks or so, adding to the fun. The need to work called, of course, but after such an extended period away neither of us was mentally ready to go back to the 8–5 grind. We lived off our savings and extended not-working for as long as we could.

After the Mexico trip we rented an apartment, and settled for awhile. Ray soon found a project to work on, and I did a couple of free-lance jobs. We were waiting for the snow in Yellowstone to melt so U.S. Highway 20 would be open. In the meantime we had traded our used Colt for a used VW camper and prepared to drive across the U.S. on highway 20. This had been on Ray's list for years. It was, at the time, the only remaining US two-lane highway from coast to coast.

We finally left in early July, driving first to the Oregon coast to fill a little glass bottle with Pacific Ocean water, to be poured into the Atlantic on arrival. It was a long, slow, enjoyable trip, passing through, or near, a number of national and state parks and monuments, and mostly small towns. We camped in or visited all the parks within reach. Our "rule" said we could leave Hwy 20 to visit a site but had to return to the same exit before continuing. An engine noise stopped us in Iowa for two nights, and given the expense of repairs we almost turned around. We sat at the stop sign, engine humming smoothly, and debated. Then we turned east. When highway 20 ended in Boston we headed north to Nova Scotia, and then west toward home.

Throughout our trip Ray—who loved talking to strangers—would ask people "do you know where, or how far, this road (highway 20) goes?" Most didn't—and Ray never said. The most common response was a variation on "Well, I know it goes to the next town, but after that, not sure." Only one person knew the correct answer, a young Amish girl, maybe 10 or 12, who was selling homemade cookies beside the road. "Yes," she said promptly. "It goes from Oregon to Massachusetts." Right on!

# 23

## THE DAWN OF A NEW MILLENNIUM

Apprehension filled the air as the New Year holiday grew closer. It would be the year 2000—a new millennium! What would happen? Would the world end? Some thought it might. The more realistic fear was the Y2k bug, a widespread worry that computers would crash, that somehow the transition from 1900 to 2000 would lead to system failures. Computer techs across the globe slogged through long hours to update and patch systems, and while we held our collective breath as the clock chimed midnight, Y2k became a non issue.

For Ray and me the millennium meant little more than another move. Our cross-country trip had ended in early fall 1999, and as previously planned we moved to Corvallis, Oregon, a small college town 30 minutes north of Eugene. We had frequented the town when our daughter was getting her masters degree at OSU, and had grown fond of it. Ray quickly found work and after some freelancing I was hired at a graphic arts and advertising firm. In late 2000 we went to France on vacation and bought a little house in a little village in Languedoc. We had fallen in love with France on our first trip in 1977 and had refused to let go of our dream. It was a crazy thing to do, but we did it.

The year 2000 was historic and busy. The first crew to live at the International Space Station moved in and it has remained occupied ever since. More important for life on Earth was the announcement of a "rough draft" of the Human Genome Project, opening new vistas for medicine and genetics that are still being explored and utilized.

Technology ruled the year, and continues to do so. Bluetooth came into wide use, as did mobile phones and their digital cameras. Online shopping became a thing, as did social media, as new networking sites were developed. And for gaming enthusiasts, Playstation 2 was released.

Pope John Paul II continued his apologia on March 12 as part of the Great Jubilee of 2000; a day of Prayer for Forgiveness of the Sins of the Church was held. On November 20, 2001, he sent his first email, apologizing for the Catholic sex abuse cases, the church-backed Stolen Generations of Aboriginal children in Australia, and to China for the behavior of Catholic missionaries in colonial times. John Paul II made, in all, official public apologies for over 100 wrongdoings. I give him much credit for that, though long overdue.[1]

In many ways the year 2000 set the stage for issues we're still dealing with 25 years later. Vladimir Putin was first elected President in Russia in 2000; his 2022 invasion of Ukraine launched a war that continues.[2] At home we remain engulfed in social media and its dilatory effects on human interactions and a degradation of trust. And despite solid, ongoing growth in alternative energy, the environmental crisis continues. Climatic changes can no longer be ignored, as hurricanes grow in strength, tornados show up in unexpected places, and the warming oceans threaten every kind of sea life around the globe. And as I write Los Angeles is burning. Some still cry "humbug!"

Women continued their upward climb in education in 2000. The number of women who completed college with a B.A. has increased since 1995, from 25 to 47 percent compared to 25 to 37 percent of males; the latter a somewhat disturbing pattern that continues.[3]

It won't surprise you to hear that median incomes do not reflect those numbers. In 2024 the Institute for Women's Policy Research reported that women earned only 84 cents for every dollar men earned—

across most industries. "At this rate," said IWPR President Jamila Taylor, "women will have to wait until 2053 for full pay equity."[4]

On December 12, 2000, the U.S. Supreme Court ruled the Florida recount of the narrow and contested 2000 presidential election be halted, and the original results certified. This ruling, which angered many, made Republican George W. Bush the winner of the 2000 election, despite losing the popular vote. The Democratic candidate, Al Gore, immediately conceded.

Nine months later, on September 11, 2001, the world collectively watched in horror as the World Trade Center's twin towers, struck by commercial airliners commanded by Islamist terrorists, collapsed in on themselves and surrendered to gravity. The terrorists called themselves al-Qaeda, an unfamiliar name we would soon learn to loathe. A third plane, flight 93, crashed in rural Pennsylvania owing to the courage of its passengers, who revolted on learning the plane's destination. All aboard were killed. A fourth plane struck the Pentagon, bringing down a section of the building. The Federal Aviation Administration immediately ordered every plane in the country grounded for an indefinite period.[5]

It was a harrowing event, and as I stood with my co-workers watching TV the huge buildings crumbled, first one, then the other; we were stupefied, gasping and speechless. "This can't be happening," we said. But it did. The attacks killed 2,977 innocent people, and cost at least $10 billion in infrastructure and property damage.[6] America, for the first time ever, invoked Article 5 of the North Atlantic Treaty, asking NATO countries for help fighting the terrorists.

The United States had promptly declared war on Al-Qaeda and the Taliban in Afghanistan, who rejected a request to expel Al-Qaeda and its leader, Osama bin Laden. This years-long war resulted in thousands of deaths, and sadly encouraged religious intolerance and hate crimes in the U.S.[7]

A wave of sympathy and loss had swept the country after the disaster, and for a period the country was united in shock and mourning. But inevitably, news from the war and the search for bin Laden eclipsed the original trauma, and within a month or two, except in the New York area, life was almost normal. But 9/11 remains a dark scar in the hearts of those who remember.

The years 2000–2010 were busy ones for us personally, and for the country. The war on terror carried on. That was followed by President Bush's war in Iraq, sparked by Saddam Hussein's "weapons of mass destruction," though no evidence was ever found. Campuses and city streets hosted anti-war demonstrations to no avail.

I remember very little of Bush's years as President except the continual news of war; though the 43rd President did accomplish some things. He initiated AIDS relief in 2003 and signed an education-reform bill, the No Child Left Behind Act. He added prescription drugs to Medicare ( Part D). And, as a result of the terrorist attack he ordered the creation of the Department of Homeland Security.

Unfortunately for women, in his second term he appointed John Roberts and Samuel Alito to the Supreme Court. He also refused to implement the Kyoto Protocol, requiring nations to reduce greenhouse gas emissions, though in 2009 he protected the world's largest marine area, the Pacific Ocean habitat. He lowered individual tax rates, but included cutting the top income rate from 39 percent to 35 percent, and lowered taxes on capital gains and dividends. His slowness over Hurricane Katrina and the confirmed torture of detainees at Abu Ghraib are black marks on his record that time can't erase.[8]

After years of chaos and death the Iraq war officially ended on December 15, 2011, but U.S. forces still, in 2025, maintain a presence in that country.

Eve's shadow has grown increasingly darker for women since 2000, despite ongoing work to make things better. For example, efforts have been made to improve the numbers of women in STEM (science, technology, engineering, and math) fields. The numbers have increased but there are still fewer female students in such classes than men, and "female students in engineering and medical majors experience sexual harassment significantly more than female students in non STEM fields."[9]

In 2008 Barack Obama was elected President, and Joe Biden Vice President. They served two terms, from 2009 to 2017. Obama was, of course, the first Black President and we cheered with friends when he won. I thought about the Black children who would finally know that someone who looked like them could be President. In my optimism I believed relations between the races would change for the better. Sadly I now believe his time in office led to increased racial animosity, aggravated in large part by the President who followed him, Donald Trump.

Obama's presidency began with the 2007–2008 financial crisis, as banks threatened to crash and people across the country lost homes and jobs. It was the Great Recession. The Recovery and Reinvestment Act of 2009 was a $787 billion stimulus package designed to save jobs and create new ones, and to provide temporary relief programs to help the country recover from the recession. Not a single House Republican voted for it.[10]

Republicans had vowed to hold Obama to one term but failed in that effort, and in his second term he signed the Affordable Care Act, a major step toward improving American health care. He negotiated a nuclear agreement with Iran, later dismantled by Trump, and normalized relations with Cuba. He oversaw the end of the Iraq War and ordered the raid that killed Osama Bin Laden. More important to this account, he appointed two women to be justices on the Supreme Court, Sonia Sotomayor, the first Hispanic American, and Elena Kagan.

While Obama was in office there was revived interest in the Equal Rights Amendment's adoption, and in 2017 Nevada became the first state to ratify after the stated deadline. Illinois followed in 2018 and Virginia in 2020. As it now stands 38 states have ratified the constitutional amendment, which is the number required for passage. (This assumes the rescindings were not legal). In 2023 a Congressional Caucus for the Equal Rights Amendment was founded by House Democrats.[11]

We can expect little help in this matter from the Supreme Court. In 2011 *The Atlantic* magazine quoted Supreme Court Justice Scalia stating, "Certainly the Constitution does not require discrimination on the basis of sex. The only issue is whether it prohibits it. It doesn't. Nobody ever thought that that is what it meant. Nobody ever voted for that. If the current society wants to outlaw discrimination by sex, hey, we have things called legislatures and they enact things called laws."[12] (Justice Scalia died February, 13, 2016.)

The election of 2016 was a strange one. Republican Donald Trump, with no previous government experience, but with 304 electoral votes, defeated the Democrat, former Secretary of State Hillary Clinton, with 227 (she also won the popular vote). Republicans retained control of Congress. Trump ran a populist campaign that was helped by the Russian government and the abundant use of misinformation, also known as lies.[13]

His Make American Great Again (MAGA) slogan meant that, in his mind, the country was currently "awful, terrible!" He held rallies for red-hatted MAGA acolytes and berated the current government and his opponent with language and lies that had never been seen in a U.S. election. He spoke against immigrants, women ("when you're a star they let you do it") and every aspect of the government that he claimed needed fixing. No one, Republican or Democrat, had ever seen such a campaign.[14]

Seven days after his inauguration he issued Executive Order 13769 restricting entry into the country by certain "foreign nationals," an action that quickly became known as the Muslim Ban. It was also immediately condemned, and airport crowds united to defend recent arrivals. State and federal courts soon halted enforcement or blocked the order.[15]

And then Covid arrived. The president first ignored it, then stated it would soon be gone, and finally pushed for quick development of a vaccine. While those on the right resisted wearing masks and downplayed the seriousness of the disease, hospitals and emergency rooms were overworked. Refrigerator trucks were brought in as temporary morgues in New York City, and thousands across the country were dying.

We wore masks, repeatedly washed our hands, and feared to leave home. Theaters cancelled events and restaurants closed. So did small businesses that depended on walk-in customers. The President passed on a suggestion about Ivermectin, an anti-parasite medication. It didn't work, and some people died taking it. Then Trump suggested an injection of disinfectant might help. Or maybe bringing bright light "inside the body." All nonsense.[16]

Surprisingly, and thanks to Trump's Operation Warp Speed, it took just over a year for an mRNA vaccine to be developed and tested, but it took longer to reach enough of us to make a difference. Schools reverted to online teaching; students fell behind anyway. Two to three years were essentially lost, as schools, churches, and businesses closed. Workers migrated from office to home offices. And as in-person meetings dwindled, loneliness and depression grew. Online buying of everything boomed, however, including home delivery of groceries, meals, and just about anything else. As the recovery finally began to take hold, prices soared and inflation set in.

In 2018 another barrier was broken when thousands of women around the world began using #MeToo on social media. Reacting to the news that more that 80 women had accused film producer Harvey Weinstein over his years of sexual abuse, women everywhere began acknowledging, often for the first time, that they had been raped, abused, or subjected to "unwanted and inappropriate" advances. The famous names were shocking, the numbers staggering. They should not have been.[17]

A poll by the *Washington Post* and ABC News in 2017 found that 54 percent of American women reported being on the receiving end of unwanted sexual advances. It's sad that what transpired so long ago during my job interview is still happening. And it's disheartening to know that despite changes in our laws and the publicity around such unwanted aggression, such events remain common. Why? What will it take to convince men to grow up and act responsibly?

It's not a casual event when a woman receives unwanted advances or worse, but that's the way it's too often treated. In 2023 the World Health Organization estimated that one-third of women worldwide had been subjected to sexual violence, and called violence against women "a major human rights violation and a global public health problem."[18]

The four years of the Trump presidency didn't help. Though #MeToo changed some minds and altered the picture somewhat, women continued to be second-class citizens, frequently demeaned and insulted by an administration that was packed with scandals, protests, investigations, lawsuits, a fake electors plot, and more. It was always going to be "infrastructure week" but never was. Trump did, unfortunately, follow the advice of the Heritage Foundation by appointing three right-wing, anti-abortion justices to the Supreme Court.

One of those justices, Brett Kavanaugh, took many of us back 26 years to the Thomas-Hill hearings. Kavanaugh too was accused of sexual misconduct by Christine Blasey Ford, a psychology professor at Palo Alto University. She claimed attempted rape when she was 15 and he 17. Her testimony made headlines. An FBI investigation was called for but found nothing; Democrats called it incomplete and worse. Despite Ford's testimony and the many ethical questions raised, Kavanaugh was passed through the Senate by a 50–48 vote.

The November, 2019 election offered positive change when the Democratic nominee, Joe Biden, received more than 81 million votes, the most ever cast for a presidential candidate. But then, of course, came January 6, 2020, and the attack on the United States Capitol, encouraged and promoted by Donald Trump, who denied the fair election.[19] Despite the attack, and calls from the crowd to "hang Mike Pence," the Vice President did what the Constitution outlined and the 2020 election was certified. After Biden's election things seemed to calm down for awhile, and he and his staff began their efforts to halt inflation and avoid the predicted recession.

Two years later, in June 2022, women's lives were suddenly upended and endangered when the U.S. Supreme Court overturned the 1993 Roe v. Wade decision, outlawing abortion and outraging women. Abortion had been a Constitutional right in the United States for 49 years. It was trashed in a 6–3 opinion written by Justice Samuel Alito, who in justifying his decision quoted English jurists William Blackstone (1723–80), Edward Coke (1552–34), and

Mathew Hale (1609–76). Hale was a strict Puritan who ordered two women executed for witchcraft and defended marital rape.

Correlating life in the 21st century with the late Middle Ages is a bit of a stretch, especially when Justice Alito knows that women in those years had no legal rights to speak of, were routinely forced to marry whomever their fathers chose and were thought to be—putting it mildly—inferior creatures. I found in Alito's decision no empathy for a raped child forced to bear another child and perhaps die as a result. Nor was there reference to the rapist, or any term in hell recommended for him. Instead Justice Alito justified his act by saying, "Roe was egregiously wrong from the start." [20]

What I find most disturbing in the aftermath of this decision (Dobbs v. Jackson Women's Health) is the growing sense of male arrogance, especially when men in positions of power appear shockingly ignorant about the birth process beyond impregnating—and know nothing about how it feels to live in a female body.

Despite their deplorable ignorance they deny women the right to make health decisions for themselves, and in 21 states where abortion is banned, deny treatment even when the woman's life is threatened. Forced to wait until they are facing death some die, denied even the most obvious care. Doctors find themselves threatened with jail or fines if they provide lifesaving treatment that includes an abortion. Clinics have closed, and travel across state lines for maternal healthcare is threatened. Even worse, if that's possible, legislators in a few states suggest abortion should legally be considered murder.

In January 2024 *Scientific American* reported on a new study released by JAMA Internal Medicine. It estimated that "more than 64,000 pregnancies resulted from rape between July 1, 2022, and January 1, 2024, in states where abortion has been banned throughout pregnancy in all or most cases. Of these, just more than 5,500 are estimated to have occurred in states with rape exceptions—and nearly 59,000 are estimated for states without exceptions. The authors calculate that more than 26,000 rape-caused pregnancies may have taken place in Texas alone."[21]

I confess my shock at those numbers, and that 64,000 doesn't include rapes where no pregnancy resulted. Has rape increased since the Dobbs decision? So far I've not been able to find such statistics. Is there, perhaps, a connection between the way women are thought of and generally treated in states with and without legal abortion? Again, no statistics. But I can hazard a guess.

Unfortunately the Dobbs ruling was based on the 14th Amendment of the Constitution which assumes our liberties include personal privacy. The right to abortion, to birth control, to marrying whomever you choose and other non-delineated liberties, all rely on that same amendment. So it is not just women who are worried. LGBTQ+ rights, voting rights, and human rights are all under threat.

The good news is that men and women are speaking out and fighting back, and will continue to do so until the first constitutional right to be renounced, is restored.

# 24

## THE RETURN OF TRUMP

As I write this in early January, 2025, President Biden will soon leave office and Donald Trump will begin again to ignore or destroy norms and laws, and put more women's lives at risk. The Biden presidency was a temporary stopgap, a parenthetical relief and correction of Donald Trump and his MAGA follower's efforts to push America backward.

The openness and acceptance of humanity's differences that appeared to grow in the nineties—accepting gay marriage, for instance—is now considered *verboten*. Organizations and companies that added DEI practices (diversity, equity, and inclusion) saw improvements in efficiency and their top lines.[1] Now some say they are halting that practice, kowtowing to the demands of the conservative right.

By the end of his first week in office Trump had issued orders terminating "illegal" DEI "mandates, policies, programs, preferences, and activities in the Federal Government, under whatever name they appear."[2] He also revoked previous executive actions of former administrations, such as environmental justice for low-income and minority populations (signed by President Clinton) and requiring "government contractors to adopt nondiscriminatory practices in hiring and employment (signed by President Lyndon Johnson). Those protections also extended to women.

Thanks to the Supreme Court's 2023 ruling ending affirmative action admissions at colleges and universities,[3] those institutions saw falling numbers of Black and brown students at a time when decreasing numbers of college applicants are causing some colleges to close. According to the website Inside Higher Ed, 16 nonprofit colleges and universities closed in 2024, most due to "financial pressures and declining enrollment."[4] This is expected to continue and does not bode well for U.S. innovation or the economy.

Meanwhile women are fearing pregnancy in ways not seen in decades. Even before the 1973 Roe v. Wade decision that allowed abortions, doctors were permitted to treat miscarriages with practices like dilation and curettage (D & Cs). Such treatment is now considered abortion and forbidden in no-abortion states. Outlawing this formerly common medical practice can, and has, led to sepsis and death.

Beyond the abortion issues, statistics support the fact that it's not our imagination, women are having a tougher time in many ways than before the 2022 ban. The Government Accountability Office (GAO) website reports that at the end of 2024, "Women are more likely to be concentrated in low-wage jobs, be responsible for care giving, and experience sexual harassment and assault. Additionally, the United States has the **highest** rates of maternal death of developed countries, with U.S. maternal mortality rates **increasing** when rates have decreased globally" (GAO emphasis). And yet another discouraging GAO statistic : "Sexual assaults in the United States increased by an estimated 64 percent from 2021 to 2022."[5]

Most of that bad news is the result of increasing fear-mongering coming from President Trump and his associates and followers over the four years he was out of office. It's encouraged too by the rise of "bro" podcasters like Andrew Tate, Joe Rogan, and others. This is a dramatic change from the 1990s acceptance mentioned above. The shadow of Eve, once optimistically pale gray, now turns to charcoal, leaving only a hint of light to hold onto.

President Biden accomplished much during his time in office (2021–25). He began his term in the dark days of Covid and worked hard to provide available, free access to the new Covid vaccines. His long service as a U.S. Senator provided the insight and experience necessary to lower inflation while keeping the economy on track for a "soft landing," something many economists declared impossible.

He signed the American Rescue Plan Act, an economic stimulus plan in response to the pandemic and job losses. He signed the bipartisan bill on Infrastructure and Manufacturing, and the Inflation Reduction Act. He oversaw the complete withdrawal of U.S. troops from Afghanistan and ended that long war, though the withdrawal itself was chaotic, with the loss of 13 service members and 170 Afghans after an attack by a suicide bomber. The removal of American forces led to the Taliban seizing control of the country.

The work President Biden did in drumming up support for Ukraine and strengthening NATO was perhaps his most critical and successful effort in foreign relations. And he selected Kamala Harris, a Black-Asian woman, as his running mate and chose another Black woman, Ketanji Brown Jackson, to fill Justice Steven Breyer's seat on the Supreme Court. Four women now hold seats on that Court.

President Biden also declared the 28th Amendment, the ERA, the law of the land, after Virginia became the 38th state to ratify it. But, say various talking heads, without the National Archives formally adding it to the Constitution it remains in limbo.

His announcement sparked multiple discussions regarding the legitimacy of that amendment. According to two of America's most esteemed law professors, Laurence Tribe, professor of constitutional law emeritus of Harvard, and his co-writer, professor of law at Harvard and Stanford, Kathleen M. Sullivan, ". . . Article V of the Constitution expressly makes any proposed Amendment to that document 'Part of this Constitution, when ratified by the Legislatures of three fourths of the several States.' Nothing in Article V makes the Constitution's binding contents depend on any further official action by any branch of the federal government, whether Congress or the Judiciary or indeed the Executive."[6]

As I've written previously, the real issue is that too many in leadership—from the founding fathers on—do not wish to see women or any "others" have rights equal to White men. It has been 102 years since that amendment was first put forward in 1923, and the country still has not accepted that women, LGBTQ+ people, people of color and others have equal constitutional rights in all endeavors, just as White men do. As President Biden said in his January 17, 2025 statement, "It is long past time to recognize the will of the American people."[7]

Unfortunately, the four years of Biden's presidency were haunted by Donald Trump's efforts to stay in the public eye and out of jail. Trump spent those four years putting himself forward in every way possible. He was frequently in court and made the most of it, talking with the waiting press and complaining about his treatment. He was daily in the news, especially after forming his own social media company. Thanks to his wealth and his lawyers, most of his legal cases were slowed by endless appeals.

Many of the delays were due to a decision by the Supreme Court made late in Biden's term. "In a historic 6–3 ruling, the justices said for the first time that 'presidents have absolute immunity from prosecution for their official acts and no immunity for unofficial acts.'"[8] They left the details to lower court judges to figure out, which produced productive delays for Trump's attorneys to use to his advantage.

On May 30, 2024 a jury in Manhattan declared Trump guilty of 34 counts of falsifying records. This was commonly known as the "hush-money case." Judge Juan Merchan, a New York State trial judge, sentenced him to "unconditional discharge" on January 10, 2025, meaning the conviction stands without penalties. This lack of monetary or other penalty was due to the numerous delays caused by various appeals, etc. and his current status as President-elect.

Trump's opponent for the office of President was Vice President Kamala Harris, who had approximately 100 days to create and run a campaign after Biden was passed over for being "too old." Both men and women worked hard to elect Harris, but Trump won with a 1.5 percent margin. After-election evaluations suggest that many normally Democratic voters stayed home, discouraged about the direction of the country maybe, or not wanting to vote for a Black or a woman. Whatever the motive of the voters, they gave Donald Trump a slim majority and he's running with it. He entered the White House as a convicted felon. The first time in our country's history.

"The will of the American people" has given way to the narcissistic will of our new President, who, on his first day in office pardoned and released approximately 1,500 prisoners who were jailed for their actions on January 6, 2020. Even the violent ones. Even their leaders.

Until the inauguration of President Trump the U.S. military had seen increased opportunities for women, with many making it a career. One of those, Admiral Linda Lee Fagan, the first female uniformed leader of an armed forces branch, the US Coast Guard, was fired by President Trump on Tuesday, January 21, apparently for her supposed DEI focus.[9]

Two other women were fired the following month by the new Defense Secretary Pete Hegseth: Chief of Naval Operations Admiral Lisa Franchetti; and Air Force Lt. General and senior military assistant to the Secretary of Defense, Jennifer Short. A third, Telita Crosland, Army Lt. General and head of the Defense Health Agency, ended her 32 year career with an abrupt retirement in February, 2025.[10]

There was no obvious need for any of these very capable women to be dismissed, but it becomes plain when the Defense Secretary is quoted as saying "The single dumbest phrase in military history is 'our diversity is our strength,'" during a town hall meeting at the Pentagon.[11] The administration's defense officials have ordered the Pentagon to erase all DEI content from its digital footprint, and ordered the end of commemorations of Black History and Women's History Months.

It's not my wish to get deeply into current politics but already President Trump is making decisions that are affecting women's lives, including immediately dismissing those four high-ranking military officers. I don't think it's too early to say that Eve's shadow has gone from charcoal to black.

One of the most riveting books I've read during the past few years is *Down Girl: The Logic of Misogyny* by Kate Manne, a professor of philosophy at Cornell University. She was writing parts of the book as the 2016 election was underway and Hillary Clinton was the Democrat's nominee, running against Trump. Given that we just came through a second female vs. Trump election, I think it's worth quoting her rather extensively.

In a section headed "Misogyny as Backlash" she writes,

> "Women are sometimes told they need to be twice as good as men, all else being equal, in order to be just as respected, successful, admired, and so on.... Such excellence in a woman may have the opposite effect on some people, resulting in her being a polarizing figure. In other words, women may be penalized for being too qualified, too competent."[12]

She expands on this in notes she'd made during the Trump-Clinton campaign.

> "[I]t is a feminist achievement of note that a woman may be the next president of the United States of America. It is not in spite of this fact, but plausibly partly because of it, that we have been seeing a lot of misogynistic backlash of late. Ironically, the fact that we might well have elected a woman president may now be the thing that prevents this from happening."[13]

It's strangely satisfying that a woman's words foreshadowed what we've all just witnessed in the 2024 election, a repeat of the performance of experience vs. misogyny. The sexism coming from the Republicans and Trump's MAGA followers was far worse in this 2024 election than 2016. Notably, they had the four years he was out of office to polish their slanders, smears, and slights. Lies, malicious gossip, and threats nicely rounded out the work of his minions, and the patriarchal-sexist-misogynistic platform he ran on.

Manne's book is filled with analysis of misogyny, sometimes brutal, often tied to specific cases of violence against women. Women, she says, are expected by our culture and by men to be giving, especially of support and attention. Some men believe they are owed.

> "[A] woman is regarded as owing her human capacities to particular people, often men or his children within heterosexual relationships that also uphold white supremacy, and who are in turn deemed entitled to her services."

A woman, she says, is "seldom her own person." She is rather someone's mother, daughter, wife, sister, grandmother. Thus her "personhood is held to be owed to others, in the form of service labor, love, and loyalty."[14] Which may explain why guilt is so common among women.

# 25
## WOMEN IN THE WORLD

No matter how women in Western countries feel about patriarchy, we do have it better than many. Women around the world are suffering under various forms of that antiquated system, supported in many cases by ultra-conservative religions. It's incumbent on us, I think, to help mitigate such circumstances. Direct intervention, however, is seldom realistic and can often be conceived as ethnocentric. What we can do is recognize and support governments and agencies working to improve or end such treatment.

### Iran

Iran and Afghanistan continue to show the modern world the most vivid examples of patriarchy and its defenders. On September 13, 2022, a young Iranian woman, 22-year-old Jina Mahsa Amini, was arrested and beaten by Iran's morality police. She later died while in custody. Her crime? Wearing her mandatory hijab (headscarf) in a way that revealed some of her hair. Her death triggered protests throughout the country and sparked a variant of revolution in Iran. Women marched, refused wearing hijabs, and sometimes burned them. The government was not gentle in its reaction, killing more than 500, using sexual violence—including rape—beatings, shootings and arrests.[1]

Months later the protest movement, known as Woman, Life, Freedom, called for the Islamic Republic's rule to end. Of course it did not end. Neither did violence against women. In a March 2023 report for NPR Fatma Tanis says, "all around the country many women are going about their business hair uncovered" despite posters "everywhere" telling women to keep their headscarves on. "A visible minority of women in Iran are refusing to wear headscarves, in defiant protest against the government."[2]

I'm in awe of these brave Iranian women who persist despite the danger and the brutality of the repression. The "morality" police, who were withdrawn after Amini's death, have been reinstated, and according to a UN September 2024 report, security forces had been beating, kicking and slapping women for failing to comply with the hijab laws. They were also said to be monitoring with drones. Iranian women were being terrorized.[3]

If you thought it couldn't get worse, the U.N. Human Rights Watch reported in the following month that Iran had passed a new law with added restrictions. This law was so extreme that public outcry caused it to be "paused." I'm including it here as an example of the very real restrictions women (and men) can be subject to.

There are "71 articles that not only strengthen the government's control over women's lives but also threaten businesses and institutions that fail to enforce these discriminatory measures with fines or closure."Among the restrictions: No dressing "immodestly" in "tight clothes" or what exposes "any part of the body below the neck, above the ankles, or above the forearms." Note that these are the same Sharia laws mentioned in Chapter 7, dating from at least 649 CE.

Men too have new restrictions; no "wearing tight clothing that exposes any part of the body below the chest and above the knee, or sleeveless shirts that expose the shoulders." All restrictions apply to online appearances as well. Fines and jail terms are listed, and are dependent on various criteria, such as how often these shameless occurrences are repeated.[4]

The President, Massoud Pezeshkian, "promised not to interfere in [women's] personal lives" during the run up to his election. A promise that obviously resonated with women. I hope and expect Iranian women will keep fighting for their human rights. I am less sanguine about the President's promise; he "is obligated to carry out parliament's resolutions."[5]

## Afghanistan

Sadly, conditions are even worse in Afghanistan. When the Taliban took over the government—after the U.S. pulled its troops out in 2021 and the old government collapsed—women were still employed, attending school, even openly protesting. But as new laws propagated and enforcement became more consistent, women's lives were increasingly limited, and fear is now overwhelming, to the point of suicide.

According to a report briefed to the United Nations Security Council on March 6, 2024 by Roza Otunbayeva, special representative of the Secretary-General for Afghanistan, there has been an erosion of basic freedoms. This is being enforced with monitoring by inspectors in "public spaces, NGO offices, mosques, bazaars, and even weddings."[6]

It's hard to imagine erosion of what was already terrible, but here's what's been happening: a June 4, 2023 report by Yogita Limaye for the BBC offered quotes from various women about the mental health situation (the women were not identified for their safety): "Most of the girls in my class have had suicidal thoughts. We are all suffering from depression and anxiety. We have no hope."

And, "Staying at home without an education or a future, it makes me feel ridiculous. I feel exhausted and indifferent to everything. It's like nothing matters anymore,' a teenage girl tells us, tears rolling down her face."

"Dr Amal [a psychologist], says she received 170 calls for help within two days of the announcement that women would be banned from universities. Now she gets roughly seven to 10 new calls for help every day. Most of her patients are girls and young women."[7]

In September 2024 the same reporter spoke with women after a new Taliban law had taken effect a month earlier. "Now," she writes, "even the small joys that were making life bearable are fraught with fear." The new law "forbids women's voices from being heard outside her home." Said one, "If we can't speak, why even live? We're like dead bodies moving around." Another, previously detained and beaten for protesting, said, "I don't want to be humiliated anymore because I'm a woman. It is better to die than to live like this."[8]

After that law was passed the European Union put out a statement, reported by EUNews.it:

> "The European Union is 'baffled' by the new law on the propagation of virtue and prevention of vice by the Taliban, which, among other things has imposed not only a strict dress code for Afghan women—requiring them not to leave any part of their bodies or faces uncovered—but also a ban on hearing their voices in singing, acting, or reading in public and, in general, in any place other than a private home. It is also forbidden for women to look directly at men who are not their relatives or family members, and vice versa."[9]

Heather Barr, associate women's rights director at Human Rights Watch, writing in the *Georgetown Journal of International Affairs* offers a stunning rebuke to governments and international organizations reactions to the crisis. "It has been disorganized, politicized, chaotic, often apathetic, and, frankly, un-feminist."

She says diplomats tend to focus on counter-terrorism, narcotics, business deals, etc., and despite pleas from Afghan women, "their rights protection agenda rarely makes it onto the priority list of diplomats. . . . If the world can learn to live with the Taliban's abuses—Afghan women being largely confined to their homes, losing their voice, their personhood, their education, their dreams, and contributions to their communities—then this is a brutal demonstration of how fragile the rights of women and girls are everywhere."[10]

A Human Rights Watch joint statement with the U.S. Policy Advocates for Afghan Women and Girls called it "gender apartheid" and criticized the international community for "gradually accepting the Taliban's violations of the rights of women and girls. This poses a dangerous trend toward the normalization of such abuses."[11]

The women in Afghanistan are trapped, voiceless, and fearful. Not because God demands it. Not because Mohammed preached it; not because an angel wrote it across the sky with a fiery sword. No. They are voiceless and fearful because men, and only men, will it.

This is patriarchal governance carried to an extreme that I doubt has ever been seen on such a scale, with the exception, perhaps, of the darkest abuses of slavery. It is nothing but outright hatred of women welded to a morbid addiction to power. And religion, once again, is an excuse for anti-woman criminal behavior. There is nothing in the Qur'an that decrees such treatment. Nothing.

## Africa

The African continent is home to 55 member states in the African Union; with one exception they are also members of the United Nations. The Union has more than 1.3 billion people and an area of around 12 million square miles (30 million sq. kilometers) and six primary working languages.[12]

To cover each country individually would take another book, and there is great variety between women's lives in, say, Morocco or Egypt, and a southern, landlocked country like Malawi. The colonial era nearly wiped out traditional village life, and the post-colonial era brought more changes, and some improvements. But poverty remains a common problem.

Significant efforts toward gender equality were made with the creation of the African (Banjul) Charter on Human and People's Rights in June 1981, and put into effect 1986. The charter encourages member states to end discrimination and violence against women. With the exception of Morocco and Burundi, all African states have adopted this charter.[13]

In some African countries girls suffer from poverty and gender-based violence, child marriage, and female genital mutilation. Girls do not receive the same educational benefits as boys, and in places where girls can attend school they often don't have access to, or can't afford, menstrual and sanitary products like pads or tampons, which leads them to stay home during their periods, or drop out altogether. This too is improving in some areas.

In sub-Saharan Africa (most of the continent) girls also continue to marry young. For instance in 2006, 45.3 percent were married before age 18; in 2021 that dropped to 35.3 percent. Girls married under age 15 in 2006 were 8.4 percent but in 2021 that rose to 13.5 percent. Early marriage and early childbirth obviously means girls and young women are subjected to birth-related health hazards, and possible long-term consequences.[14] It doesn't take much imagination to believe young girls would rather be kids, go to school, and have a life.

It's not a pretty picture, but it's not bleak either. So many African women have succeeded in so many fields—including politics, writing, human rights work—that it's been impossible for me to choose which to highlight; and they keep coming. Here are just three who have made names for themselves: Wangari Maathai, a Kenyan environmental activist, won a Nobel Peace Prize in 2004;[15] so did Ellen Johnson Sirleaf of Liberia in 2011.[16] She was her country's first female elected President (2006–2018). Chimamanda (Amada) Ngozi is a Nigerian author and activist who was on Time magazine's 2015 list of the 100 most influential people. She received a MacArthur Fellowship in 2008 and many, many awards.[17] I've no doubt African women will continue to stand up for women's rights and will keep winning awards. In the meantime we can support the efforts being made to strengthen women's progress in education and in life.

When President Trump closed the highly respected USAID organization thousands, if not millions of people in Africa lost critical food and medical support provided by USAID workers. In early March, 2025 I checked their website hoping to find more information, but found only a February 23, 2025 "Notification of Administrative Leave." A link to the agency's Office of Inspector General lists several reports. After scanning them I can't justify including what appears to me as unjustified and/or unsupported actions. [18]

## Sri Lanka

On an island off the tip of southern India, once known as Ceylon, life is looking up for women. Dr. Harini Amarasuriya, a woman, is the new Prime Minister of Sri Lanka, appointed to the post in September 2024, by the new male President, Anura Kumara Dissanayake. She is "a sociologist and activist" who received her doctorate in social anthropology from the University of Edinburgh. She's the "first woman to hold such a high post in South Asia who is not the wife or daughter of a previous top leader."

The leftist party in Sri Lanka succeeded in ousting the former leader with the help of women who protested the hardships they were facing as the country's economy steeply declined. Women were the majority of registered voters, at 56 percent, electing the new president as well as a parliament where "in many districts, women won handily." The country's new leaders are committed to improving life for women, and have established regional women's committees with the hope that more women will become involved in Sri Lanka's political life.

The country has a long economic climb ahead of it, but the party "is focused on entrenching its mobilization of women to get more of them into leadership positions."[19]

For Sri Lankan women to win seats in parliament and have a female Prime Minister is real change, especially after living through a 26-year civil war that ended in 2009. It will be interesting to see how these woman and the country fares. Maybe we can learn something from them.

## South Korea

From Sri Lanka we travel northeast to South Korea where a very different story is playing out. I stumbled across it in a *Forbes* article by Mark Travers, a psychologist. It's all about the 4B movement and the women searching for a means of control over their lives, vis-à-vis their patriarchal culture. Apparently women in the U.S., especially young women, are listening too.

In Korean the prefix bi means no. Thus: no dating (biyeonae), no marriage (bihon), no sex (bisekseu), no children with men (bichulsan).[20]

Travers emphasizes that this movement is not the result of females unable to date or find partners, but a positive choice for women who are fed up with men and their treatment of women. Some, he says, are even shaving their heads in opposition to the beauty standards they're expected to adhere to. His article offers three reasons for the rise of 4B:

"(1) Women do not want to put up with mistreatment. (2) Women do not get the reproductive care they deserve. (3) Women genuinely enjoy their own company."[21]

In a National Public Radio article, writer Rachel Treisman interviewed Ju Hui Judy Han, a gender studies professor at the University of California Los Angeles, who described 4B "as a relatively small movement that began as an offshoot of the growing feminist movement in South Korea, driven by structural misogyny and gender discrimination."[22]

"South Korea ranked 99 out of 146 in the World Economic Forum's 2024 Global Gender Gap Index" writes Treisman, and The Economist "ranked South Korea the worst OECD country for working women in 2022." It also has the lowest fertility rate in the world.

"It would be a stretch to blame 4B for causing the decline in childbirths," says Han, who sees it as a response to conditions, such its "culture of compulsory marriage." A number of events, including "the 2016 murder of a 23-year-old woman in a public bathroom" raised the ire of women after the murderer said he did it because "women have always ignored me."

4B spread quickly on social media and word of mouth. "What I think is most important," says Han, "is that it's about women recognizing that they're in a collective struggle, and that there's a collective sense of frustration."[23]

We already know that since 2022 American women aren't all getting the reproductive care they need and deserve, and that many have died from lack of treatment. Travers sites several 2018 statistics including that "one in six American women experience attempted or completed rape in her lifetime with 54 percent of victims under 30."

Given the "anti-woman" attitudes growing more prevalent every day in the U.S. it does not surprise me that women are taking control of their lives with or without 4B. No one deserves not to be safe in their own home. Travers adds that women who decide to remain single "often report higher levels of happiness than single men, and are less likely to seek romantic relationships."[24]

CNN reports that "Young liberal women across TikTok and Instagram are discussing and sharing information about the South Korean feminist movement . . . saying they are enraged and fed up after a majority of their male counterparts voted for a candidate who was found liable for sexual abuse. . . . In response, they say they're swearing off men—and they're encouraging others around the country to join them."[25] Whether female Trump voters feel the same is an open question.

One woman reported that after posting on social media about her decision to join the 4B movement, "men flooded her DMs with death threats and hateful comments about her appearance. 'It doesn't exactly entice you to re-enter the dating pool.'"[26]

# 26

## WHERE DO WE GO FROM HERE?

I had hoped when starting this book that by the time it was finished our new president might be a U.S. historical first, a woman. That hope died with the second election of Donald Trump. But that isn't—that can't be—the end of our story.

History in its simplest form is a continual recording of events. Tomorrow's historians will study leaders that we praise or decry today. They will analyze, poke, and prod for meaning long after the actors are gone. But we needn't wait for history's final word, we are living witnesses to an exceptional moment in time. A time when norms are replaced by memes, and rapid changes retard comprehension. An uneasy time, when the arc of the moral universe bends, but can't find justice.

Nor will justice be found in the mythology of Eve or the story of Pandora, though injustice abounds. So does inequity, brutality and exploitation. Eve's mythology has done unimaginable damage to the minds and souls of millions of women. I could fill multiple pages with quotes from women who, throughout time, have felt the weight generated by those myths. From the unknown to the notable, their words declaim the memory of centuries of hate, mistrust and humiliation.

The issue is no longer who is to blame for what has happened but rather what will happen now? We like to think we are more sophisticated now, more scientific, less easily swayed by superstition and cant. And yet . . .

One of President Trump's first acts was to declare that there are only two sexes: male and female.[1] It doesn't matter to him that every year children are born with sex characteristics that do not fit normal patterns, such as atypical chromosomes, gonads, or hormones. It doesn't matter that gender dysphoria is a real thing.[2] Nor does he care about the issues trans children or adults might have to deal with as a result of his mandate.

He cares about stopping all diversity, equity, and inclusion (DEI).[3] Why? Because he does not care that DEI makes life easier for everyone. He doesn't understand that when all of us work together we learn to care about and respect one another. He doesn't accept that companies say DEI training programs have helped their bottom lines.[4]

The president issued orders demanding that those three words and others like them be removed from all government web pages and documents. He illegally cut funding to DEI programs across all agencies. He wants to eliminate anyone who is in anyway different from what he considers "normal," and of course that includes women of every color. Because throughout time men have been and still are the norm that sets the standard.

We women, while making progress in many ways over the last few hundred years, now find ourselves slipping backwards rather rapidly. There are, unfortunately, signals that suggest this may not be temporary. For instance, a *Psychology Today* article quotes Keegan Hankes, an analyst for the Southern Poverty Law Center (SPLC) saying, "male supremacy had become impossible to ignore." They began monitoring male supremacist hate groups in 2018 and found that "Those misogynistic beliefs, so depressingly familiar and widespread, have hardened into a more distinct force in recent years, and have been fueled by the election of Donald Trump and the resurrection of white supremacist groups in American political life."[5]

According to the SPLC, male supremacy represents all women as "genetically inferior, manipulative, and stupid beings who exist primarily for their reproductive and sexual functions."[6] Of course we know all this by now. But these mistaken ideas are part of a growing movement often linked to white supremacists, who claim they are better than everyone, including any woman.

"Why won't you go out with me?" is apparently a frequent complaint, and one that resulted in multiple deaths in a 2014 shooting by Elliot Rodger, a 22-year-old man. This is an infamous case that occurred on the campus of UC Santa Barbara. Kate Manne has a full account of it in *Down Girl* where she quotes part of a video he made before the shooting, speaking of his unhappiness because "girls have never been attracted to me. Girls gave their affection and sex and love to other men but never to me . . . It has been very torturous." He continues with more of the same, and says, "I'll take great pleasure in slaughtering all of you [in the sorority]. You will finally see that I am, in truth, the superior one—the true alpha male."[7]

Obviously not all young men are Elliot Rodger. But the SPLC report states that "Like white supremacy, male supremacy is both an extremist ideology as well as a part of the social fabric that informs every aspect of American life. . . . However, the omnipresent nature of misogyny and its far-reaching influence on American society means the extent of the problem is often hidden in plain sight."[8]

And nowhere is that sight plainer than inside the oval office where the president is firmly in the patriarchal/misogyny camp. And outside those walls men are listening. Masculinity is a popular topic these days because apparently it's being threatened. By whom? Oh yes, by weak, stupid, inferior women. And this bothers men why?

Back in the mid '80s I worked on a project about women and guilt—a broad subject. We sent about 500 six-page surveys to women in the U.S., England, and Australia and had a 40 percent return. This was more than surprising; most surveys get somewhere between 10–20 percent returns—at least at that time, and I doubt it has changed. What didn't surprise was that nearly all who participated admitted feeling guilty. About what? Everything.

At the time I described this kind of guilt as "a nagging, nebulous emotion evolving from routine events and relationships, usually disproportionate to its cause."

Girls who grew up in the late '40s to mid '60s were taught it was a woman's responsibility to nurture—everyone. "Have you had enough to eat?" "Take your coat, it's cold outside!" "Are you feeling okay?" "Can I get you anything?"

In the survey women reported guilt over children and child-rearing, husbands, parents, friends, and co-workers. Collectively, most guilt arose from those relationships. But what drew the highest number— 77 percent—was "failure to live up to one's own expectations." Two expectations were described: those representing the internalized demands of others (achieving the feminine ideal, the superwoman syndrome) and those we set for ourselves; career goals and others.

Every kind of guilt imaginable surfaced in that survey, and it all led to diminished self-esteem, which I found and find deeply saddening. As if to rub it in, a fiercely misogynist book by John Carroll came out in 1985. *Guilt, the Grey Eminence* blamed society's ills on matriarchal guilt and "momism"—whatever that means.

I haven't surveyed young women today so I can't say guilt is still a problem, or as heavy as it was when housewifely perfection was thought to be every woman's goal. I'd be surprised though, to learn it's nonexistent. It is, after all, chiefly a product of our patriarchal culture, along with the evil Eve mythology. Most women seem to outgrow it as they age, but as long as there's someone around to nurture or not, guilt will be waiting to pounce.

I suffered a '50s flashback a few days ago when I saw a commercial that confirmed the guilt-ready wife is still around: A man enters a kitchen and picks up a small bottle from the counter. He turns to his wife who is entering the room and says "Have you taken your vitamins today?" She smiles and says "That's my job." No. It's not. If you're feeling guilty please get over it.

The mythology of Eve has for more than 3000 years fed this kind of female guilt, which is one reason it's used so often. Author Beth Allison

Barr explains why she believes Eve's story is so tied to patriarchy. She quotes the Latin Vulgate Bible regarding Eve's punishment: "In sorrow shalt thou bring forth children, and thou shalt be under thy husband's power and he shall have dominion over thee." But says Barr, "Patriarchy wasn't what God wanted; patriarchy was a result of human sin."[9]

Much as I respect Barr and her amazing book I disagree. For believing Christians, Muslims, and others, this story dates to the very creation of the world and is a true telling. In my opinion it's simply a myth, like Pandora only more successful. A myth used as an excuse to blame women. "Sin" just upped the ante.

Perhaps it's enough to hope that women will never again become the victims of superstition as they once were. But just as the holocaust haunts our memories with all those murdered in World War II, so the memory of centuries of hate and mistrust and humiliation dwell deep in the hidden recesses of a woman's mind. It is that memory, that flawed image of woman, that demands acknowledgement and correction. That will happen when men and women can define and recognize themselves as equal partners. Partners in life and partners in all the work that faces humanity, and in all the joy that comes with working together on a shared goal.

Unfortunately, the misogyny embedded in American soil is crippling us. The first settlers carried it aboard their ships and released it, like a virus, into the new world. It was firmly established when Abigail Adams wrote to her husband, pleading for a soupçon of power for women in the new country, but all she got in return was "petticoat despotism."

It was carried across the continent in covered wagons, where it scooped up a few native versions. It was present in 1920 when women finally won the vote after more than 150 years of trying. It rode in the first Ford Model A to roll off the newly invented assembly line. It was with the military during two world wars, was boosted by the media, and traveled hidden in duffle bags to Vietnam and Afghanistan and Iraq.

Patriarchy was well established in Washington D.C. when Ronald Reagan came to town, and it continues to be fed and petted by a good number of our representatives and senators. And of course it has been actively promoted for more than two thousand years by the Roman Catholic Church, and by competing religions and sects taking up the call. But as historian Barr reminds us, "The subjugation of women is indeed a historical constant—but that doesn't make it divinely ordained."[10]

I'm not here to say that women are better than men. We're not. But neither are men better than women. We developed together over millions of years of joint evolution. Men didn't evolve faster or better, and neither did women. We did it together as we created generation after generation. Do women think differently? Undoubtedly. That doesn't mean one sex is more brilliant than the other. As Leonard Sax reports in *Psychology Today,* "Researchers have long since established that there are, in fact, no differences in average intelligence between men and women."[11] So let's agree that men and women share equally in all the attributes necessary to build a nation. Or rebuild one.

Throughout our long history on this planet men and women have sought to make life easier for themselves and for the ones they loved. There is evidence that early men and women lived together happily without either being dominant. But whenever land was procured, when trade became a way of bettering yourself, when couples were divided in their efforts, equity was lost. And slowly but inevitably the idea of power over others evolved, and centuries passed. Women were no longer equal partners in life but were subject to laws that, in some places, reduced them to little more than slaves.

Eve's shadow has been with us throughout this book and at this moment I feel its darkness weighing heavily. But that shadow represents more than an imaginary tool for measuring patriarchal misogyny. Her shadow proves the light. Light that I believe is waiting for us, but in a future only men and women together can create. The poet Rainer Maria Rilke offers us a path in his *Letters to a Young Poet.* Written over a period beginning about 1903, his ideas about gender strike a surprisingly modern tone. In Letter 4 he writes:

"Perhaps the genders are more closely related than people think. The great renewal of the world will perhaps consist in this: that male and female, freed from all false feelings and disinclinations, do not seek each other as objects but rather as siblings and neighbors; to become human together simply, seriously, and patiently helping each other bare the burden that sexuality has placed on them."[12]

He expands on this idea in Letter 7: "Women, who know a more immediate, fruitful, and trustful relation to life must, after all, have become more humane than men, who have not gone through the hardship of giving birth, and who, rash and arrogant, undervalue what they mean to love. . . . One day the girl and the woman, who don't define themselves in masculine terms but as something in themselves—female humans—will require no other completion. This enormous shift will transform the character of love, which is hampered today by the resistance of men, and generate a relationship from human to human, not from man to woman."[13]

Obviously I can't predict the future. But unless global warming finally destroys life as we know it, or a plague devastates humanity, or a meteor smashes the planet to smithereens, the United States will probably continue to exist in some form. No matter how determined the president and his minions are to destroy democracy, Americans, I believe, will rise again to recreate what we have lost. And this time women—who are, remember—as strong, determined, and intelligent as males—must share leading roles.

If we can decouple power and wealth from the values we claim to honor—life, liberty, and the pursuit of happiness—and if we can acknowledge and accept that diversity is one of humanity's greatest strengths, our country could exist and even stand proudly for as long as a thousand years, just like Çatalhöyük.

It's time to live up to our own expectations.

## ACKNOWLEDGEMENTS

No book is written alone and I could not have completed this one without the support of many. First, thank you to Sally Petersen who read and commented on each chapter draft; her support was critical. Thank you also to my "writer support" group who supplied ongoing moral support: Kim Cook, Louise Lague, Diane Lund, Glennis McNeal, Jim Petersen, and Martha Ragland. Nadine Fiedler, poet and former co-worker, did heroic work as my primary editor, and my daughter Jennifer Gilden served as chief proofer and willing listener.

Many thanks to Joanne McLennan, an old friend and my former boss who designed and built the amazing cover, and granddaughter Melina Holmes who created the perfect graphic that's used throughout. Thanks also to friends who put up with my frequent absences and unanswered calls. I am deeply indebted to all.

Every book is a process and none is without its flaws and failures. *Eve and Me* is no exception to that rule, though I've tried to be accurate in all things. The views and ideas expressed here, as well as the errors, are mine alone.

# APPENDIX

## National and International Organizations
### Supporting Women.

**Amnesty International:** https://www.amnesty.org/en/
**Association for Women's Rights in Development**(AWID): https://www.awid.org/
**Center for Reproductive Rights:** https://reproductiverights.org/
**Equality Now:** https://equalitynow.org/
**European Institute for Gender Equality:** https://eige.europa.eu/
**Gender at Work:** https://genderatwork.org/
**Global Fund for Women:** https://www.globalfundforwomen.org/
**Human Rights Watch—UN organization:** www. hrw.org
**International Alliance for Women** (IAW): https://womenalliance.org/
**International Women's Development Agency** (IWDA): https://iwda.org.au/
**National Organization for Women:** https://now.org
**Office of Violence Against Women** (OVW): https://www.justice.gov/ovw
**Grants for Women:** https://www.federalgrants.com/federal-grants-for-women.htm
**Save the Children:** https://www.savethechildren.net/
**UN Women** organization for women's human rights: https://www.unwomen.org/en
**U.S. Policy Advocates for Afghan Women and Girls:** https://www.amnestyusa.org/
**US Agency for International Development:** https://www.usaid.gov/
**USA for UNFPA -United Nations sexual and reproductive rights agency:** usaforunfpa.org

**The following organizations furnish sanitary products to African schoolgirls and women who can't afford or don't have access to them. All accept donations.**

**Huru International:** https://www.huruinternational.org/
**Africa Bags:** https://www.africabags.org/
**Menstruation Foundation:** https://menstruation.foundation/

# REFERENCES


**1**

1. Kate Manne, Down Girl: The Logic of Misogyny (New York: Oxford University Press 2018) 88.

**2**

1. "Göbekli Tepe." Wikipedia. https://en.wikipedia.org/wiki/Göbekli_Tepe
2. Çatalhöyük Research (online) https://www.catalhoyuk.com/
3. Ian Hodder. Çatalhöyük: A 9000-Year-Old Town." Video. Universita di Catania, August 2018) Last accessed June 13, 2025 https://t.co/0awEYfmmoV
4. Ankara Museum of Anatolian Civilizations. https://turkiyetoday.com/culture/must-see-artifacts-at-ankara-museum-of-anatolian-civilizations-90814/?s=1
5. Hodder Çatalhöyük
6. Barbara Walker, *Women's Encyclopedia of Myths and Secrets* (San Francisco: Harper & Row) 635.
7. "Marija Gimbutas" Wikipedia. https://en.wikipedia.org/wiki/Marija_Gimbutas
8. Angela Saini, *The Patriarchs: The Origins of Inequality* (Boston: Beacon Press 2023) 72.
9. Saini, *Patriarchs*, 85–86.
10. Gimbutas, *The Civilization of the Goddess: The World of Old Europe* (SanFrancisco: Harper Collins, 1991) viii.
11. Gimbutas, *Civilization*, xiii–x.
12. Gimbutas, *Civilization*, x.
13. Saini, *Patriarchs*, 90.
14. Rosalind Miles, *Who Cooked the Last Supper? The Women's History of the World.* (New York: Three Rivers Press 1988, 2001) 31.
15. Will Durant, *Our Oriental Heritage: The Story of Civilization, Vol. 1.* (New York: Simon and Schuster 1954) 34-35.
16. Barbara G.Walker, "Hera": *Woman's Encyclopedia of Myths and Secrets* (San Francico: Harper & Row) 392.
17. Franz Cumont. *Oriental Religions in Roman Paganism.* (New York: Dover Publications 1956) 83. Cited in *Woman's Encyclopedia*, n17, 455.
18. Jack Lindsay. The Origins of Astrology (New York: Barnes & Noble Inc. 1971) 132. Cited in *Woman's Encyclopedia,* n1, 169.

19. Francis Legge, *Forerunners and Rivals of Christianity* (Vol.2). (New York: University Books, Inc. 1964) 64. Cited in Walker, *Woman's Encyclopedia* n2 951–953.
20. Hans Jonas, *The Gnostic Religion* (Boston, Beacon Press 1963) 204. Cited in Walker, *Women's Encyclopedia*, 951, n4.
21. Walker, *Woman's Encyclopedia.* 951.
22. Hagia Sophia is now a Moslem grand mosque. The minarets were added in the 15th –16th centuries. It was declared a museum by the secular Atatürk in 1935. The current President Erdoğan reclaimed it as a mosque in 2020, a move that was condemned by UNESCO (it is a world heritage site), the World Council of Churches, and many other organizations and national leaders.
23. Donald Attwater, *The Penguin Dictionary of Saints.* (Baltimore: Penguin Books, Inc. 1965) 127, 312.
24. Beth Allison Barr, *The Making of Biblical Womanhood* (Brazos Press: Grand Rapids, Michigan) 33.

**3**

1. Stephen Greenblatt, *The Swerve: How the World Became Modern* (New York: W.W. Norton & Company), 82.
2. Merlin Stone, *When God Was a Woman* (San Diego: Harcourt Brace Jovanovich, 1976) 196–198.
3. 1 Kings 15:5 and 2 Kings 9:31 (Revised Standard Version, 1952)
4. Stone, *When God was a Woma*n, 218–219.
5. Barbara Walker, "Demeter," *Woman's Encyclopedia of Myths and Secrets.* (San Francisco: Harper and Row 1983), 218–220.
6. Brian Muraresku, *The Immortality Key: The Secret History of the Religion With No Name (*New York: St. Martin's Press), 129–130.
7. Muraresku, *Immortality Key.* 27.
8. Muraresku, *Immortality Key.* 28.
9. "Ergot: The Psychoactive Fungus that Changed History," US Department of Agriculture; Forest Service. Accessed March 15, 2025. https://www.fs.usda.gov/wildflowers/ethnobotany/Mind_and_Spirit/ergot.shtml
10. Muraresku, *Immortality Key,* 26–27.
11. "Poppy goddess" Wikipedia. Theocritus (Idyll vii 157) n7. https://en.Wikipedia.org.org/wiki/Poppy_goddess.
12. Walker, *Woman's Encyclopedia*, 236.
13. Muraresku, *Immortality Key,* 35–36.
14. J. B. Russell, *Witchcraft in the Middle Ages.* (Ithaca, NY: Cornell University Press, 1972) 235; cited in *Woman's Encyclopedi*a, n15, 234.

15. Will Durant, *Our Oriental Heritage, The Story of Civilization Part 1* (New York: Simon and Schuster 1954) 35.

16. Leonard Shlain, *The Alphabet and the Goddess: The Conflict Between Word and Image* (New York: Viking 1998) 52.

17. Durant, *Oriental Heritage*, 246.

18. Shlain, *Alphabet* 7.

19. Shlain, *Alphabet*, 129.

20. "Pandora." *Brittanica.* Last accessed 8/22/2025. https://www.britannica.com/topic/Pandora-Greek-mythology.

21. *The Book of Knowledge, Vol 13–14* (New York: The Grolier Society, 1944) "Pandora's box," Adapted from Nathaniel Hawthorne's *Wonder Book.* 5259.

**4**

1. Genesis 1:27, 2:21 (Revised Standard Version, 1952).

2. Gen. 3:6.

3. *Father Knows Best.* Wikipedia. https://en.wikipedia.org/wiki/Father_Knows_Best.

4. Betty Cornell, *Betty Cornell's Teen-Age Popularity Guide* (New York: Prentice Hall, Inc. 1953).

**5**

1. Karen Jo Torjesen. *When Women Were Priests: Women's Leadership in The Early Church and The Scandal of Their Subordination in The Rise of Christianity.* (New York: HarperOne, 1993) 82.

2. Catherine Nixey. *The Darkening Age: The Christian Destruction of The Classical World* (NewYork: Mariner Books, Houghton Mifflin Harcourt, 2019) 66.

3. Nixey, *Darkening*, 67.

4. Nixey, *Darkening*, 63.

5. Note: Other films: *The Ten Commandments 1956; Ben Hur* 1959; *Spartacus* 1960; *The Greatest Story Ever Told* 1965; *The Bible: In the Beginning* 1966.

6. Will Durant, *The Age of Faith: The Story of Civilization Part IV.* (New York: Simon and Schuster, 1950) 9.

7. Brian C. Muraresku, *The Immortality Key: The Secret History of The Religion With No Name* (New York: St. Martin's Press, 2020) 288.

8. Durant, *Age of Faith*, 75.

9. Barbara G. Walker, ed., "Attis." *The Woman's Encyclopedia of Myths and Secrets,* (San Francisco: Harper and Row, 1983) 77–79.

10. Nixey, *Darkening*, xxviii.

11. Nixey, *Darkening*, 48–49.
12. Nixey, *Darkening*, 145–146. See also Stephen Greenblatt, *The Swerve* (New York: Norton 2011) 91–93.
13. Durant, *Age of Faith*, 13–21.
14. Durant, *Age of Faith*, 43.
15. James Trager, Ed., *The People's Chronology: A year-by-year Record of Human Events from Prehistory to the Present* (New York: Holt, Rinehart and Winston) 50–51.
16. Durant, *Age of Faith*, 42.

**6**

1. Timothy 2:11 (Revised Standard Version, 1952).
2. Beth Allison Barr, *The Making of Biblical Womanhood: How the Subjugation of Women Became Gospel Truth.* (Grand Rapids: Brazos Press, 2021) 56–57, 63.
3. 1 Peter, 3:1 (Revised Standard Version, 1952),
4. Mary Daly, *The Church and the Second Sex* (Boston: Beacon Press 1968, 1975, 1985) 87.

5–6. Daly, *Church*, 85.

7. Daly, *Church*, 89.
8. Barr, *Biblical Womanhood*, 46.
9. Lisa Isherwood and Dorothea McEwan, *Introducing Feminist Theology*, second edition (Sheffield, England: Sheffield Academic Press, 2001) 61.
10. Rosalind Miles, *Who Cooked the Last Supper?: The Women's History of the World* (New York: Three Rivers Press, 1988, 2001) 89.

**7**

1. Will Durant, *The Age of Faith: The Story of Civilization, Vol. 4* (New York: Simon and Schuster 1950) 461–471.
2. Durant, *Faith*, 458–460. See also "Moors" at Wikipedia.org.
3. Durant, *Faith*, 181.
4. Durant, *Faith* 180.
5. Glassé, Cyril (1989). *The Concise Encyclopaedia of Islam.* (London: Stacey International) 413. Cited in "Women in Islam," Wikipedia.org, n47. https://en.wikipedia.org/wiki/Women_in_Islam.
6. Liana Aghajanian, "The Complicated History of Headscarves" Racked.com, December 20, 2016. Accessed March 22, 2026. https://wrapunzel.com/racked-the-complicated-history-of-headscarves-by-liana-aghajanian/
7. To fully appreciate that number, the world population estimates in 1300 AD vary between 500 million to 301 million. We're now over 8 billion. See "Estimates of historical world population" at Wikipedia.org. or ourworldindata.org.

8. Barbara W. Tuchman, *A Distant Mirror* (New York: Alfred A. Knopf, 1978) 9.

9. Tuchman, *Mirror*, 32.

10. Tuchman, *Mirror*, 29.

11. Tuchman, *Mirror*, 53.

**8**

1. Shulamith Shahar, *The Fourth Estate: A History of Women in the Middle Ages,* translated by Chaya Galai (London: Methuen & Co, Ltd, 1983) 1–3.

2. Barbara W. Tuchman, *A Distant Mirror* (New York: Alfred A. Knopf, 1978), 216.

3. Gilden, Karen and Ray, *Tea & Bee's Milk: Our Year in a Turkish Village* (Portland: Artha Press, 2008) 94–95.

4. Shahar, *Fourth Estate*, 3.

5. Tuchman, *Mirror*, 211.

6-7. Tuchman, *Mirror*, 219.

8. Prudence Allen, *The Concept of Woman: The Early Humanist Reformation,* 1250–1500, page 469. Cited in "Margery Kempe" Wikipedia. n39. Accessed May 6, 2025. https://en.wikipedia.org/wiki/Margery_Kempe

9. Jone Johnson Lewis, "Julian of Norwich Quotes: From the English Mystic." ThoughtCo.com. Updated March 21, 2018. http://thoughtco.com/julian-of-norwich-quotes-3530114.

10. Jone Johnson Lewis, "Biography of Hildegard of Bingen, Mystic, Writer, Composer, Saint." ThoughtCo.com. Updated March 21, 2018. https://www.thoughtco.com/hildegard-of-bingen-3529308.

11. "The Preservation of Women's Words," 15th Century Feminist (Substack), June 5, 2025. https://15thcfeminist.substack.com/p/the-preservation-of-womens-words-e87.

12. Shahar, *Fourth Estate,* 64.

13–14. Tuchman, *Mirror*, 214.

15. O'Shea, Stephen, *The Perfect Heresy: The Revolutionary Life and Death of the Medieval Cathars.* (New York: Walker & Company, 2000) 80-81. Cited in "Catharism," n72. https://en.wikipedia.org/wiki/Catharism.

16. Mike Magee, "The Catholic Inquisition, Methods and Torture and Victims." https://churchandstate.org.uk/2026/03/the-catholic-inquisition-methods-of-torture-and-victims/

17. Rosa Rubicondior. "Lesson from France—The Bloody Extermination of the Cathars at Béziers." Church and State, July 23, 2023. https://churchandstate.org.uk/2024/06/lesson-from-france-the-bloody-extermination-of-the-cathars-at-beziers-kill-them-all-for-the-lord-knoweth-them-that-are-his/.

## 9

1. "List of papal bulls." Wikipedia. https://wikipedia.org/wiki/List_of_papal_bulls.
2. "Tomas-de-Torquemada." Britannica online. Accessed 4/25/25. https://www.britannica.com/biography/
3. Sister Antoinette Marie Pratt, A.M. "The Attitude of the Catholic Church Towards Witchcraft and the Allied Practices of Sorcery and Magic," Dissertation. (Catholic University of America, Washington D.C. (June, 1915) page 10. Via Google Books. https://www.google.com/books/edition/The_Attitude_of_the_Catholic_Church_Towa/gG61OAHgOXkC?hl=en&gbpv=1&bsq=woman in collusion voluntarily.
4. Pratt, "Attitude Toward Witchcraft," 10–11.
5. Will Durant, *The Reformation, The Story of Civilization Part VI* (New York: Simon and Schuster, 1957) 459–460.
6. Durant, *Reformation*, 415.
7. Will Durant, *The Age of Faith, The Story of Civilization, Part IV* (New York: Simon and Schuster, 1950) 784.
8. Beth Allison Barr, *The Making of Biblical Womanhood: How the Subjugation of Women Became Gospel Truth,* (Grand Rapids: Brazos Press 2021) 154.
9. Joseph Klaits, *Servants of Satan: The Age of the Witch Hunts,* (Indiana University Press: 1985) 52.
10. Klaits, *Servants*, 53.
11. Klaits, *Servants*, 56–57.
12. Jacob Springer and Heinrich Kraemer, *Malleus Maleficarum* (*The Hammer of Witches*) 1487. Article revised and updated by Amy Tikkanen. Britannica. https://www.britannica.com/topic/Malleus-maleficarum.
    This is a "detailed legal and theological document regarded as the standard handbook on witchcraft. . . . The *Malleus* went through 28 editions between 1486 and 1600 and was accepted by Roman Catholics and Protestants alike as an authoritative source of information concerning Satanism and as a guide to Christian Defense."
13. "Salem witch trials." Wikipedia.Accessed April 24, 2025. https://en.wikipedia.org/wiki/Salem_witch_trials.

## 10

1. "Betttisia Gozzadini," Wikipedia. Last modified November 9, 2024, https://en.wikipedia.org/wiki/ Bettisia_Gozzadini.
2. "Lucy Stanton (abolitionist)" Wikipedia. Last modified March 10 2025 https://en.wikipedia.org/wiki/Lucy_Stanton_(abolitionist).

3–4. Will Durant, *The Renaissance. The Story of Civilization,* Vol. 5 (New York: Simon & Schuster 1953) 5.

5. Stephen Greenblatt, *The Swerve: How the World Became Modern* (New York: W. W. Norton & Company, 2011) 7.

6. Durant, *Renaissance,* 86.

7. Durant, *Renaissance,* 255.

8. Durant, *Renaissance,* 582.

9. Durant, *Renaissance,* 584–585.

10 . Durant, *Renaissance,* 585.

11. Durant, *Renaissance,* 585–586.

12. Durant, *Renaissance,* 582.

13. Shulamith Shahar, *The Fourth Estate: A History of Women in the Middle Ages.* (London and New York: Methuen & Co. 1983) 169-170.

14. Deborah G. Felder, *A Bookshelf of Our Own: Works that Changed Women's Lives* (New York: Citadel Press Books, 2005) 7.

15. Beth Allison Barr, *The Making of Biblical Womanhood: How the Subjugation of Women Became Gospel Truth.* (Grand Rapids: Brazos Press, 2021) 77.

**11**

1–2. Will Durant, *The Age of Reason Begins, The Story of Civilization,* Vol VII (New York: Simon and Schuster, 1961) 5.

3–4. Durant, *Reason,* 11.

5. Durant, *Reason,* 35–36.

6. Jane Austin, *Pride and Prejudice,* (New York: E. P. Dutton and Company, Inc., 1976) 173.

7. James Trager, ed., *The People's Chronology: A Year-by-Year Record of Human Events from Prehistory to the Present* (New York: Holt, Rinehart and Winston, 1979) 189–190.

8. Virginia Woolf, *A Room of One's Own* (New York & London: Harcourt Brace Jovanovich, 1929) 69.

9. Dale Spender, *Women of Ideas: And What Men Have Done to Them* (London: Unwin Hyman Limited, 1988) 34.

10. Spender, *Women,* 35.

11. Spender, *Women,* 37.

12. Spender, *Women,* 41.

13. Woolf, *A Room,* 68.

14.–15. Durant, *Reason*, 479.

16. "Anna Maria van Schurman." Wikipedia. https://en.wikipedia.org/wiki/Anna_Maria_van_Schurman. n13.

17. "Maria Tesselschade Visscher" Wikipedia. Updated 19 March 2025. https://en.wikipedia.org/wiki/Maria_Tesselschade_Visscher,

## 12

1. Dale Spender, *Women of Ideas: And What Men Have Done to Them* (London: Unwin Hyman Limited, 1988) 68–69.
2. Spender, *Women*, 73.
3. Spender, Women, 78–79, quoting from a 1976 Facsimile Reprint of the Bentham Press, 1739.
4. "Lady Mary Wortley Montagu" Wikipedia. Last modified 17 June 2025. https://en.wikipedia.org/wiki/Lady_Mary_Wortley_Montagu.
5. Robert Halsband and Christopher Pick, eds. *Embassy to Constantinople: The Travels of Lady Mary Wortley Montagu,* Introduction by Dervla Murphy. (New York: New Amsterdam Books, 1988) 12–21.
6. Spender, *Women*, 71.
7. "Lady Mary Wortley Montagu." Wikipedia.
8. Helen Chapin Metz, ed., *Turkey: A Country Study* (Federal Research Division, Library of Congress, 5th edition, 1996) 37.
9. "Mîna Urgan." Wikipedia. Last modified 24 April 2025, at 16:40 (UTC). https://en.wikipedia.org/wiki/Mîna_Urgan.
10. Suzanne Massie, *Land of the Firebird: The Beauty of Old Russia.* (New York: Simon and Schuster, 1980) 133.
11. Note: According to the *Atlas of Russian History* (Martin Gilbert, Marlboro Books, 1972) only 3,000 of the 30,000 native Aleuts survived the 83 years of Russian rule, which ended when Alaska was sold to the United States in 1867.
12. Robert K. Massie, *Peter the Great: His Life and World.* (New York: Alfred A.Knopf, 1980) 390–391.
13. Klier JD. "The Ambiguous Legal Status of Russian Jewry in the Reign of Catherine II." *Slavic Review 35, no. 3 (*1976): 504–517. n116. Cited in Wikipedia. org. https://en.wikipedia.org/wiki/Catherine_the_Great

## 13

1. Leslie Stephen and Sidney Lee, eds. *Dictionary of National Biography,* Oxford University Press, 1973, p. 921. Quoted in *Women of Ideas and What Men Have Done to Them.* (London: Pandora Press 1988) 96.

2. Elizabeth Eger. *Bluestockings: Women of Reason from Enlightenment to Romanticism.* (London: Palgrave Macmillan, 2010) 206. Cited at Wikipedia. org, n10. https://en.wikipedia.org/wiki/Bluestocking

3–4. Will and Ariel Durant, *The Age of Napoleon, The Story of Civilization,* Vol XI, (New York: Simon and Schuster 1975) 366.

5. Wikipedia.org., "*William Godwin, Memoirs of the Author of A Vindication of the Rights of Woman*" (1798) https://en.wikipedia.org/wiki/Memoirs_of_the_Author_of_A_Vindication_of_the_Rights_of_Woman.

6. Durant, *Napoleon*, 52.

7. Durant, *Napoleon*, 65–66.

8. Olympe de Gouges, *Declaration of the Rights of Woman and of the Female Citizen* (Madison, WI: Handcar Press, 2024) 15–16. (Original copyright 1791.)

9. Arthur Young, *Travels in France and Italy During the Years 1787, 1788 and 1789.* (New York: Everyman's Library, E. P. Dutton. [n.d.,1792.] 146.

10. Young, *Travels*, 126.

11. Young, *Travels*, 172.

12. Young, *Travels*, 336.

13. Curtis Cate, *George Sand: A Biography* (Boston: Houghton Mifflin Company, 1975) 190–191.

14. Cate, *Sand*, 203.

15. Cate, *Sand* nd, x.

16. Cate, *Sand*, xix.

17. Cate, *Sand*, ix.

18. Wikipedia.org., "George Eliot" https://en.wikipedia.org/wiki/George_Eliot. Last accessed March 30, 2025.

## 14

1. Dale Spender, *Women of Ideas: And What Men Have Done to Them* (London: Routledge and Kegan Paul Ltd., 1982) Pandora Press 1988. 278.

2. "Amelia Bloomer." Wikipedia. Accessed March 29, 2025 https://en.wikipedia.org/wiki/Amelia_Bloomer.

3. Abigail Adams, letter to John Adams, March 31, 1776. National Constitution Center. https://constitutioncenter.org/the-constitution/historic-document-library/detail/abigail-adams-to-john-adams-1776

4. Margaret Townsend, *Our Paper,* Vol. XXVII. Massachusetts Reformatory, Concord Junction, MA, August 26, 1911, 407. Via Google books.

5. Louis Coffin, ed. *The Coffin Family* (Nantucket: Nantucket Historical Association, 1962) 73.

6. Allen Coffin, *The Life of Tristram Coffyn Of Nantucket, Mass.* (Nantucket: Husey & Robinson, 1881) 56–57.
7. Townsend, *Our Paper*, 407.
8. Elizabeth Cady Stanton, Susan B. Anthony, and Matilda Joslyn Gage, "Lucretia Mott" In *History of Woman Suffrage, Vol 1* 407. https://www.google.com/books/edition/History_of_woman_suffrage_Vol_1_3_ed_by/s9X8RI0L5-8C?hl=en&gbpv=0, Vol. 1. New York: Susan B. Anthony / Charles Mann, 1861, 407.
9. Stanton, et al. *History*, 411–412.
10. Stanton, et al. *History*, 416–417.
11. Stanton, et al. *History*, 421–422.
12. Carol Faulkner, *Lucretia Mott's Heresy: Abolition and Women's Rights in Nineteenth Century America* (Philadelphia: University of Pennsylvania Press, 2011) 7.f
13. Stanton, et al. *History*, 414.
14. Spender, *Women of Ideas,* 318.
15. Spender, *Women of Ideas,* 382.
16. Matilda Joslyn Gage, *Woman, Church and State: The Original Exposé of Male Collaboration Against the Female Sex.* 238. [Original publication 1893.] Reprinted in Troutdale, Oregon 05/05/2024.
17. "Women's Loyal National League." Wikipedia.org. See "History" https://en.wikipedia.org/wiki/Women's_Loyal_National_League.
18. Spender, *Women of Ideas,* 188.
19. Spender, *Women of Ideas*, 559.
20. "Emmeline Pankhurst." Wikipedia.org., https://en.wikipedia.org/wiki/Emmeline_Pankhurst.

**15**

1. "Frederick Douglass." Women's Rights National Historical Park (website). https://www.nps.gov/wori/learn/historyculture/frederick-douglass.htm.
2. Martha C. Wright, Letter to her daughter on December 30, 1860, Women's Rights National Historical Park. https://www.nps.gov/wori/learn/historyculture/martha-c-wright.htm.
3. Note: Wyoming 1890; Colorado (partial) 1893; Idaho 1896; Washington 1910; California 1911; Oregon, Arizona, and Kansas 1912; Alaska Territory 1913, Montana and Nevada 1914.

4–5. Catherine Clinton, *Harriet Tubman: The Road to Freedom* (New York: Little, Brown and Company, 2015) 157.

6. Clinton, *Harriet Tubman* 167.
7. Clinton, *Harriet Tubman* 17–18.

8. Clinton, *Harriet Tubman*, 212.

9. "Sojourner Truth," Women's Rights National Historical Park. https://www.nps.gov/wori/learn/historyculture/sojourner-truth.htm.

10–11. "Sojourner Truth," Women's Rights NP.

12. Elizabeth Cady Stanton, Susan B. Anthony, and Matilda Joslyn Gage. *History of Woman Suffrage, 3 vols.* New York, Susan B.Anthony; Charles Mann, 1861, Volume 1:115–117. https://www.google.com/search?udm=36&q=History+of+Woman+Suffrage.

13. Stanton et al., *History*, (1876) 2:193.

14. Stanton et al., *History*, (1861) 1:567.

15. Stanton et al., *History*, (1885) 3:531–532.

16. Caitlin Dickerson "Ida B. Wells, Who Took on Racism in the Deep South With Powerful Reporting on Lynchings." *The New York Times* (online) Amisha Padnani and Jessica Bennett (eds.) *New York Times* online, March 8, 2018, retrieved April 22, 2018. https://www.nytimes.com/interactive/2018/obituaries/overlooked-ida-b-wells.html.

17. "Ida B. Wells, Anti-lynching campaign," Wikipedia.org. https:/en.wikipedia.org/wiki/Ida_B._Wells

18. Nikole Hannah-Jones, Caitlin Roper, Elena Silverman, and Jake Silverstein Eds. *The 1619 Project,* (New York: New World, 2021) 453.

19. 'Ethel Payne." Obituary. *New York Times.* June 1, 1991. https://www.nytimes.com/1991/06/01/obituaries/ethel-payne-79-dies-was-a-correspondent.html.

20. Gwen Ifill, "Black journalist Ethel Payne changed the national agenda with coverage of civil rights." PBS News Hour, February 26, 2015. https://www.pbs.org/newshour/show/black-journalist-ethel-payne-changed-national-agenda.

21. Ifill, PBS News Hour.

22. "Ethel L. Payne." Wikipedia. Accessed April 18, 2025 https://en.wikipedia.org/wiki/Ethel_L._Payne. Last accessed April 18, 2025.

23. Nicole Hannah-Jones, *The 1619 Project* (New York: One World, 2021) 464.

24. Hannah-Jones, *1619 Project* 476.

**16**

1. "Into the Intro: The Outbreak of theFirst World War," Cambridge University Press blog, July 21, 2014. https://cambridgeblog.org/2014/07/into-the-intro-the-outbreak-of-the-first-world-war/

2. Guy Hartcup. World War 1" *The War of Invention: Scientific Developments, 1914–18.* (Brassey's Defence Publishers, 1988), 82–86. n325. Cited in "World WarI," Wikipedia.org. https://en.wikipedia.org/wiki/World_War_I.

3. Julie M. Powell, "November 11, 1918: The End of World War I?" Origins: Current Events in Historical Perspective. Ohio State University. https://origins.osu.edu/milestones/wwi-armistice-centennial-armisticeday-november-11-1918-worldwarone-surrender

4. Kirstin Downey, *The Woman Behind the New Deal: The Life and Legacy of Frances Perkins, FDR's Secretary of Labor and His Moral Conscience.* (NewYork: Anchor Books, 2010) 120–123.

5. Downey, *The Woman*, 34–35.

6. Geraldine H. Murray, "New York's New Citizen Makes Good as an Officeholder and Paves the Way for Future Appointments." *New-York Tribune.* August 3, 1919. ISSN 1941-0646.

7. "Remembering The 1911 Triangle Factory Fire" a Lecture by Frances Perkins at Cornell University, School of Industrial and Labor Relations, 30 September 1964. https://trianglefire.ilr.cornell.edu/primary/lectures/FrancesPerkinsLecture.html.

8. Rose Schneiderman. Full speech: Leon Stein, ed., *Out of the Sweatshop: The Struggler Industrial Democracy* (New York: Quadrangle/New Times Book Company, 1977) 196–197. https://www2.umbc.edu/che/tahlessons/pdf/historylabs/The_Triangle_Sh_student:_RS15.pdf.

**17**

1. William Shirer. *The Rise and Fall of the Third Reich: A History of Nazi Germany* (New York: Simon and Schuster 1960). *The Nightmare Years, Vol II, 20th Century Journey: A Memoir of a Life and the Times* (Boston: Little, Brown and Company, 1984).

2. "World War II casualties," Wikipedia. https://en.wikipedia.org/wiki/World_War_II_casualties.

3. Shirer, *The Rise and Fall of the Third Reich:* 967.

4. "Rosie the Riveter." history.com, Last updated February 27, 2025. https://www.history.com/articles/rosie-the-riveter.

5. Thalia Ertman, "The Lanham Act and Universal Childcare During World War II" Friends of the National WWII Memorial. https://www.wwiimemorialfriends.org/blog/the-lanham-act-and-universal-childcare-during-world-war-ii

**18**

1. "Potsdam Declaration" https://en.wikipedia.org/wiki/Potsdam_Declaration

2. Note: "Evidence of redlining is the systematic denial of mortgages, insurance, loans, and other financial services based on location—and that area's default history—rather than on an individual's qualifications and credit worthiness. Notably, the practice of redlining is felt most by residents of minority neighborhoods. Redlining is illegal." https://www.investopedia.com/terms/r/redlining.asp.

3. David McCullough. *Truman.* New York: Simon & Schuster, 1992) 657.

4. Erin Blakemore, "How 'Queen for a Day' Turned Unhappy Housewives into Royalty." History.com, July 19, 2017, updated March 4, 2025. https://www.history.com/articles/this-midcentury-show-turned-unhappy-housewives-into-tv-royalty.

5. Judith Thurman, *Introduction to The Second Sex* (New York: Vintage Books, 2011) x

6. Lisa Appignanesi, "Did Simone de Beauvoir's open 'marriage' make her happy?" *The Guardian.* (10 June 2005) London. https://www.theguardian.com/world/2005/jun/10/genderpoliticsphilosophyandsociety

7. Simone de Beauvoir, *The Second Sex*, trans. Constance Borde and Sheila Malovany-Chevallier (New York: Vintage Books, 2009) 82 and 87.

8. Marcelo Gleiser, *The Dawn of a Mindful Universe: A Manifesto for Humanity's Future.* (New York: HarperCollins Publishers, 2023) 78 and 203.

9. de Beauvoir, *Second Sex,* 751.

10. Dale Spender, *Women of Ideas* (London, Pandora Press, 1988) 719.

11. Spender, *Women of Ideas,* 722.

12–13. Sally Petersen, "A Woman, a Time, a Place: A Mid-Century Memoir." Unpublished memoir (2022) 45.

14. "Ruth Bader Ginsberg." Wikipedia.org. https://en.wikipedia.org/wiki/Ruth_Bader_Ginsburg.

**19**

1. "U.S.. President's Commission on the Status of Women Records." John F. Kennedy Presidential Library and Museum. https://www.jfklibrary.org/assetviewer/archives/uspcsw.

2. "Addressing Political Violence: Lessons from the 1960s." GovFacts.org https://govfacts.org/history/addressing-political-violence-lessons-from-the-1960s/

3. Doris Kearns Goodwin, *An Unfinished Love Story: A Personal History of the 1960s* (New York: Simon & Schuster, 2024) 182.

4–5. Goodwin, 218–219.

6. "Vietnam War: Casualties." Wikipedia. https://en.wikipedia.org/wiki/Vietnam_War.

**20**

1. "Kent State shootings." Wikipedia. https://en.wikipedia.org/wiki/Kent_State_shootings.

2. "The Equal Rights Amendment." Wikipedia. https://en.wikipedia.org/wiki/Equal_Rights_Amendment#CITEREFMansbridge.

3. Angela Saini. *The Patriarchs: The Origin of Inequality* (Boston: Beacon Press, 2023) 49

4. Jane J. Mansbridge, *Why we lost the ERA* (University of Chicago Press, 1986) p 110. Cited in "The Equal Rights Amendment," n74, Wikipedia.org. https://en.wikipedia.org/wiki/Equal_Rights_Amendment.

5. Gilden, Karen *Camping With the Communists: The Adventures of an American Family in the Soviet Union* (Sister, OR: Artha Press, 2013) 3–4.

6. Wikipedia.org., "Richard Nixon," https://wikipedia.org/wiki/Richard_Nixon.

7. Jeff Stein, "Trump Ambassador Beat and 'Kidnapped' Woman in Watergate Cover-up: Reports." *Newsweek* December 11, 2017. https://www.newsweek.com/2017/12/29/donald-trump-watergate-stephen-king-martha-mitchell-richard-nixon-john-744823.html

8. Carl Bernstein and Bob Woodward, *All the President's Men* (New York: Simon & Schuster, 1974). See also wikipedia.org/

9. "Select Committee on Presidential Campaign Activities 1973–1974." U.S. Senate. https//www.senate.gov/about/powers-procedures/investigations/watergate.htm.

10. Jesse Greenspan, "Battle of the Sexes': When Billie Beat Bobby." History.com. https://www.history.com/articles/billie-jean-king-wins-the-battle-of-the-sexes-40-years-ago

11. Wikipedia.org., "Jimmy Carter," https://en.wikipedia.org/wiki/Jimmy_Carter

12. Jimmy Carter, *Our Endangered Values: America's Moral Crisis,* (Simon & Schuster, 2005) 93.

13. Jimmy Carter, "Losing My Religion for Equality," *The Age* online, July 15, 2009. https://www.theage.com.au/politics/federal/losing-my-religion-for-equality-20090714-dk0v.html.

14. Lou Cannon (2003). *Governor Reagan: His Rise to Power*. Public Affairs. 209–214. ISBN 978-1-58648-030-1.

15. "Ronald Reagan." Wikipedia. https://en.wikipedia.org/wiki/Ronald_Reagan.

**21**

1. Vladimir Bukovsky, *To Build a Castle: My Life as a Dissenter.* [Originally published in Russian, Novelpress 1977] Translated into English. (New York: Viking Press, 1978) 141.

2. Gilden, Karen, *Camping With the Communists: An American Family in the Soviet Union,* (Sisters, OR, Artha Press, 2013) 189.

3. "A History of Black Feminism in the United States" at Race, Racism and the Law (website). https://racism.org/articles/intersectionality/gender/8223-but-some-of-us-are-brave?start=5.

## 22


1. "Anita Hill." Wikipedia. https://en.wikipedia.org/wiki/Anita_Hill.
2. David Rosenbaum. "No-Comment Is Common at Hearings for Nominees." *New York Times* (July 12, 2005). https://www.nytimes.com/2005/07/12/politics/politicsspecial1/nocomment-is-common-at-hearings-for-nominees.html
3. "Opening Statement: Sexual Harassment Hearings Concerning Judge Clarence Thomas." Infoplease.com. Updated September 23, 2019. https://www.infoplease.com/primary-sources/government/court/opening-statement-sexual-harassment-hearings-concerning-judge.
4. "Clarence Thomas Supreme Court nomination" Wikipedia. https://en.wikipedia.org/wiki/Clarence_Thomas_Supreme_Court_nomination
5. Marcus, Ruth. "One Angry Man." *The Washington Post.* October 3, 2007
6. "Clarence Thomas Supreme Court nomination." Wikipedia. https://en.wikipedia.org/wiki/Clarence_Thomas_Supreme_Court_nomination
7. Note: The Civil Rights Act of 1964 had prohibited employment discrimination. The first case to award the victim of sexual harassment was Barnes v. Costle when in 1977 the U.S.Court of Appeals (DC) reversed an early decision [wenzelfenton.com]. It wasn't until 1980 that the EEOC issued regulations defining sexual harassment. The Civil Rights Act of 1991 finally expanded the rights of women to sue and collect damages for discrimination or harassment [https://www.congress.gov/bill/102nd-congress/senate-bill/1745].
8. Kuczynski, Alex; Glaberson, William (June 27, 2001). "Book Author Says He Lied in His Attacks on Anita Hill in Bid to Aid Justice Thomas," *The New York Times* https://www.nytimes.com/2001/06/27/us/book-author-says-he-lied-his-attacks-anita-hill-bid-aid-justice-thomas.html.
9. "Year of the Woman." Senate Historical Office 2018. https://www.senate.gov/artandhistory/history/minute/year_of_the_woman.htm.
10. "History of the Violence Against Women Act." Justice.gov. https://www.justice.gov/archive/ovw/docs/history-vawa.pdf
11. Berners-Lee, Tim; Mark Fischetti. *Weaving the Web: The Original Design and Ultimate Destiny of the World Wide Web.* (London: Orion Business, 1999).
12. Gilden, Karen and Ray. *Tea & Bee's Milk: Our Year in a Turkish Village* (Portland, OR, Artha Press: 2008).
13. "Presidency of Bill Clinton." Wikipedia. https://en.wikipedia.org/wiki/Presidency_of_Bill_Clinton.
14. "Pope John Paul II." Wikipedia. https://en.wikipedia.org/wiki/Pope_John_Paul_II

## 23

1. "List of apologies made by Pope John." Wikipedia. https://en.wikipedia.org/wiki/List_of_apologies_made_by_Pope_John_Paul_II.
2. "Vladimir Putin." Biography.com. https://www.biography.com/political-figures/vladimir-putin.
3. Kiley Hurst, "U.S. women are outpacing men in college completion, including in every major racial and ethnic group." Pew Research Center (November 18, 2024) https://www.pewresearch.org/short-reads/2024/11/18/us-women-are-outpacing-men-in-college-completion-including-in-every-major-racial-and-ethnic-group/
4. Dr. Jamila K. Taylor, "Women Earn Less than Men in All Occupations." Institute for Women's Policy Research, March 7, 2024) https://iwpr.org/new-report-women-earn-less-than-men-in-all-occupations-even-ones-commonly-held-by-women/
5. "9/11 Timeline." History.com, updated August 20, 2024. https://www.history.com/topics/21st-century/9-11-timeline.
6. "September 11 Attacks," History.com. Accessed June 30, 2025. https://www.history.com/articles/9-11-attacks.
7. Note: Biden brought the troops home from Afghanistan August 31, 2021, based on an agreement made by Trump with the Taliban to withdrawn troops by May 1. It was a chaotic departure with an airport attack on August 26 that killed 13 U.S. military personnel and 70–170 Afghan citizens. The Afghan government collapsed soon after. (Aljazeera, "Kabul bombings: 13 US army personnel killed in attacks at airport," August 26, 2021; updated August 27, 2021.)
8. Brian Duignan. "Presidency of George W. Bush." Britannica.com. Last updated February 11, 2025. https://www.britannica.com/biography/George-W-Bush/Presidency
9. National Academies of Sciences, Engineering, and Medicine. "Sexual Harassment of Women: Climate, Culture, and Consequences in Academic Sciences, Engineering, and Medicine." https://doi.org/10.17226/24994. Washington, DC: The National Academies Press, 2018.
10. Steven E. Schier. ed. *Debating the Obama Presidency,* (Lanham, MD Rowman & Littlefield Publishers 2016) Cited in "America Recovery and Reinvestment Act of 2009," n5. Wikipedia. https://en.wikipedia.org/wiki/American_Recovery_and_Reinvestment_Act_of_2009.
11. "Equal Rights Amendment," Wikipedia. https://en.wikipedia.org/wiki/Equal_Rights_Amendment.
12. Max Fisher. "Scalia Says Constitution Doesn't Protect Women From Gender Discrimination." *The Atlantic.* January 4, 2011. https://www.theatlantic.com/politics/archive/2011/01/scalia-says-constitution-doesn-t-protect-women-from-gender-discrimination/342789/

13. Robert S. Mueller III. "Report on The Investigation into Russian Interference in the 2016 Presidential Election, Vol. II." Special Counsel's Office, March 2019 https://www.govinfo.gov/app/details/GPO-SCREPORT-MUELLER/.

14. "2016 United States presidential election." Wikipedia. https://en.wikipedia.org/wiki/2016_United_States_presidential_election

15. Tom Kertscher, "Is Donald Trump's executive order a 'Muslim ban'?" Politifact.com, February 3, 2017. https://www.politifact.com/article/2017/feb/03/donald-trumps-executive-order-muslim-ban/.

16. E. Kiely, L. Robertson,R. Rieder, and D. Gore, "Timeline of Trump's COVID-19 Comments." FactCheck.org, October 2, 2020. https://www.factcheck.org/2020/10/timeline-of-trumps-covid-19-comments/.

17. Gary Langer. "Unwanted sexual advances not just a Hollywood, Weinstein story, poll finds." ABC News. https://abcnews.go.com/Politics/unwanted-sexual-advances-hollywood-weinstein-story-poll/story?id=50521721.

18. World Health Organization. "Violence Agaist Women." Fact Sheet. Geneva: WHO, March 2024. https://www.who.int/news-room/fact-sheets/detail/violence-against-women

19. Final Report of the Select Committee to Investigate the January 6th Attack on the United States Capitol. Or: *The January 6th Report: of the Congressional Select Committee* (New York: Celedon Books, 2022)] https://www.govinfo.gov/app/details/GPO-J6-REPORT/context

20. Maria Cramer, "Key Passages from the Leaked Supreme Court Draft Opinion." (*New York Times*, May 3, 2022). https://www.nytimes.com/2022/05/03/us/supreme-court-abortion-opinion-draft.html

21. Tanya Lewis, ed. Dean Visser, "64,000 Pregnancies Caused by Rape Have Occurred in States with a Total Abortion Ban." (*Scientific American*, January 25, 2024). https://www.scientificamerican.com/article/64-000-pregnancies-caused-by-rape-have-occurred-in-states-with-a-total-abortion-ban-new-study-estimates/

**24**

1. Note: Costco, among others, is fighting back. "Our board has considered this proposal and believes that our commitment to an enterprise rooted in respect and inclusion is appropriate and necessary," Costco's board of directors said in a December 2025 statement mentioned by CNN.

2. Andrea Hsu. "Trump calls DEI programs 'illegal.'"NPR, January 23, 2025. https://www.npr.org/2025/01/23/nx-s1-5271588/trump-dei-diversity-equity-inclusion-federal-workers-government.

3. Amy Howe, "Supreme Court Strikes Down Affirmative Action Programs in College Admissions," SCOTUSblog, June 29, 2023. https://www.scotusblog.com/2023/06/supreme-court-strikes-down-affirmative-action-programs-in-college-admissions/

4. Josh Moody, "The Year in Closures and Mergers," Inside Higher Ed, (online). December 13, 2024. https://www.insidehighered.com/news/business/financial-health/2024/12/13/2024-has-seen-more-college-closures-last-year.

5. Note: Interestingly, when I went back to the GAO website to confirm that information in early May, 2025, the report could not be found. I searched every category. Almost every available report was dated 2025, after the new administration had taken office. I did a search for the word "women" on each page of the site and found nothing. Unfortunately this is indicative of the administration not only ignoring women and their history, but other areas of public interest as well.

6. Lawrence Tribe and Kathleen M. Sullivan, "The Equal Rights Amendment at Long Last," The Contrarian (Substack). January 17, 2025. https://contrarian.substack.com/p/the-equal-rights-amendment-at-long.

7. Betsy Klein and Arlette Saenz, CNN (website) "Biden says Equal Rights Amendment is ratified. . ." CNN, January 17, 2025. https://www.cnn.com/2025/01/17/politics/joe-biden-equal-right-amendment

8. Mark Sherman, "Supreme Court: Trump's immunity case goes back to lower court," Associated Press, published on PBS News Hour, July 1, 2024. https://www.pbs.org/newshour/politics/supreme-court-trumps-immunity-case-goes-back-to-lower-court.

9. Idrees Ali, Phil Stewart, and David Shepardson, "Trump removes US Coast Guard Chief, Official Ties DEI Focus." Reuters January 21, 2025. https://www.reuters.com/world/us/trump-fires-coast-guard-commandant-over-dei-security-fox-news-reports-2025-01-21/.

10. Konstantin Torpin and Steve Beynon. "No More Female 4-Stars: Franchetti Firing Leaves Top-Ranks Filled by Men. Military.com, February 27, 2025. https://www.military.com/daily-news/2025/02/27/no-more-female-4-stars-franchetti-firing-leaves-top-ranks-filled-men.html

11. Phil Stewart, "Pentagon's Hegseth: 'Diversity is Our Strength' is Dumbest Phrase in Military History." Reuters, February 7, 2025. https://www.reuters.com/world/us/pentagons-hegseth-diversity-is-our-strength-is-dumbest-phrase-military-history-2025-02-07/

12–13. Manne, Kate, *Down Girl: The Logic of Misogyny,* 2018, Oxford University Press, 102, 103

14. Mann, *Down Girl,* 173.

**25**

1. Lipika Pelham, "Mahsa Amini: Iran Responsible for 'Physical Violence' Leading to Death, UN says. (BBC: March 8, 2024) https://www.bbc.com/news/world-middle-east-68511112.

2. Fatma Tanis, "Women Across Iran are Refusing to Wear Headscarves, in Open Defiance of the Regime." National Public Radio: March 2023. https://www.npr.org/sections/pictureshow/2023/03/13/1157657246/iran-hijab-protest-regime-politics-religion-mahsa-amini.

3. Hasan Almasi, "Iran: Repression of Women "intensifying," Two Years on from Mass Protests." (United Nations News: September 13, 2024). https://news.un.org/en/story/2024/09/1154306.

4. "Iran: New Hijab Law Adds Restrictions and Punishments." Human Rights Watch: October 14, 2024. https://www.hrw.org/news/2024/10/14/iran-new-hijab-law-adds-restrictions-and-punishments.

5. Jiyar Gol, "Iran Pauses Controversial New Dress Code Law." BBC, December 16, 2024. https://www.bbc.com/news/articles/c0mv83m4z7vo.

6. Roza Otunbayeva, "Special Representative Urges de Facto Authorities Reverse Repressive Policies Towards Women." United Nations, March 6, 2024 https://press.un.org/en/2024/sc15612.doc.htm.

7. Yogita Limaye, "Afghan Women in Mental Health Crisis over Bleak Future." (British Broadcasting Corporation, June 4, 2023) https://www.bbc.com/news/world-asia-65765399.

8. Yogita Limaye, "'If We Can't Speak, Why Live?' BBC Meets Women After New Taliban law." BBC, September 11, 2024.

9. Francesco Bortoletto, "Brussels Condemns Taliban's Law Prohibiting Afghan Women's Public Expression." EU News: August 26, 2024. https://www.eunews.it/en/2024/08/26/brussels-condemns-talibans-law-prohibiting-afghan-womens-public-expression/.

10. Heather Barr, "The Taliban and the Global BacklashAgainst Women's Rights." *Georgetown Journal of International Affairs,* February 6, 2024. https://gjia.georgetown.edu/2024/02/06/the-taliban-and-the-global-backlash-against-womens-rights/.

11. "Marking 3 Years of Taliban Oppression." Joint Statement. Human Rights Watch, August 16, 2024) https://www.hrw.org/news/2024/08/16/joint-statement-marking-3-years-taliban-oppression.

12. "African Union." Wikipedia. https://en.wikipedia.org/wiki/African_Union.

13. "African Charter on Human and Peoples' Rights." Wikipedia. https://en.wikipedia.org/wiki/African_Charter_on_Human_and_Peoples'_Rights.

14. UN statistical commission, "2022 GlobalSurvey of National Gender Statistics Programs." https://unstats.un.org/unsd/iaeggs/Meetings/Online_December_2022/docs/4_UNSD.pdf." United Nations, 2022.

15. Wangari Maathai, "The Nobel Peace Prize 2004: Press Release." Nobel Foundation, October 8, 2004. Archived at the Wayback Machine March 13, 2009. https://www.nobelprize.org/prizes/peace/2004/press-release/.

16. Ellen Johnson Sirleaf, "The Nobel Peace Prize 2011 – Press Release." Nobel Foundation. Retrieved October 7, 2011. https://www.nobelprize.org/prizes/peace/2011/press-release/

17. Chimamanda Ngozi Adichi, Wikipedia. https://en.wikipedia.org/wiki/Chimamanda_Ngozi_Adichie.

18. US Agency for International Development: https://www.usaid.gov/.

19. Mujib Mashal and Pamodi Waravita, "Where a Strongman Failed, Women Are Now Fueling a Democratic Revival" (*New York Times*: February 4, 2025). https://www.nytimes.com/2025/02/04/world/asia/sri-lanka-politics-women.html

20–21. Travers, Mark, "Why the '4B Movement Resonates With Women Worldwide—by a Psychologist."*Forbes,* December 24, 2024) https://www.forbes.com/sites/traversmark/2024/12/24/why-the-4b-movement-has-women-breaking-up-with-men-by-a-psychologist/.

22. Rachel Treisman, "Boycott men? South Korea's 4B Movement Gains Traction in the U.S. after Trump's win. NPR, November 8, 2024. https://www.npr.org/2024/11/08/nx-s1-5182888/4b-movement-trump-south-korea

23. Treisman, "Boycott Men?"

24–25 Travers, "Why 4B"

26. Harmeet Kaur, "After Trump's Win, Some Women are Considering the 4B Movement." CNN: November 13, 2024 https://www.cnn.com/2024/11/09/us/4b-movement-trump-south-korea-wellness-cec/index.html

## 26

1. Mike Wendling and Kayla Epstein "Trump makes 'two sexes' official and scraps DEI policies," January 20, 2025. BBC.com. https://www.bbc.com/news/articles/czx84en1yp4o

2. "Gender Dysphoria," Mayo Clinic. https://www.mayoclinic.org/diseases-conditions/gender-dysphoria/symptoms-causes/syc-20475255

3. Fernanda Figueroa, Ayanna Alexander, and Cory Williams. "Trump order ending federal DEI programs leaves agencies and stakeholders on uncertain ground." (AP News: January 23, 2025) https://apnews.com/article/trump-dei-executive-order-diversity-inclusion-f67ea86032986084dd71c5aa0c6b8d1d

4. Tim Paradis, "The companies fighting back against Trump's war on DEI (Business Insider, (online) January 25, 2025) https://www.businessinsider.com/jpmorgan-costco-keeping-dei-despite-trump-executive-orders-2025-1?op=1

5–6. Rosaline C. Barnett, and Caryl Rivers, "Are Some Men Becoming HostileTowards Women?" *Psychology Today* (online), September 12, 2023. https://www.psychologytoday.com/us/blog/a-womans-place/202309/are-some-men-becoming-hostile-towards-women

7. Kate Manne, *Down Girl: The Logic of Misogyny,* (New York: Oxford University Press, 2018) 35.

8. "How Male Supremacy Provided the Foundation for Hate in 2023," Report:

Dismantling White Supremacy Southern Poverty Law Center, June 4, 2024) https://www.splcenter.org/resources/reports/male-supremacy-dangers/

9. Beth Allison Barr, *The Making of Biblical Womanhood: How the Subjugation of Women Became Gospel Truth* (Grand Rapids: Brazos Press 2021) 28–29.

10. Beth Allison Barr, *Biblical Womanhood.* 127.

11. Leonard Sax, "New Research Finds Huge Differences Between Male and Female Brains." *Psychology Today* (online) May 24, 2024. https://www.psychologytoday.com/us/blog/sax-on-sex/202405/ai-finds-astonishing-malefemale-differences-in-human-brain

12. Rainer Maria Rilke, *Letters to a Young Poet: A New Translation and Commentary.* Translated by Anita Barrows and Joanna Macy (Boulder, CO: Shambhala Publications, 2021) 36–37.

13. Rilke, *Letters to a Young Poet* 59–60.

# BIBLIOGRAPHY

Barr, Beth Allison. *The Making of Biblical Womanhood: How the Subjugation of Women Became Gospel Truth.* Grand Rapids: Brazos Press, 2021.

Beauvoir, Simone de, *The Second Sex.* Translated by Constance Borde and Sheila Malovany-Chevallier. 2009. New York: Vintage Books, 2011. Original copyright 1949, Introduction by Judith Thurman, 2010.

Bukovsky, Vladimir, *To Build a Castle: My Life as a Dissenter.* New York: Viking Press, 1979. Previous copyrights by Novelpress 1977, Viking Press 1978.

Carter, Jimmy. *Our Endangered Values: America's Moral Crisis.* New York: Simon & Schuster Paperbacks, 2006.

Cate, Curtis. *George Sand: A Biography.* Boston: Houghton Mifflin, 1975.

Clinton, Catherine. *Harriet Tubman: The Road to Freedom.* New York: Backbay Books, 2004.

Coffin, Allen. *The Life of Tristram Coffyn Of Nantucket, Mass.* Nantucket: Husey & Robinson, 1881.

Coffin, Louis editor. *The Coffin Family.* Nantucket: Nantucket Historical Association, 1962.

Collins, Paul. *The Sumerians.* London: Reaction Books Ltd., 2021.

Daly, Mary. *The Church and the Second Sex.* Boston: Beacon Press, 1968, 1975, 1985.

de Gouges, Olympe. *Declaration of the Rights of Woman and of the Female Citizen.* Madison, Wisconsin: Handcar Press, 2024. ISBN 9781941892800

Downey, Kirstin. *The Woman Behind the New Deal: The Life and Legacy of Frances Perkins*—Social Security, Unemployment Insurance, and the Minimum Wage. New York: Anchor Books, 2009.

Durant, Will. *Our Oriental Heritage: The Story of Civilization: Part I.* New York: Simon and Schuster, 1954.

Durant, Will. *The Age of Faith: A History of Medieval Civilization—Christian, Islamic, and Judaic—from Constantine to Dante: A. D. 325–1300. Part IV.* New York: Simon and Schuster, 1950.

Durant, Will. *The Renaissance: A History of Civilization in Italy from 1304–1576 A.D. Part V.* New York: Simon and Schuster, 1953.

Durant, Will. *The Reformation: A History of European Civilization from Wyclif to Calvin: 1300–1564. Part VI.* New York: Simon and Schuster, 1957.

Durant, Will. *The Age of Reason Begins: A History of European Civilization in the Period of Shakespeare, Bacon, Montaigne, Rembrandt, Galileo, and Descartes: 1558–1648. Part VII.* New York: Simon and Schuster, 1961.

Durant, Will and Ariel. *The Age of Napoleon: A History of European Civilization from 1789 to 1815. Part XI.* Simon and Schuster, 1975.

Faulkner, Carol. *Lucretia Mott's Heresy: Abolition and Women's Rights in Nineteenth Century America.* Philadelphia: University of Pennsylvania Press, 2011.

Gage, Matilda Joslyn. *Woman, Church & State: The Original Exposé of Male Collaboration Against the Female Sex.* Originally published 1893. Copy of the original printed in Troutdale, Oregon, May 2024. ISBN 9798580276601.

Gilbert, Martin. *Atlas of Russian History.* Marlboro Books, 1984. Originally published in Great Britain as Russian History Atlas, 1972, ISBN 0-88029-018-8

Gilden, Karen and Ray. *Tea and Bee's Milk: Our Year in a Turkish Village.* Portland: Artha Press, 2008.

Gilden, Karen. *Camping With the Communists: An American Family in the USSR.* Sisters, OR, Artha Press 2013

Gimbutus, Marj. *The Civilization of the Goddess: The World of Old Europe.* SanFrancisco: Harper Collins, 1991.

Gleiser, Marcelo. *The Dawn of a Mindful Universe: A Manifesto for Humanity's Future.* New York: Harper Collins, 2023.

Goodwin, Doris Kearns, *An Unfinished Love Story: A Personal History of the 1960s.* New York: Simon & Schuster, 2024.

Gouges, Olympe de. *Declaration of the Rights of Woman and of the Female Citizen.* Madison: Handcar Press, 2024.

Greenblatt, Stephen. *The Swerve: How the World Became Modern.* New York: W. W. Norton & Company, 2011.

Greenblatt, Stephen. *The Rise and Fall of Adam and Eve.* New York: W .W .Norton & Company, 2017.

Hannah-Jones, Nikole. *The 1619 Project: A New Origin Story.* New York: One World, 2021.

Lisa Isherwood, Dorothea McEwan. *Introducing Feminist Theology.* Second edition Sheffield, England: Sheffield Academic Press, 2001.

Manne, Kate. *Down Girl: The Logic of Misogyny.* New York: Oxford University Press, 2018.

Massie, Robert K. *Peter the Great: His Life and World.* New York: Alfred A.Knopf, 1980.

Massie, Suzanne. *Land of the Firebird: The Beauty of Old Russia.* New York: Simon and Schuster, 1980.

Metz, Helen Chapin, Editor. *Turkey: A Country Study,* Federal Research Division, (Dept. of the Army) Library of Congress, U. S. Government Printing Office, 1996.

Miles, Rosalind. *Who Cooked the Last Supper? The Women's History of the World.* New York: Three Rivers Press, 1988, 2001.

Montagu, Lady Mary Wortley. *Embassy to Constantinople: The Travels of Lady Mary Wortley Montagu.* Edited by Roert Halsband and Christopher Pick. New York: New Amsterdam Books, 1988.

Muraresku, Brian C. *The Immortality Key: The Secret History of the Religion With No Name.* New York: St. Martin's Press, 2020.

Nixey, Catherine. *The Darkening Age: The Christian Destruction of the Classical World.* Boston: Mariner Books, 2017.

Penaluna, Regan. *How to Think Like a Woman: Four Women Philosophers Who Taught Me How to Love the Life of the Mind.* New York: Grove Press, 2023.

Rilke, Rainer Maria. *Letters to a Young Poet: A New Translation and Commentary.* Translated by Anita Barrows and Joanna Macy. Boulder, CO: Shambhala Publications, 2021.

Saini, Angela. *The Patriarchs: The Origins of Inequality.* Boston: Beacon Press, 2023.

Shahar, Shulamith. *The Fourth Estate: A History of Women in the Middle Ages.* Translated by Chaya Galai. London and New York: Methuen, 1983.

Shirer, William L. *The Rise and Fall of the Third Reich: A History of Nazi Germany.* New York: Simon and Schuster, 1960.

Shirer, William L. *The Nightmare Years 1930–1940.* Boston: Little Brown & Company, 1984

Shlain, Leonard, *The Alphabet Versus the Goddess: The Conflict Between Word and Image.* New York: Viking Penguin, 1998.

Solzhenitsyn, Aleksandr I. Translated by Thomas P Whitney. *The Gulag Archipelago 1918–1956: An Experiment in Literary Investigation I-II.* New York: Harper & Row, 1973.

Spender, Dale. *Women of Ideas: And What Men Have Done to Them.* London: Routledge and Kegan Paul, 1982. Paperback by Pandora Press, Unwin Hyman Limited, 1988.

Stanton, Elizabeth Cady. "Lucretia Mott," *History of Woman's Suffrage, Vol 1, Chapter 11,* 1887.

Stone, Merlin. *When God Was a Woman: The Landmark Exploration of the Ancient Worship of the Great Goddess and the Eventual Suppression of Women's rites.* New York: Harper Collins, 1976.

Torjesen, Karen Jo. *When Women Were Priests: Women's Leadership in the Early Church & the Scandal of their Subordination in the Rise of Christianity.* New York: Harper Collins, 1993.

Trager, James, Editor *The People's Chronology: A Year-by-Year Record of Human Events from Prehistory to the Present.* New York: Holt, Rinehart and Winston, 1979.

Tuchman, Barbara W. *A Distant Mirror: The Calamitous 14th Century.* New York: Alfred A. Knopf, 1978.

Walker, Barbara G. *The Woman's Encyclopedia of Myths and Secrets.* San Francisco: Harper & Row, 1983.

Woolf, Virginia. *A Room of One's Own.* New York: Harcourt, Brace & World, Inc., 1957.

Young, Arthur. *Travels in France & Italy During the Years 1787, 1788 and 1789.* New York: E. P. Dutton. No copyright date is provided.

# INDEX

# ABOUT THE AUTHOR

Karen began freelancing in 1978 and her articles have appeared in local and national publications. *Eve and Me* is her fifth book.

She loves spending time outdoors, walking, reading, swimming, travel, and trees—especially the Redwoods, and she's been blogging since 2006. Follow her at karengilden.substack.com.

www.ingramcontent.com/pod-product-compliance
Lightning Source LLC
La Vergne TN
LVHW091120080826
845145LV00008B/1995
* 9 7 8 1 8 8 6 9 2 2 0 9 9 *